Texts and Monographs in Computer Science

Texts and Monographs in Computer Science

String-Rewriting Systems

Ronald V. Book
Friedrich Otto

Springer-Verlag

New York Berlin Heidelberg London Paris
Tokyo Hong Kong Barcelona Budapest

Ronald V. Book
Department of Mathematics
University of California
Santa Barbara, CA 93106
USA

Friedrich Otto
Fachbereich Mathematik/Informatik
Gesamthochschule Kassel
Postfach 10 13 80
3500 Kassel
Germany

Series Editor:
David Gries
Department of Computer Science
Cornell University
Upson Hall
Ithaca, NY 14853
USA

Library of Congress Cataloging-in-Publication Data
Book, Ronald V.
    String-rewriting systems/Ronald V. Book, Friedrich Otto.
      p.   cm.—(Texts and monographs in computer science)
    Includes bibliographical references and index.
    ISBN 0-387-97965-4
    1. Rewriting systems (Computer science)   I. Otto, Friedrich.
    II. Title. III. Series.
    QA267.B66   1993
    005.13′1—dc20   92-37370

Printed on acid-free paper.

Production managed by Natalie Johnson; manufacturing supervised by Vincent Scelta.
Photocomposed using the authors' LaTeX files.
Printed and bound by R.R. Donnelley & Sons, Inc., Harrisonburg, VA.
Printed in the United States of America.

9 8 7 6 5 4 3 2 1

ISBN 0-387-97965-4 Springer-Verlag New York Berlin Heidelberg
ISBN 3-540-97965-4 Springer-Verlag Berlin Heidelberg New York

Preface

The subject of this book is string-rewriting systems. It is generally accepted that string-rewriting was first introduced by Axel Thue in the early part of this century. In the 1960's and early 1970's, it received renewed attention due to interest in formal language theory. In the 1980's and 1990's, it has received more interest since it can be viewed as a special case of term-rewriting, a subject that has become important in the study of automated deduction. Today, string-rewriting is studied by researchers in theoretical computer science and also by researchers interested in the foundations of artificial intelligence. A sketch of the way that the subject has developed is contained in Chapter 0, and the reader is advised to begin with that chapter.

Both authors have been active in the field and have lectured on the subject in several universities. Lecture notes have been produced and distributed. This monograph is a result of revising and rewriting those notes. It represents an attempt by the authors to present the concepts that the authors consider to be most fundamental and to gather together the most useful results in such a way that they can be understood and used in studies relating to more general rewriting, to automated deduction, and to algorithmic problems of algebraic structures.

This monograph is written for independent study by researchers in theoretical computer science or in the foundations of artificial intelligence. While it has not been written as a textbook, it can be used that way for a lecture course at the advanced undergraduate/beginning graduate level (USA interpretation), or as a supplement to a course in rewriting theory or foundations of artificial intelligence. The authors feel that it is easier for some students to learn about the concepts (e.g., the word problem, confluence) in the context of string-rewriting before they meet the same ideas in the study of term-rewriting. As prerequisites, mastery of the material in a good course covering automata, formal languages, and computability is sufficient; an alternative prerequisite might be a course in logic, particularly computational logic.

The authors' gratitude goes to many. The first author was introduced to the subject by Maurice Nivat. Jürgen Avenhaus and Klaus Madlener greatly influenced the second author's interest in algorithmic problems in algebra and in rewriting. Much encouragement was given by Deepak Kapur, Robert F. McNaughton, and Paliath Narendran. Over the years the authors also benefited from many valuable discussions with Günter Bauer, Volker Diekert, Matthias Jantzen, Colm Ó'Dúnlaing, Geraud Senizergues, and Craig Squier.

Both authors have worked with Celia Wrathall on problems in this area, and she demanded that we finish this work. It is likely that without her constant attention and encouragement, the first author would have given up the whole idea of completing this manuscript.

Leslie Wilson typed some of the lecture notes upon which this monograph is based, and Frau R. Kohl at Kaiserslautern and Frau E. Djawadi at Kassel typed several preliminary versions of various chapters of this monograph.

The production of this monograph would not have been completed without the extraordinary efforts of Shilo Brooks. Both of the authors are grateful for her assistance.

Over the period of the first author's work in this area and on this book, his research was supported in part by grants from the Computer Research Division of the National Science Foundation. The second author also wants to express his gratitude to the Deutsche Forschungsgemeinschaft (DFG) for a grant that gave him the opportunity to spend the 1982/83 academic year as a postdoctoral researcher at the Department of Mathematics of the University of California, Santa Barbara. It was there and then that he met the first author, who introduced him to the field of string-rewriting systems.

Ronald V. Book   Friedrich Otto
Santa Barbara   Kassel

Contents

0

Introduction

0.1 Historical Development

In the early part of the twentieth century, Axel Thue [Thu14] discussed the following problem: Suppose one has a set of objects and a set of transformations ("rules") that when applied to these objects yield objects in the same set. Given two objects x and y in the set, can x be transformed into y, or is there perhaps a third object z such that both x and y can be transformed into z?

This problem came to be known as the "word problem." Thue established some preliminary results about strings of symbols (that is, elements of a free monoid), and he suggested that one might be able to extend this approach to more structured combinatorial objects such as graphs or trees. Indeed, if Thue were doing this work today, he might have considered a set of data structures of some particular type as an appropriate set of objects.

Thue wanted to develop a "calculus" to decide the word problem, that is, a set of procedures or algorithms that could be applied to the given objects to obtain the correct answer to the question. In modern terminology, he wanted a general algorithm to solve the word problem in a variety of different settings.

At approximately the same time, Dehn [Deh11] was working on what became the underpinnings of combinatorial group theory and he introduced the word problem for finitely presented groups. It is reasonable to consider these problems as part of what was to become "Hilbert's Program."

Apparently Thue's work was ignored for many years, but it did come to the surface in the 1930's when logicians attempted to provide formal definitions of notions such as "algorithm" and "effective procedure" (see [Dav58]). This was quite natural since Thue wanted to know whether the word problem was decidable. It is well known that there can be no calculus to solve the word problem in its most general form, and that in a number of specific domains such as finitely presented groups and monoids the word problem is undecidable.

In the mid-1950's and in the 1960's, the notion of a semi-Thue system was studied in mathematical linguistics and in formal language theory since it was very useful in mathematical models for phrase-structure grammars. These grammars were exhaustively studied in the context of the problem of machine translation of natural languages. At the same time that increases in the size of computer memories and in the speed of machine computations suggested to some that machine translation might be possible, logicians began to look to the computer as a tool for studying problems in mathematics and began to consider new proof methods that might be implemented on real machines. This led to the development of automated deduction (mechanical theorem-proving).

In the 1960's there were many interesting theoretical developments in automated deduction and some led to the development of new concepts that have proven to be extremely enlightening [BlLo83], [SiWr83]. Concepts such as resolution and unification inspired much new work. A particularly influential role was played by a paper by Knuth and Bendix [KnBe70] that described an automatic procedure for solving word problems in abstract algebras.

In the 1970's the notion of term-rewriting systems played an increasingly important role in the study of automated deduction. A (presently) biannual international conference with emphasis on automated deduction and its foundations was begun in the 1970's and a biannual international conference on rewriting techniques and their applications began in 1985 (see [Jou87]).

What happened to Thue systems? While semi-Thue systems played an important role in the development of formal language theory in the 1960's, the corresponding algebraic approach did not receive very much attention with the exception of the French school (who have always emphasized the relationships between algebra and formal language theory). Much of the work in France was carried out by the school of Nivat who, following the lead of Schützenberger, emphasized the relationship between Thue congruences and formal language theory (see [Ber77]). However, the work of the French school in the 1970's did not emphasize the role of algorithmic solution to certain problems or the complexity of algorithms and the inherent computational difficulty of the problems. As far as Thue systems and Thue congruences are concerned, the algorithmic approach with its corresponding attention to the complexity of problems and algorithms has been the work of the 1980's.

Thus, Thue systems and their applications have been studied in several contexts: combinatorial rewriting systems for strings and other types of objects; specification of monoids and groups; specification of formal languages by means of formal grammars; and automated deduction and mechanical theorem-proving. We will refer to Thue systems and semi-Thue systems as "string-rewriting systems." This is consistent with the view that such systems can be considered to be special cases of term-rewriting systems where there are only function symbols of arity one, that is, symbols that represent unary functions, and there are no constants. In addition, ground-term rewriting systems can be seen as special cases of string-rewriting systems (since ground-terms are variable-free).

0.2   An Outline of Recent Developments

Now we turn to a brief review of developments on string-rewriting systems in the 1980's.

The French school emphasized rewriting in the sense of formal language theory and, in particular, considered rewriting rules that when applied caused a string to be rewritten as a shorter string. It was in this way that the idea of "confluence" was initially studied in the context of string-rewriting systems. However, this property had been previously studied in the context of the lambda-calculus [ChRo39] and combinatorial reasoning and abstract rewriting [New43], [Hue80]. In addition, rewriting properties other than confluence were studied and for some time the definitions were unsettled. Following Berstel's survey [Ber77] of the results of the French school, Book [Boo82a] considered the word problem for finite string-rewriting systems where the notion of "reduction" was based on rewriting strings as shorter strings. He showed that for any confluent system of this type, there is a linear-time algorithm to solve the word problem; the linear-time bound depends very heavily on the fact that the notion of "reduction" was based on rewriting strings as shorter strings. In addition, the algorithm described by Book was used to show for finite confluent string-rewriting systems whose rewriting rules had a specific form ("monadic" systems), that each congruence class is a deterministic context-free language, and that the class of such deterministic context-free languages forms a Boolean algebra.

Using a technique developed in [Boo82a], Book and O'Dúnlaing [BoÓ'Dú81b] showed that there is a polynomial-time algorithm to test whether a finite string-rewriting system is confluent. The same technique was used by Book, Jantzen, and Wrathall [BJW82] and by Ó'Dúnlaing [Ó'Dú81, 83b] in their studies of the specification of formal languages through finite (and also infinite) monadic and confluent string-rewriting systems.

String-rewriting systems can be viewed as presentations of monoids in the sense that they define a quotient of the free monoid modulo the Thue congruence that they generate. Thus, it is reasonable to consider various combinatorial decision problems about the monoid so presented. Ó'Dúnlaing [Ó'Dú83a] studied some undecidability results relating to finite string-rewriting systems and the congruences specified by such systems; in particular, he studied properties that could be classified as "Markov properties." On the other hand, Book [Boo83] developed a uniform decision procedure for a large class of problems about finite string-rewriting systems that are confluent and monadic and about the monoids presented by such systems. Then the limits of Book's decision procedure were explored by Otto [Ott84a].

If the notion of reduction in a string-rewriting system is not based on length but on a more general ordering, then the simple connection between the length of reductions or derivations (that is, the "derivational complexity") and the inherent computational difficulty of the word problem is not necessarily true. This is shown by results of Madlener and Otto [MaOt85] and Bauer and Otto [BaOt84] who showed that there are string-rewriting systems with the following two properties: (i) the word problems are decidable by means of fast algorithms; (ii) the derivational complexity is as great as any given recursive function.

Independent of the development outlined above, Gilman [Gil79] considered a procedure that, from a finite string-rewriting system, attempts to construct an equivalent string-rewriting system that is "noetherian" and confluent, that is, a string-rewriting system such that every congruence class has a unique "irreducible" string. This procedure appears to be a modification of the "completion procedure" developed by Knuth and Bendix [KnBe70] in the setting of term-rewriting systems (however, it appears that Gilman was unaware of the work of Knuth and Bendix). Later Kapur and Narendran [KaNa85b] showed how the Knuth-Bendix completion procedure could be adapted to the setting of string-rewriting systems (but it appears that they in turn were not aware of Gilman's work). As part of their study, Kapur and Narendran introduced the notion of "reduced" or "normalized" string-rewriting system, a notion that was independently considered by Avenhaus and Madlener [AvMa83] in a special context. These were important steps in the study of string-rewriting systems where reduction is not based on length but on a more general ordering.

Since a string-rewriting system presents a monoid, there have been a number of studies investigating questions such as whether a monoid so presented is in fact a group or whether it is a free monoid or .... In particular, decision procedures for such questions are of great interest. Related to this theme is the study of algebraic characterizations of monoids and/or groups by syntactic characterizations of presentations. There are a number of interesting contributions to this area, such as Otto [Ott85, Ott86b], Narendran and Otto [NaOt88a], Gilman [Gil84], Avenhaus, Madlener, and Otto [AMO86], Cochet [Coc76], and Autebert, Boasson, and Senizergues [ABS87].

The question of which Thue congruences (the congruences on free monoids induced by Thue systems) and which monoids admit finite, noetherian, and confluent string-rewriting systems received much attention. It is known that there exist finitely generated Thue congruences that cannot be generated by such systems even though there do exist such systems over a different alphabet (set of generators) that do present the same monoid. Thus, there are finite string-rewriting systems with decidable word problems that have no "equivalent systems" (that is, systems generating the same Thue congruence over the original alphabet) that are finite, noetherian, and confluent. Such results were obtained by Kapur and Narendran [KaNa85a] and by Jantzen [Jan81, Jan85]; in fact, such systems arise in the study of string-rewriting systems presenting abelian groups [Die86]. More recently, a surprising result was obtained by Squier [Squ87b]. By establishing the fact that each monoid that can be presented by some finite, noetherian, and confluent string-rewriting system satisfies a certain homological finiteness condition, and by exhibiting examples of finitely presented monoids that have decidable word problems but do *not* satisfy this condition, Squier proved that there exist finitely presented monoids with decidable word problems that cannot be presented by string-rewriting systems that are finite, noetherian, and confluent.

In some of these studies, it has been extremely useful to consider systems that are confluent only on specific congruence classes; examples of this can be seen in Dehn's work on the word problem and on "small cancellation theory." Otto [Ott87] and Otto and Zhang [OtZh91] investigated such systems and their congruences with emphasis on decision procedures for certain combinatorial properties. Recently, specialized completion procedures for such systems have been considered.

One of the properties which appears to be related to that of confluence of string-rewriting systems is that of "preperfect" systems. This property arises not only in string-rewriting systems but more generally in term-rewriting systems, where it corresponds to the notion of "confluence modulo an equivalence relation" as studied by Jouannaud and Kirchner [JoKi86]. In contrast to the fact that confluence for string-rewriting systems (where reduction is based on length) is decidable in polynomial time, Narendran and McNaughton [NaMc84] showed that it is undecidable whether a given string-rewriting system is preperfect.

While the context of most of the work in string-rewriting has been a finitely generated free monoid, some very interesting work has been done when rewriting is carried out in a free partially commutative monoid and a free partially commutative group (that is, in structures where some but not all pairs of generators commute). The original motivation for this work was purely combinatorial [CaFo69], essentially being part of the study of combinatorics on words. However, it was shown later that this notion can be used in modelling certain aspects of parallel computation [Maz77]. It is trivial to note that the word problem for a finitely generated free monoid is decidable in linear time. It is known that this property is shared by finitely generated free partially commutative monoids [BoLi87]. Since a finitely generated free group can be presented by a finite confluent string-rewriting system where reduction is based on length, its word problem is again decidable in linear time. Consider a finitely generated free partially-commutative group; each such group has a presentation by a finite preperfect string-rewriting system. Wrathall [Wra88] has shown that once again the word problem is decidable in linear time. Currently, there is much interest in rewriting in free partially commutative monoids and groups.

0.3   Contents of the Monograph

To a large extent the present monograph represents an attempt by the authors to gather together the most fundamental results of the 1980's on string-rewriting systems. The goal is to explain these results in such a way that they can be understood and used in studies relating to more general rewriting, automated deduction, and algorithmic problems of algebraic structures.

Chapter 1 contains preliminary notions that are required for much of the remainder of the text. It is frequently the case that when mathematical concepts are involved, it is easier to understand a concept in an abstract setting rather than a specific concrete setting. This is precisely the case when considering reduction systems. In Sections 1.1 and 1.2 we follow Huet [Hue80] in the presentation of the basic notions of reduction and replacement. We consider a set of abstract objects and binary relations on that set. Reduction and replacement are described in terms of these binary relations. These notions form the basis for the discussion of rewriting and reduction in the later chapters. The other sections of Chapter 1 contain material with which the reader familiar with automata, formal languages, and computability should be comfortable, and such a reader need only scan Sections 1.3 and 1.4 until the need arises to refer to a specific term or result.

String-rewriting systems are defined and studied in Chapter 2. An algorithm for computing irreducible strings is introduced in Section 2.2; this algorithm is used frequently in the remaining sections of the monograph. In Section 2.3 we develop an algorithm for testing for "local confluence," which in the context of noetherian rewriting is equivalent to testing for confluence (as shown in Section 1.1). Then the Knuth-Bendix completion procedure as adapted for string-rewriting systems is presented. We close this chapter by establishing some undecidable properties of string-rewriting systems.

In Chapter 3 we consider the setting where reduction of the length of strings is the basis for reduction in the rewriting procedure. In this context the algorithm for computing irreducible strings introduced in Section 2.2 becomes a linear-time algorithm and, hence, if the system is confluent, then the word problem becomes decidable in linear time. In addition, the property of being confluent becomes decidable in polynomial time based on the test for local confluence developed in Section 2.3. Other topics of Chapter 3 include a development of undecidability results for Markov properties of Thue congruences, as well as a discussion of Church-Rosser congruences, and a brief survey of the properties of non-confluent systems where reduction is based on length.

The topic of Chapter 4 is monadic string-rewriting systems. Basic properties are discussed, including the use of such systems in order to specify formal languages. But the main thrust of Chapter 4 lies in Section 4.3 where a decision procedure is introduced. The decision procedure applies to string-rewriting systems that are finite, monadic, and confluent. Certain combinatorial or algebraic questions about the congruence generated by such a system (or the monoid so presented or even about specific elements of this monoid) are of interest; for example, (i) given two elements, is the first a power of the second?, and (ii) is the monoid actually a group? The questions must be presented by asking whether a logical sentence is or is not true about the congruence; the syntax of the sentence is very narrowly specified. The decision procedure is guaranteed to operate within polynomial work space (and to solve PSPACE-complete problems), but very frequently it operates in polynomial time. After presenting the decision procedure in Section 4.3, we describe a number of applications in Section 4.4. Then in Section 4.5 we describe some of the limitations of the decision procedure by giving examples that violate the conditions described in Section 4.3 and to which the decision procedure does not apply.

In Chapter 5 we describe properties of string-rewriting systems that are length-reducing but are not monadic. It is shown there that every recursively enumerable set can be represented by such systems and so many of the properties that are decidable when the system is confluent and monadic are undecidable in this context.

In Chapter 6 we show how results developed in Chapters 1–4 can be used to present the results of Dolev and Yao [DoYa83] on secure protocols for public-key crypto-systems. These results fit very nicely into the "algebraic" framework of congruences specified by string-rewriting systems that are finite, monadic, and confluent, and so we refer to them as "algebraic protocols." The inclusion of these results is intended to be one illustration of how the ideas relating to string-rewriting systems are applied.

We have noted that string-rewriting systems can be viewed as presentations of monoids in the sense that they define a quotient of the free monoid modulo the Thue congruence that they generate. This suggests that string-rewriting systems may be studied in the context of combinatorial group theory or, better, combinatorial monoid theory. This is precisely what is done in Chapter 7.

We make no claim that the results presented here represent all of the important results in the theory of string-rewriting systems. However, we do think that the results developed in Chapters 1–4 are the principal results to be understood if one is to use results about string-rewriting systems to investigate more general rewriting systems, particularly term-rewriting systems, and their application to automated deduction and to the study of algorithmic problems of algebraic structures.

We recommend that on first reading the reader devote her/his attention to Section 1.1 and Chapters 2, 3, and 4 in that order. Section 1.2 is not needed until Section 3.6. Sections 1.3 and 1.4 should be referred to only as needed. Chapters 5, 6, and 7 depend on Chapter 4 and can be read independently of each other.

1

Preliminaries

In this chapter we present basic notions on which the entire monograph is based. In the first section we consider rewriting in the abstract sense, discussing the idea of a set of objects with a binary relation that illustrates the properties that rewriting relations should have. It is in this setting that notions such as "confluence" are introduced, and this chapter is essential for the remainder of the book. It should be the first section to be read carefully. Since the second section extends the first but is aimed at material that is not needed until 3.6, the reader is advised to wait until Section 3.6 is reached before addressing Section 1.2. In Section 1.3 we describe basic properties of strings, languages, and automata (with which we anticipate that the reader is familiar), and this section should be referred to only as needed. This chapter closes with a description of some basic Turing machine constructions, which again should be referred to only as needed.

1.1   Abstract Reduction Systems

In mathematics it is sometimes the case that ideas are most easily understood when explained in an abstract setting. This appears to be true in the case of reduction and replacement systems. There have been several such studies; we have chosen to follow the approach of Huet.

Notation 1.1.1 *Let* $\mathbf{B}$ *be a set of objects and let* $\to$ *be a binary relation on* $\mathbf{B}$. *Let* $\to^{-1}$ *be the inverse of* $\to$, *and let* $\circ$ *denote composition of relations.*

(a) $\overset{0}{\to}$ *is the identity relation.*

(b) $\overset{n}{\to} = \to \circ \overset{n-1}{\to}$ *for* $n > 0$.

(c) $\overset{*}{\to} = \bigcup_{n \geq 0} \overset{n}{\to}$ *and* $\overset{+}{\to} = \bigcup_{n > 0} \overset{n}{\to}$.

(d) $\leftrightarrow = \to \cup \to^{-1}$.

(e) $\overset{0}{\leftrightarrow}$ *is the identity relation.*

(f) $\overset{n}{\leftrightarrow} = \leftrightarrow \circ \overset{n-1}{\leftrightarrow}$ *for* $n > 0$.

(g) $\overset{+}{\longleftrightarrow} = \bigcup_{n > 0} \overset{n}{\leftrightarrow}$ *and* $\overset{*}{\longleftrightarrow} = \bigcup_{n \geq 0} \overset{n}{\leftrightarrow}$.

The relation $\overset{*}{\to}$ is reflexive and transitive, and the relation $\overset{*}{\longleftrightarrow}$ is an equivalence relation on **B**. In fact, it is the smallest equivalence relation on **B** that contains $\to$.

Definition 1.1.2 *Let* **B** *be a set of objects and let* $\to$ *be a binary relation on* **B**.

(a) *The structure* $S = (\mathbf{B}, \to)$ *is a* **reduction system** *and the relation* $\to$ *is the* **reduction relation**.

(b) *If* $x \in$ **B** *and there is no* $y \in$ **B** *such that* $x \to y$, *then* x *is* **irreducible**; *otherwise,* x *is* **reducible**. *The set of all irreducible elements of* **B** *with respect to* $\to$ *is denoted* $IRR(S)$.

Definition 1.1.3 *Let* $(\mathbf{B}, \to)$ *be a reduction system. If* x, $y \in$ **B** *and* $x \overset{*}{\to} y$, *then* x *is an* **ancestor** *of* y *and* y *is a* **descendant** *of* x. *If* x, $y \in$ **B** *and* $x \overset{*}{\longleftrightarrow} y$, *then* x *and* y *are* **equivalent**.

(a) The **common ancestor problem** for $(\mathbf{B}, \to)$ is the following:

   Instance: x and y in **B**.

   Question: does there exist $w \in$ **B** such that w is an ancestor of both x and y?

(b) The **common descendant problem** for $(\mathbf{B}, \to)$ is the following:

   Instance: x and y in **B**.

   Question: does there exist $z \in$ **B** such that z is a descendant of both x and y?

(c) The **word problem** for $(\mathbf{B}, \to)$ is the following:

   Instance: x and y in **B**.

   Question: are x and y equivalent under $\overset{*}{\longleftrightarrow}$?

Notation 1.1.4 *Let* $(\mathbf{B}, \to)$ *be a reduction system.*

(a) For each $x \in$ **B**, let $\Delta(x) = \{y \mid x \to y\}$, $\Delta^+(x) = \{y \mid x \overset{+}{\to} y\}$, and $\Delta^*(x) = \{y \mid x \overset{*}{\to} y\}$. Thus, $\Delta^*(x)$ is the set of descendants of x. For each $A \subseteq$ **B**, let $\Delta(A) = \cup_{x \in A}\Delta(x)$, $\Delta^+(A) = \cup_{x \in A}\Delta^+(x)$, and $\Delta^*(A) = \cup_{x \in A}\Delta^*(x)$.

(b) For each $x \in$ **B**, let $\nabla(x) = \{y \mid y \to x\}$, $\nabla^+(x) = \{y \mid y \overset{+}{\to} x\}$, and $\nabla^*(x) = \{y \mid y \overset{*}{\to} x\}$. Thus, $\nabla^*(x)$ is the set of ancestors of x. For each $A \subseteq$ **B**, let $\nabla(A) = \cup_{x \in A}\nabla(x)$, $\nabla^+(A) = \cup_{x \in A}\nabla^+(x)$, and $\nabla^*(A) = \cup_{x \in A}\nabla^*(x)$.

(c) For each $x \in \mathbf{B}$, let $[x] = \{y \mid y \stackrel{*}{\longleftrightarrow} x\}$ so that $[x]$ is the equivalence class of x. For each $A \subseteq \mathbf{B}$, let $[A] = \cup_{x \in A}[x]$.

Thue discussed the notion of rewriting systems for strings. Furthermore, he wanted to deal with graphs and trees instead of only strings and wanted to investigate algorithms to deal with very general notions of combinatorial objects that today we would consider to be data structures. In theoretical computer science it has become clear that operations such as "delete" or "insert" play an important role when considering a variety of data structures, such as graphs and trees. One would like to have a formal calculus in order to decide questions such as the common ancestor problem, the common descendant problem, or the word problem. In general these problems are undecidable; we will see a specific case of the undecidability of the word problem in the next chapter. However, there are situations where some of these questions are decidable; in many of these situations, certain notions of "normal form" play a significant role and we will develop such things here.

Definition 1.1.5 *Let* $(\mathbf{B}, \rightarrow)$ *be a reduction system. For* $x, y \in \mathbf{B}$, *if* $x \stackrel{*}{\longleftrightarrow} y$ *and* y *is irreducible, then* y *is a* **normal form** *for* x.

Suppose that for every object in $\mathbf{B}$ there is a unique normal form. Then for every x, $y \in \mathbf{B}$, $x \stackrel{*}{\longleftrightarrow} y$ if and only if the normal form of x is identically equal to the normal form of y. Suppose that, in addition, there is an algorithm that allows one to compute for every given $w \in \mathbf{B}$ the unique normal form in $[w]$, and that there is an algorithm to determine whether two objects are identically equal. Then there is an algorithm to decide the word problem. This fact provides the motivation for much of our approach.

Now we consider conditions that guarantee the existence of unique normal forms in the abstract setting.

Definition 1.1.6 *Let* $S = (\mathbf{B}, \rightarrow)$ *be a reduction system.*

(a) S *is* **confluent** *if for all* w, x, $y \in \mathbf{B}$, $w \stackrel{*}{\rightarrow} x$ *and* $w \stackrel{*}{\rightarrow} y$ *imply that there exists a* $z \in \mathbf{B}$, $x \stackrel{*}{\rightarrow} z$ *and* $y \stackrel{*}{\rightarrow} z$.

(b) S *is* **locally confluent** *if for all* w, x, $y \in \mathbf{B}$, $w \rightarrow x$ *and* $w \rightarrow y$ *imply that there exists a* $z \in \mathbf{B}$, $x \stackrel{*}{\rightarrow} z$ *and* $y \stackrel{*}{\rightarrow} z$.

(c) S *has the* **Church-Rosser property** *if for all* $x, y \in \mathbf{B}$, *if* $x \stackrel{*}{\longleftrightarrow} y$, *there exists a* $z \in \mathbf{B}$, *such that* $x \stackrel{*}{\rightarrow} z$ *and* $y \stackrel{*}{\rightarrow} z$.

Thus, a system has the Church-Rosser property if the word problem is equivalent to the common descendant problem. Frequently, we will say that a system "is Church-Rosser" when we mean that it has the Church-Rosser property.

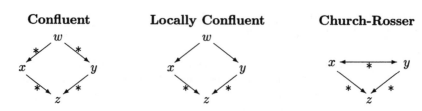

Confluent   **Locally Confluent**   **Church-Rosser**

Lemma 1.1.7 *Let $S = (\mathbf{B}, \rightarrow)$ be a reduction system. Then S is Church-Rosser if and only if it is confluent.*

Proof. It is trivial that every Church-Rosser system is confluent. Thus, assume that $S = (\mathbf{B}, \rightarrow)$ is confluent. We must show that for every x, $y \in \mathbf{B}$, if $x \overset{*}{\longleftrightarrow} y$, then there exists $z \in \mathbf{B}$ such that $x \overset{*}{\rightarrow} z$ and $y \overset{*}{\rightarrow} z$. We proceed by induction on the number n of applications of $\leftrightarrow$ used in obtaining $x \overset{*}{\longleftrightarrow} y$.

If $x \overset{0}{\longleftrightarrow} y$, then $x = y$, so let $z = x = y$.

Assume that for all choices of x, $y \in \mathbf{B}$ and for some $n \geq 0$, if $x \overset{n}{\longleftrightarrow} y$, then there exists $z \in \mathbf{B}$ such that $x \overset{*}{\rightarrow} z$ and $y \overset{*}{\rightarrow} z$. Consider x, $y \in \mathbf{B}$ such that $x \overset{n+1}{\longleftrightarrow} y$. Then there exists $x_1 \in \mathbf{B}$ such that $x \longleftrightarrow x_1 \overset{n}{\longleftrightarrow} y$, and so the induction hypothesis implies that $x_1 \overset{*}{\rightarrow} z_1$ and $y \overset{*}{\rightarrow} z_1$ for some $z_1 \in \mathbf{B}$. If $x \rightarrow x_1$, then $x \overset{*}{\rightarrow} z_1$, so let $z = z_1$. If $x \leftarrow x_1$, then S being confluent implies that there exists $z \in \mathbf{B}$ such that $x \overset{*}{\rightarrow} z$ and $z_1 \overset{*}{\rightarrow} z$. Since $\overset{*}{\rightarrow}$ is transitive, $y \overset{*}{\rightarrow} z_1$ and $z_1 \overset{*}{\rightarrow} z$ imply that $y \overset{*}{\rightarrow} z$.

Proof of Lemma 1.1.7 when $x \leftarrow x_1$ □1.1.7

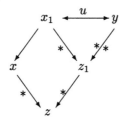

Corollary 1.1.8 *Let $S = (\mathbf{B}, \rightarrow)$ be a reduction system that is confluent. Then for each $x \in \mathbf{B}$, $[x]$ has at most one normal form.*

This result guarantees that in reduction systems that are Church-Rosser, normal forms will be unique when they exist. Now we consider conditions under which normal forms are guaranteed to exist.

Definition 1.1.9 *Let $(\mathbf{B}, \rightarrow)$ be a reduction system. The relation $\rightarrow$ is* **noetherian** *if there is no infinite sequence $x_0, x_1, \ldots \in \mathbf{B}$ such that for all $i \geq 0, x_i \rightarrow x_{i+1}$.*

Lemma 1.1.10 *Let* $(\mathbf{B}, \rightarrow)$ *be a reduction system. If* $\rightarrow$ *is noetherian, then for every* $x \in B$, $[x]$ *has a normal form.*

Proof. If x is irreducible, then x is a normal form for $[x]$. If not, there is a y such that $x \rightarrow y$. Thus, there is a sequence $y_0, y_1, y_2, \ldots$ such that $y_0 = x$ and $y_i \rightarrow y_{i+1}$. Since $\rightarrow$ is noetherian, this sequence is finite and there is some k such that y_k is irreducible. Since $x \xrightarrow{*} y_k$, y_k is a normal form for $[x]$.   □1.1.10

In our study of string-rewriting systems, the definition of reduction will satisfy the properties (1) of being acyclic and (2) being such that for every $x, \Delta^*(x)$ is finite. It is left to the reader to show that these conditions are sufficient to show that the reduction is noetherian.

Combining the conditions of being confluent and noetherian yields an important property.

Definition 1.1.11 *If* $S = (\mathbf{B}, \rightarrow)$ *is a reduction system such that* S *is confluent and* $\rightarrow$ *is noetherian, then* S *is* **convergent**.

Theorem 1.1.12 *Let* $S = (\mathbf{B}, \rightarrow)$ *be a reduction system. If* S *is convergent, then for every* $x \in \mathbf{B}$, $[x]$ *has a unique normal form.*

In general, it is undecidable whether a reduction system is confluent. However, if the reduction itself is noetherian, then there is a necessary and sufficient condition that is quite useful.

Theorem 1.1.13 *Let* $S = (\mathbf{B}, \rightarrow)$ *be a reduction system. Suppose that* $\rightarrow$ *is noetherian. Then* S *is confluent if and only if* S *is locally confluent.*

To prove Theorem 1.1.13 we depend on the notion of "noetherian induction."

Definition 1.1.14 *Let* $S = (\mathbf{B}, \rightarrow)$ *be a reduction system. For any predicate* P *on* $\mathbf{B}$, P *is* $\rightarrow$**-complete** *if for every* $x \in \mathbf{B}$ *the following implication holds: if* $P(y)$ *is true for every* $y \in \Delta(x)$, *then* $P(x)$ *is true.*

Notice that if P is $\rightarrow$-complete, then for every normal form x, $P(x)$ is true since $\Delta(x)$ is empty.

Theorem 1.1.15 *Let* $S = (\mathbf{B}, \rightarrow)$ *be a reduction system such that* $\rightarrow$ *is noetherian. If* P *is a predicate that is* $\rightarrow$*-complete, then for all* $x \in \mathbf{B}$, $P(x)$ *is true.*

Proof. Let $A = \{x \in \mathbf{B} \mid P(x) \text{ is true}\}$. If $A \neq \mathbf{B}$, consider any $y \in \mathbf{B} - A$ with the property that there is no $z \in \mathbf{B} - A$ such that $y \rightarrow z$; such a y will exist since $A \neq \mathbf{B}$ and $\rightarrow$ is noetherian. Since $y \in \mathbf{B} - A$, y is not a normal form, and so $\Delta(y)$ is not empty. But $\Delta(y) \subseteq A$ by choice of y.

Since P is $\to$-**complete**, $\Delta(y) \subseteq A$ implies $y \in A$, contrary to the choice of $y \in \mathbf{B} - A$. Hence, $\mathbf{B} - A$ is empty. $\square$1.1.15

Theorem 1.1.15 is a version of the "principle of noetherian induction."
Now let us return to Theorem 1.1.13.

Proof of Theorem 1.1.13

That confluence implies local confluence is trivial. Conversely, assume that $S = (\mathbf{B}, \to)$ is locally confluent and that $\to$ is noetherian.

Let $P(x)$ be the predicate that is true if and only if for all $y, z \in \mathbf{B}$, $x \overset{*}{\to} y$ and $x \overset{*}{\to} z$ imply that for some $w \in \mathbf{B}$, $y \overset{*}{\to} w$ and $z \overset{*}{\to} w$. If we show that P is $\to$-complete, then we have our result by means of noetherian induction.

Choose $x \in \mathbf{B}$ arbitrarily. We must show that $P(x)$ holds if $P(y)$ holds for all $y \in \Delta(x)$. Suppose that there exist $y, z \in \mathbf{B}$ such that $x \overset{*}{\to} y$ and $x \overset{*}{\to} z$. If $x = y$ or $x = z$ or $y = z$, then the result follows trivially. Otherwise, let $x \overset{m}{\to} y$ and $x \overset{n}{\to} z$ with $m, n > 0$. Thus, for some $y_1, z_1 \in \mathbf{B}$, $x \overset{1}{\to} y_1 \overset{m-1}{\to} y$ and $x \overset{1}{\to} z_1 \overset{n-1}{\to} z$. Since S is locally confluent, if $x \overset{1}{\to} y_1$ and $x \overset{1}{\to} z_1$, then there exist $u \in \mathbf{B}$ such that $y_1 \overset{*}{\to} u$ and $z_1 \overset{*}{\to} u$.

Since $x \overset{1}{\to} y_1$ and $x \overset{1}{\to} z_1, y_1, z_1 \in \Delta(x)$ and so we may assume that $P(y_1)$ and $P(z_1)$ hold. Thus, $y_1 \overset{*}{\to} y$ and $y_1 \overset{*}{\to} u$ imply that for some $v \in \mathbf{B}$, $y \overset{*}{\to} v$ and $u \overset{*}{\to} v$ since $P(y_1)$ holds. Since $\overset{*}{\to}$ is transitive, $z_1 \overset{*}{\to} u$ and $u \overset{*}{\to} v$ imply that $z_1 \overset{*}{\to} v$. Thus, $z_1 \overset{*}{\to} v$ and $z_1 \overset{*}{\to} z$, implying that for some $w \in \mathbf{B}$, $v \overset{*}{\to} w$ and $z \overset{*}{\to} w$ since $P(z_1)$ holds. Since $\overset{*}{\to}$ is transitive, $y \overset{*}{\to} v$ and $v \overset{*}{\to} w$ imply $y \overset{*}{\to} w$. This yields $y \overset{*}{\to} w$ and $z \overset{*}{\to} w$, as desired.

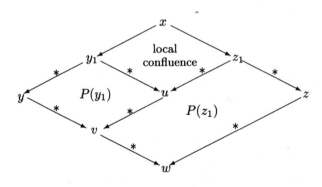

$\square$1.1.13

Corollary 1.1.16 *Let $S = (\mathbf{B}, \to)$ be a reduction system. Suppose that $\overset{+}{\to}$ is acyclic and for every $x \in \mathbf{B}$, $\Delta^*(x)$ is finite. Then S is confluent if and only if S is locally confluent.*

The result of Corollary 1.1.16 will be an important tool in our study of string-rewriting systems. Often the notion of reduction will depend on reduction of the length of strings so that for every x, $\Delta^*(x)$ will be finite.

With this notion of reduction, the property of being (locally) confluent is decidable (in fact, tractable) for finite string-rewriting systems as we shall see in Chapter 2.

1.2   Reduction Modulo an Equivalence Relation

Consider the situation that we have a reduction system $S = (\mathbf{B}, \rightarrow)$ together with an equivalence relation $\approx$ on $\mathbf{B}$ which is not assumed to be compatible with $\rightarrow$, that is, for $x, y \in \mathbf{B}$, $x \approx y$ does not necessarily imply that $x \xleftrightarrow{*} y$. Then the relations $\rightarrow$ and $\approx$ can be seen as two different parts of a generating set for the combined relation $\equiv \; : = (\longleftrightarrow \cup \approx)^*$, that is, $\equiv$ is the least equivalence relation on $\mathbf{B}$ containing both $\rightarrow$ and $\approx$. Now this combined relation $\equiv$ might be much too complicated to be dealt with directly. In this situation we would try to consider the relations $\rightarrow$ and $\approx$ separately. For doing so the following notions are important.

Definition 1.2.1 *Let $S = (\mathbf{B}, \rightarrow)$ be a reduction system, let $\approx$ be an equivalence relation on $\mathbf{B}$, and let $\equiv = (\longleftrightarrow \cup \approx)^*$.*

(a) We say that $\rightarrow$ is **Church-Rosser modulo** $\approx$ if for all $x, y \in \mathbf{B}$, $x \equiv y$ implies that for some $\overline{x}, \overline{y} \in \mathbf{B}$, $x \xrightarrow{*} \overline{x}$ and $y \xrightarrow{*} \overline{y}$ and $\overline{x} \approx \overline{y}$.

(b) We say that $\rightarrow$ is **confluent modulo** $\approx$ if for all $x, y, x', y' \in \mathbf{B}$, $x \approx y$ and $x \xrightarrow{*} x'$ and $y \xrightarrow{*} y'$ imply that for some $\overline{x}, \overline{y} \in \mathbf{B}$, $x' \xrightarrow{*} \overline{x}$ and $y' \xrightarrow{*} \overline{y}$ and $\overline{x} \approx \overline{y}$.

Church-Rosser modulo $\approx$ **confluence modulo** $\approx$

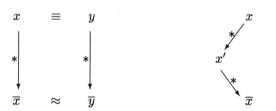

The Church-Rosser property modulo $\approx$ states that the relation $\equiv$ can be reduced to the equivalence relation $\approx$ by using the reduction relation $\rightarrow$. In fact, under a slight restriction on the reduction relation $\rightarrow$ the above two notions coincide.

Lemma 1.2.2 *Let $S = (\mathbf{B}, \rightarrow)$ be a reduction system and let $\approx$ be an equivalence relation on $\mathbf{B}$. Suppose that for every $x \in \mathbf{B}$ there exists a normal form y such that $x \xrightarrow{*} y$. Let $\equiv = (\leftrightarrow \cup \approx)^*$. Then $\rightarrow$ is confluent modulo $\approx$ if and only if the following condition holds: (*) for every $x, y \in \mathbf{B}$ and every irreducible u and v, if $x \equiv y$ and $x \xrightarrow{*} u$ and $y \xrightarrow{*} v$, then $u \approx v$.*

Proof. The reader should note that $\equiv$ is an equivalence relation since it is the reflexive, transitive closure of the relation $\leftrightarrow \cup \approx$ which is symmetric (but is not necessarily an equivalence relation). The proof that condition (*) holds if $\rightarrow$ is confluent modulo $\approx$ follows immediately from the definitions. For the proof in the other direction, it suffices to notice that if $x \equiv y$, $x \overset{*}{\rightarrow} x'$, and $y \overset{*}{\rightarrow} y'$, then there exist normal forms u and v such that $x' \overset{*}{\rightarrow} u$ and $y' \overset{*}{\rightarrow} v$. Hence, from (*) we can conclude that $u \approx v$.   □1.2.2

Notice that the requirement about normal forms in Lemma 1.2.2 is satisfied if $\rightarrow$ is noetherian.

In certain applications we want to be able to test a system for the property of being confluent modulo some specific equivalence relation. This is a very difficult, if not impossible, task to perform if one attempts to approach the problem on a global basis. Thus, we introduce a property similar to "local confluence."

Condition α   **Condition β**

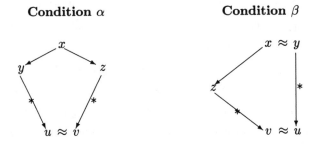

Definition 1.2.3 *Let $S = (\mathbf{B}, \rightarrow)$ be a reduction system and let $\approx$ be an equivalence relation on $\mathbf{B}$. The relation $\rightarrow$ is **locally confluent modulo** $\approx$ if each of the following conditions is satisfied:*

α: *for every $x, y, z \in \mathbf{B}$, if $x \rightarrow y$ and $x \rightarrow z$, then there exist u, v such that $y \overset{*}{\rightarrow} u$, $z \overset{*}{\rightarrow} v$, and $u \approx v$;*

β: *for every $x, y, z \in \mathbf{B}$, if $x \approx y$ and $x \rightarrow z$, then there exist u, v such that $y \overset{*}{\rightarrow} u$, $z \overset{*}{\rightarrow} v$, and $u \approx v$.*

We will prove the following result:

Lemma 1.2.4 *Let $S = (\mathbf{B}, \rightarrow)$ be a reduction system and let $\approx$ be an equivalence relation on $\mathbf{B}$. Suppose that $\rightarrow$ is noetherian. Then $\rightarrow$ is confluent modulo $\approx$ if and only if it is locally confluent modulo $\approx$.*

To prove Lemma 1.2.4 we define a relation $\Rightarrow$ on $\mathbf{B}^2 = \mathbf{B} \times \mathbf{B}$ based on the reduction $\rightarrow$. Define the following:

(a) $(x, y) \Rightarrow_a (x', y')$ if $x \rightarrow x'$ and $y = y'$;

(b) $(x, y) \Rightarrow_b (x', y')$ if $x \rightarrow x'$ and $x \rightarrow y'$;

(c) $(x,y) \Rightarrow_c (x',y')$ if $x = x'$ and $y \rightarrow y'$;

(d) $(x,y) \Rightarrow_d (x',y')$ if $y \rightarrow x'$ and $y \rightarrow y'$;

(e) $\Rightarrow_e = \Rightarrow_a \cup \Rightarrow_b$;

(f) $\Rightarrow_f = \Rightarrow_c \cup \Rightarrow_d$.

Then define $\Rightarrow$ as $\Rightarrow_e \cup \Rightarrow_f$.

It will be useful to show the following:

Claim. If $\rightarrow$ is noetherian, then $\Rightarrow$ is noetherian.

Proof. Since $\rightarrow$ is noetherian, $\xrightarrow{+}$ is a well-founded partial ordering on $\mathbf{B}$, that is, $\xrightarrow{+}$ does not admit an infinite descending sequence of the form $x_0 \xrightarrow{+} x_1 \xrightarrow{+} \ldots$. On $\mathbf{B}^2$ consider the multi-set ordering $\gg$ induced by $\xrightarrow{+}$, that is, $(x,y) \gg (x',y')$ if and only if $\exists U \subseteq \{x,y\}$ such that $U \neq \emptyset$ and $\exists V \subseteq \{x',y'\}$ such that $\{x',y'\} = (\{x,y\} - U) \cup V$, and for each $v \in V$ there is some $u \in U$ such that $u \xrightarrow{+} v$. Then $(x,y) \Rightarrow (x',y')$ obviously implies that $(x,y) \gg (x',y')$. Since $\xrightarrow{+}$ is well-founded, so is $\gg$, and hence, $\Rightarrow$ is noetherian. $\qquad\qquad \Box$Claim.

Proof of Lemma 1.2.4 Let $S = (\mathbf{B}, \rightarrow)$ be a reduction system and let $\approx$ be an equivalence relation on $\mathbf{B}$. Suppose that $\rightarrow$ is noetherian. If $\rightarrow$ is confluent modulo $\approx$, then certainly $\rightarrow$ is locally confluent modulo $\approx$; it is the converse that must be shown.

Let $\rightarrow$ be locally confluent modulo $\approx$. Let P be the property defined for $(x,y) \in \mathbf{B}^2$ as follows: $P(x,y)$ if and only if $x \approx y$ implies [for all x', y', if $x \xrightarrow{*} x'$ and $y \xrightarrow{*} y'$, then there exist u,v such that $x' \xrightarrow{*} u$, $y' \xrightarrow{*} v$, and $u \approx v$]. We show that P is $\Rightarrow$-complete. Let $x,y,x',y' \in \mathbf{B}$ be such that $x \approx y$, $x \xrightarrow{n} x'$, and $y \xrightarrow{m} y'$. We will show the existence of $\overline{x},\overline{y}$ such that $x' \xrightarrow{*} \overline{x}$, $y' \xrightarrow{*} \overline{y}$, and $\overline{x} \approx \overline{y}$.

If $n = 0$ or $m = 0$, then the result is trivial, so we assume without loss of generality that $n \neq 0$. Thus, for some $x_1 \in \mathbf{B}$, we have $x \rightarrow x_1 \xrightarrow{*} x'$. By hypothesis $\rightarrow$ is locally confluent modulo $\approx$ so that, in particular, property β holds. Since $x \approx y$ and $x \rightarrow x_1$, there exist u and v such that $x_1 \xrightarrow{*} u$, $y \xrightarrow{*} v$, and $u \approx v$. We consider two cases based on the value of m.

Case 1. $m = 0$.

We have $x \approx y = y'$, $x \rightarrow x_1 \xrightarrow{*} u$, $x \rightarrow x_1 \xrightarrow{*} x'$, $y \xrightarrow{*} v$, and $u \approx v$. Since $x_1 \in \Delta(x)$, we have $(x,y) \Rightarrow (x_1,x_1)$ so that $P(x_1,x_1)$ holds by the induction hypothesis. Let $\overline{x}'$ be an irreducible descendant of x' and let $\overline{u}$ be an irreducible descendant of u ($\overline{x}'$ and $\overline{u}$ must exist since $\rightarrow$ is noetherian). By $P(x_1,x_1)$, $x_1 \approx x_1$ implies $\overline{x}' \approx \overline{u}$ since both of these strings are irreducible. Similarly, since $u \in \Delta^+(x)$, $P(u,v)$ holds by the induction hypothesis. Thus, if $\overline{v}$ is an irreducible descendant of v, then $\overline{u} \approx \overline{v}$. Since $\overline{x}'$ and $\overline{v}$ are irreducible, $x' \xrightarrow{*} \overline{x}'$, $y = y' \xrightarrow{*} \overline{v}$, and $\overline{x}' \approx \overline{u} \approx \overline{v}$, we have $P(x,y)$.

Case 2. $m > 0$. Let y_1 be such that $y \rightarrow y_1 \xrightarrow{m-1} y'$.

There are two subcases.

subcase 2.1. $v = y$.

Now $u \approx y$ and $y \to y_1$. By hypothesis $\to$ is locally confluent modulo $\approx$ so that property β can be applied to u, y, and y_1. Thus, there exist $w, z \in \mathbf{B}$ such that $u \overset{*}{\to} w$, $y_1 \overset{*}{\to} z$, and $z \approx w$. Since $w \in \Delta^+(x)$ and $z \in \Delta^+(y)$, the induction hypothesis applies so that $P(w, z)$ holds, and this means that $\overline{w} \approx \overline{z}$ where $\overline{w}$ is an irreducible descendant of w and $\overline{z}$ is an irreducible descendant of z. As in Case 1, we have $P(x_1, x_1)$ so that $\overline{x}' \approx \overline{w}$ is an irreducible descendant of x'. Also, notice that $P(y_1, y_1)$ holds since $y_1 \in \Delta(y)$, so that $\overline{y}' \approx \overline{z}$ where $\overline{y}'$ is an irreducible descendant of y'. Thus, $\overline{x}' \approx \overline{w} \approx \overline{z} \approx \overline{y}'$.

subcase 2.2. $v \neq y$.

Let t be such that $y \to t \overset{*}{\to} v$. By hypothesis $\to$ is locally confluent modulo $\approx$ so that property α can be applied to y, y_1 and t. Thus, there exist w, z such that $t \overset{*}{\to} w$, $y_1 \overset{*}{\to} z$, and $w \approx z$. As in the other cases we apply the induction hypotheses $P(x_1, x_1)$, $P(u, v)$, $P(t, t)$, $P(w, z)$, and $P(y_1, y_1)$ so that $\overline{x}' \approx \overline{u} \approx \overline{v} \approx \overline{w} \approx \overline{z} \approx \overline{y}'$ where $\overline{x}'$, $\overline{u}$, $\overline{v}$, $\overline{w}$, $\overline{z}$, and $\overline{y}'$ are the appropriate irreducible descendants.

This completes the proof of subcase 2.2 and, hence, of Case 2.

It is clear that the induction hypothesis $P(\ ,\ )$ was applied only to pairs that were proper $\Rightarrow$ descendants of (x, y). Since $\Rightarrow$ is noetherian from the Claim (and the fact that $\to$ was assumed to be noetherian), Theorem 1.1.15 (noetherian induction) can be applied so that $P(x, y)$ is true for all choices of x and y. This yields the desired result.

Diagrams for the Proof of Lemma 1.2.4

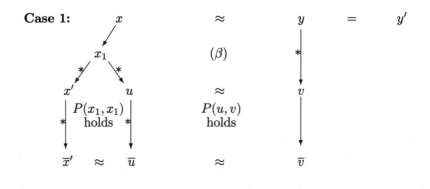

$$\overline{x}',\ \overline{u},\ \overline{v} \in \mathrm{IRR}(\to)$$

Diagrams continued

Case 2.1:

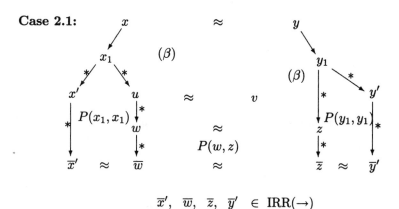

$$\overline{x}',\ \overline{w},\ \overline{z},\ \overline{y}' \in \mathrm{IRR}(\rightarrow)$$

Case 2.2:

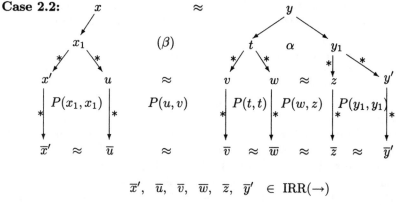

$$\overline{x}',\ \overline{u},\ \overline{v},\ \overline{w},\ \overline{z},\ \overline{y}' \in \mathrm{IRR}(\rightarrow)$$

□1.2.4

There is one additional technical tool that is most easily discussed in the abstract setting. Instead of dealing with an equivalence relation $\approx$, we wish to restrict attention to a symmetric relation, say $\vdash\!\dashv$, such that $\approx$ is the transitive, reflexive closure of $\vdash\!\dashv$. This will be useful in Section 3.6 when we consider the congruence relation on the free monoid that is generated by a given relation that is finite but symmetric.

We will prove the following result.

Lemma 1.2.5 *Let $S = (\mathbf{B}, \rightarrow)$ be a reduction system, let $\vdash\!\dashv$ be a symmetric relation on $\mathbf{B}$, and let $\approx$ be the transitive, reflexive closure of $\vdash\!\dashv$. Suppose that $\rightarrow \circ \approx$ is noetherian. Then $\rightarrow$ is confluent modulo $\approx$ if and*

Condition γ

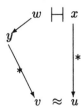

only if properties α and γ are satisfied, where property (γ) is defined as follows:

γ: *for all w, x, y, if $w \vdash x$ and $w \rightarrow y$, then there exist u, v such that $x \xrightarrow{*} u$, $y \xrightarrow{*} v$, and $u \approx v$.*

If $x \approx y$, then define $\delta(x, y)$ as the least k such that $x \overset{k}{\vdash} y$, where $\overset{k}{\vdash}$ denotes k applications of $\vdash$.

To prove Lemma 1.2.5 we define a relation $\mapsto$ on $\mathbf{B}^2$ based on the reduction $\Rightarrow$ on $\mathbf{B}^2$ and the equivalence relation $\approx$. Define the following: $(x, y) \mapsto (x', y')$ if either (i) $(x, y) \Rightarrow (x', y')$ or (ii) $x \approx y \approx x' \approx y'$ and $\delta(x, y) > \delta(x', y')$.

Since the range of δ is included in the set of natural numbers, it is easy to see that there can be no infinite chain of applications of the relation $\mapsto$ which are based only on part (ii) of the definition. Thus, we see that if $\rightarrow \circ \approx$ is noetherian, then $\rightarrow$ is confluent modulo $\approx$ if and only if properties α and γ are satisfied.

Proof of Lemma 1.2.5 It is clear that if $\rightarrow$ is confluent modulo $\approx$, then properties α and γ are satisfied so it is the converse that must be shown. We use noetherian induction on $\mathbf{B}^2$ by showing that the predicate P is $\mapsto$ complete where $P(x, y)$ holds if $x \approx y$ implies that [for all x', y', if $x \xrightarrow{*} x'$ and $y \xrightarrow{*} y'$, then there exist u, v such that $x' \xrightarrow{*} u$, $y' \xrightarrow{*} v$, and $u \approx v$].

Let $x, y, x', y' \in \mathbf{B}$ be such that $x \approx y$, $x \xrightarrow{n} x'$, and $y \xrightarrow{m} y'$.

Case 1. $x = y$.

If $n = 0$ or $m = 0$, then the proof is trivial. If $n > 0$ and $m > 0$, let u and v be such that $x \rightarrow u \xrightarrow{*} x'$ and $y \rightarrow v \xrightarrow{*} y'$. Since $x = y$, we can apply property α to x, u, and v; thus, there exist w and z such that $u \xrightarrow{*} w$, $v \xrightarrow{*} z$, and $w \approx z$. Since u, v, w, and z are proper descendants of $x(= y)$, the induction hypothesis applies to pairs chosen appropriately from this collection of four elements. Let $\overline{x}'$, $\overline{w}$, $\overline{z}$, and $\overline{y}'$ be irreducible descendants of x', w, z, and y' respectively. Applying the induction hypotheses $P(u, u)$, $P(w, z)$, and $P(v, v)$ just as in the proof of Lemma 1.2.4, we obtain $\overline{x}' \approx \overline{w} \approx \overline{z} \approx \overline{y}'$.

Case 2. $x \neq y$ so that $\delta(x, y) > 0$.

If $n = 0$ and $m = 0$, then $x' = x \approx y = y'$. If not, assume that $n > 0$ so there exists u such that $x \to u \xrightarrow{*} x'$. Let v be such that $x \mathrel{\mathpalette\@mathbin{|}} v \approx y$ with $\delta(v, y) = \delta(x, y) - 1$. Property γ can be applied to x, v, and u to obtain w and z such that $u \xrightarrow{*} w$, $v \xrightarrow{*} z$, and $w \approx z$. The induction hypotheses $P(u, u)$, $P(w, z)$, and $P(v, y)$ are applicable so that (just as in Case 1) we obtain $\overline{x}' \approx \overline{w} \approx \overline{z} \approx \overline{y}'$ where $\overline{x}', \overline{w}, \overline{z}$, and $\overline{y}'$ are irreducible descendants of x', w, z, and y' respectively.

Diagrams for the Proof of Lemma 1.2.5

Case 1:

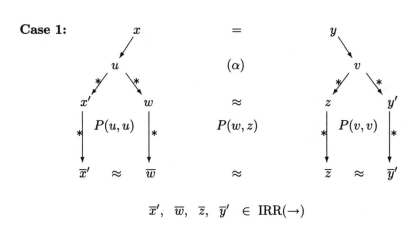

$$\overline{x}', \ \overline{w}, \ \overline{z}, \ \overline{y}' \ \in \ \mathrm{IRR}(\to)$$

Case 2:

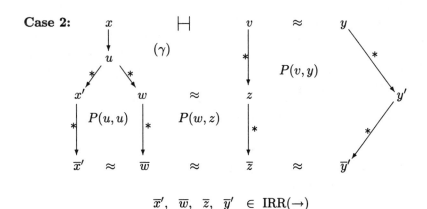

$$\overline{x}', \ \overline{w}, \ \overline{z}, \ \overline{y}' \ \in \ \mathrm{IRR}(\to)$$

□1.2.5

1.3   Strings, Languages and Automata

Here we give formal definitions of strings, languages, automata, etc., and establish notation. There is nothing new in this section; its purpose is to state the starting point for the reader.

For any set Σ of symbols, Σ^* denotes the set of all strings of symbols over Σ, including the empty string e. Thus, Σ^* denotes the free monoid generated by Σ under the operation of concatenation with the empty string serving as identity. In this setting, Σ is called the "alphabet." Sometimes it is useful to refer to the set Σ^*-$\{e\}$, and this set will be denoted by Σ^+, that is, Σ^+ denotes the set of nonempty strings in Σ^*.

If $w \in \Sigma^*$, then the **length** of w, denoted $|w|$, is defined as follows: $|e| := 0$, $|a| := 1$ for each $a \in \Sigma$, and $|wa| := |w| + 1$ for $w \in \Sigma^*$ and $a \in \Sigma$. For each $n \in \mathcal{N}$, Σ^n denotes the set of strings of length n, that is, $\Sigma^n := \{w \in \Sigma^* \mid |w| = n\}$. If $w \in \Sigma^*$ and $a \in \Sigma$, the **a-length** of w is defined to be the number of occurrences of the letter a in w and is denoted by $|w|_a$. Also, $\mathrm{alph}(w) := \{a \in \Sigma \mid |w|_a \geq 1\}$.

To simplify notation strings are sometimes written using exponents: for $w \in \Sigma^*$, $w^0 := e$, $w^1 := w$, and $w^{n+1} := ww^n$ for $n \geq 1$. In addition, w^R denotes the **reversal** of w : $e^R := e$, $a^R := a$, and $(wa)^R := aw^R$ for $w \in \Sigma^*$ and $a \in \Sigma$. The operation of concatenation conc: $\Sigma^* \times \Sigma^* \to \Sigma^*$, $\mathrm{conc}(u,v) := uv$, can be extended to subsets of Σ^*: if $A, B \subseteq \Sigma^*$, then the concatenation of A and B, denoted AB, is the set $\{uv \mid u \in A, \ v \in B\}$. Furthermore, if $A \subseteq \Sigma^*$, then we define $A^0 := \{e\}$, $A^1 := A$, $A^{n+1} := AA^n$ for $n \geq 1$, $A^+ := \bigcup_{i \geq 1} A^i$, and $A^* := \bigcup_{i \geq 0} A^i$.

It is clear that if $A \subseteq \Sigma^*$, then A^* is the submonoid of Σ^* generated by A, that is, $A^* = \{u_1 u_2 \ldots u_n \mid n \geq 1, \ u_1, u_2, \ldots, u_n \in A\} \cup \{e\}$. Recall that if Σ is a finite alphabet, then the class $REG(\Sigma)$ of regular subsets of Σ^* is the smallest class of subsets of Σ^* that contains the finite subsets and that is closed under the operations of union, concatenation, and star (*).

Since the subsets of Σ^* are also called (formal) languages on Σ, the above is a characterization of the class of regular languages on Σ. We shall encounter regular languages over and over again in the following. We give an additional characterization of this class and fix notation. (For details the reader is asked to consult a book on formal language theory.)

Definition 1.3.1

(a) *A* **finite state acceptor** *$\mathcal{A}$ is specified by a 5-tuple $\mathcal{A} = (Q, \Sigma, \delta, q_0, F)$, where*

  Q is a finite set, the elements of which are called states,

  Σ is a finite alphabet (the input or tape alphabet),

  $\delta : Q \times \Sigma \to 2^Q$ is the transition relation,

$q_0 \in Q$ is the initial state, and

$F \subseteq Q$ is the set of accepting states.

(b) *The transition relation $\delta : Q \times \Sigma \to 2^Q$ of a finite state acceptor $\mathcal{A}$ can be extended to $Q \times \Sigma^*$ as follows:*

$$\delta(q, e) \;=\; \{q\},$$
$$\delta(q, wa) \;=\; \cup_{p \in \delta(q,w)} \delta(p, a).$$

(c) *A string $w \in \Sigma^*$ is accepted by $\mathcal{A}$ if $\delta(q_0, w) \cap F \neq \emptyset$. The language $L(\mathcal{A}) := \{w \in \Sigma^* \mid w$ is accepted by $\mathcal{A}\}$ is called the **language accepted by $\mathcal{A}$**.*

If $q \in Q$ and $a \in \Sigma$, then $\delta(q, a)$ is the set of states that $\mathcal{A}$ can reach from q reading a. Thus, if $|\delta(q, a)| > 1$, then $\mathcal{A}$ has several possible moves in this situation. Hence, finite state acceptors as defined above are nondeterministic automata, and therefore they are also called **nondeterministic** finite state acceptors (nfa).

Definition 1.3.2 *A finite state acceptor $\mathcal{D} = (Q, \Sigma, \delta, q_0, F)$ is **deterministic** if $|\delta(q, a)| = 1$ holds for all $q \in Q$ and $a \in \Sigma$, that is, δ can be written as a function $\delta : Q \times \Sigma \to Q$. Its extension to $Q \times \Sigma^*$ is defined by*

$$\delta(q, e) \;=\; q,$$
$$\delta(q, wa) \;=\; \delta(\delta(q, w), a).$$

*A string $w \in \Sigma^*$ is accepted by $\mathcal{D}$ if $\delta(q_0, w) \in F$, and the language $L(\mathcal{D}) := \{w \in \Sigma^* \mid w$ is accepted by $\mathcal{D}\}$ is called the **language accepted by $\mathcal{D}$**.*

If $q \in Q$ and $w \in \Sigma^*$, then $\delta(q, w)$ denotes the state that the deterministic finite state accceptor (dfa) $\mathcal{D}$ reaches from q reading w. The following is a fundamental result from formal language theory.

Theorem 1.3.3 *Let $L \subseteq \Sigma^*$. Then the following statements are equivalent:*

(1) *L is regular;*

(2) *there exists a nfa $\mathcal{A}$ such that L is accepted by $\mathcal{A}$;*

(3) *there exists a dfa $\mathcal{D}$ such that L is accepted by $\mathcal{D}$.*

In fact, given a nfa $\mathcal{A}$ one can effectively construct a dfa $\mathcal{D}$ such that $\mathcal{A}$ and $\mathcal{D}$ accept the same language. However, if $\mathcal{A}$ contains n states, then $\mathcal{D}$ may contain up to 2^n states, and in general constructing $\mathcal{D}$ from $\mathcal{A}$ takes time $0(2^n)$, that is, this construction is rather inefficient, and one should try to avoid it whenever possible. Finite state acceptors are very useful specifications of regular languages. Using them one can easily prove that the class of regular languages is closed under various operations like intersection and complementation. Also they allow one to solve various decision problems efficiently for this class of languages.

Theorem 1.3.4 *Each of the following problems is decidable:*

Instance: *A deterministic or nondeterministic finite-state acceptor $\mathcal{D}$*

(a) *The* **membership problem***: for a string x, is x a member of $L(\mathcal{D})$?*

(b) *The* **emptiness problem***: is $L(\mathcal{D})$ empty?*

(c) *The* **finiteness problem***: is $L(\mathcal{D})$ finite?*

The membership problem is decidable in linear time (linear in $|x|$), the emptiness problem is decidable in quadratic time (quadratic in the size of $\mathcal{D}$, that is, the length of the string of symbols that specifies $\mathcal{D}$), and the finiteness problem is decidable in cubic time (cubic in the size of $\mathcal{D}$).

Another class of languages that will be needed is the class of context-free languages. Usually context-free languages are specified by "context-free grammars," that is, a generating device, but they can also be characterized through "pushdown automata," that is, an accepting device. Here we will only be interested in the latter; therefore, we only restate this characterization.

Definition 1.3.5

(a) *A* **pushdown automaton** *(pda) $\mathcal{A}$ is specified by a 7-tuple $\mathcal{A} = (Q, \Sigma, \Gamma, \delta, q_0, \#, F)$, where*

Q *is a finite set of states,*

Σ *is a finite alphabet, the* input *alphabet,*

Γ *is a finite alphabet, the* stack *alphabet,*

$\delta: Q \times (\Sigma \cup \{e\}) \times \Gamma \to 2^{Q \times \Gamma^*}$ *is the transition function, where $\delta(q, a, b)$ is a finite set for each $q \in Q$, $a \in \Sigma \cup \{e\}$, and $b \in \Gamma$,*

$q_0 \in Q$ *is the initial state,*

$\# \in \Gamma$ *is the bottom marker of $\mathcal{A}$'s stack, and*

$F \subseteq Q$ *is the set of final (or accepting) states.*

The symbol $\#$ cannot be generated by $\mathcal{A}$, that is, if $q \in Q$, $a \in \Sigma \cup \{e\}$, $b \in \Gamma$, and $(p, z) \in \delta(q, a, b)$, then $|z|_\# = 0$ or $z \in \{\#\}(\Gamma - \{\#\})^*$ and $b = \#$.

(b) *A* **configuration** *of $\mathcal{A}$ is a triple (q, u, v), where $q \in Q$, $u \in \Sigma^*$, and $v \in (\{\#\}(\Gamma - \{\#\})^*) \cup \{e\}$. The pda $\mathcal{A}$ induces a single-step computation relation $\vdash_\mathcal{A}$ on the set of configurations.*

The reflexive and transitive closure $\overset{*}{\vdash}_{\mathcal{A}}$ *of this relation is called the* **computation relation** *induced by* $\mathcal{A}$. *If* $(q, u, v) \overset{*}{\vdash}_{\mathcal{A}} (p, x, y)$, *then* (p, x, y) *is a* **successor configuration** *of* (q, u, v).

(c) *A string* $w \in \Sigma^*$ *is accepted by* $\mathcal{A}$ *if there exist a final state* $p \in F$ *and a string* $z \in \Gamma^*$ *such that the* **final configuration** (p, e, z) *is a successor of the* **initial configuration** $(q_0, w, \#)$, *that is,* $(q_0, w, \#) \overset{*}{\vdash}_{\mathbf{A}}$ (p, e, z). *The language* $L(\mathcal{A}) := \{w \in \Sigma^* \mid w \text{ is accepted by } \mathcal{A}\}$ *is called the* **language accepted** *by* $\mathcal{A}$.

The pushdown automaton is obtained from the nondeterministic finite state acceptor by adding a stack (or pushdown store) as a storage device.

Definition 1.3.6 *A language* $L \subseteq \Sigma^*$ *is* **context-free** *if there exists a pda* $\mathcal{A} = (Q, \Sigma, \Gamma, \delta, q_0, \#, F)$ *that accepts exactly the language* L.

The languages $L_1 := \{a^n b^n \mid n \geq 0\}$ and $L_2 := \{ww^R \mid w \in \{a, b, c\}^*\}$ are typical examples of context-free languages, while $L_3 := \{a^n b^n c^n \mid n \geq 0\}$ is not context-free.

Definition 1.3.7 *A pda* $\mathcal{A} = (Q, \Sigma, \Gamma, \delta, q_0, \#, F)$ *is* **deterministic** *if the following two conditions are satisfied:*

(i) $\forall q \in Q \quad \forall a \in \Sigma \cup \{e\} \quad \forall b \in \Gamma : \ |\delta(q, a, b)| \leq 1$, *and*

(ii) $\forall q \in Q \quad \forall a \in \Sigma \quad \forall b \in \Gamma : \ if \ \delta(q, e, b) \neq \emptyset, \ then \ \delta(q, a, b) = \emptyset$.

Thus, if $\mathcal{A}$ is a deterministic pushdown automaton (dpda), then the induced single-step computation relation $\overset{*}{\vdash}_{\mathcal{A}}$ is a partial function.

Definition 1.3.8 *A language* $L \subseteq \Sigma^*$ *is* **deterministic context-free** *if there exists a dpda* $\mathcal{A} = (Q, \Sigma, \Gamma, \delta, q_0, \#, F)$ *that accepts exactly the language* L.

The languages $L_1 := \{a^n b^n \mid n \geq 0\}$ and $L_4 := \{wdw^R \mid w \in \{a, b, c\}^*\}$ are typical examples of deterministic context-free languages, while $L_2 := \{ww^R \mid w \in \{a, b, c\}^*\}$ is context-free but is not deterministic context-free.

To capture the notions of recursive and recursively enumerable languages (that is, languages for which the membership problem is effectively decidable and languages that can be effectively enumerated) we consider a more general type of automaton, the Turing machine. Finite state acceptors and pushdown automata are restricted versions of Turing machines.

Definition 1.3.9

(a) *A* **Turing machine** *(TM)* $\mathcal{M}$ *is given through a 5-tuple* $\mathcal{M} = (Q, \Sigma, \delta, q_0, q_a)$, *where*

Q is a finite set of states,

Σ is a finite alphabet, the so-called input alphabet not containing the blank symbol b, and $\Sigma_b = \Sigma \cup \{b\}$ is the tape alphabet of $\mathcal{A}$,

$q_0 \in Q$ is the initial state,

$q_a \in Q$ is the halting (or accepting) state, and

$\delta : (Q - \{q_a\}) \times \Sigma_b \rightarrow (Q \times (\Sigma_b \cup \{R, L\}))$ is the transition function.

(b) A **configuration** of $\mathcal{M}$ is an element of $\Sigma_b^* \cdot Q \cdot \Sigma_b^*$, that is, it is a string of the form uqv, where $u, v \in \Sigma_b^*$ and $q \in Q$. The string uv is the **tape inscription** and q is the **state** corresponding to the configuration uqv. In an obvious way the TM $\mathcal{M}$ induces a single-step computation relation $\vdash_{\mathcal{M}}$ on the set of configurations. If $u_1 q_1 v_1 \vdash_{\mathcal{M}} u_2 q_2 v_2$, then $u_2 q_2 v_2$ is an immediate successor configuration of $u_1 q_1 v_1$. The reflexive and transitive closure $\vdash_{\mathcal{M}}^*$ of $\vdash_{\mathcal{M}}$ is called the **computation relation** of $\mathcal{M}$. If $u_1 q_1 v_1 \vdash_{\mathcal{M}}^* u_3 q_3 v_3$, then $u_3 q_3 v_3$ is a successor configuration of $u_1 q_1 v_1$. A configuration uqv is **final** (or **halting**) if it has no immediate successor configuration, that is, if $q = q_a$. For $w \in \Sigma^*$, the configuration $q_0 w$ is the **initial configuration** on input w.

(c) A string $w \in \Sigma^*$ is **accepted** by $\mathcal{M}$ if $q_0 w \vdash_{\mathcal{M}}^* u q_a v$ for some $u, v \in \Sigma_b^*$, that is, if $\mathcal{M}$ halts eventually on input w. The language $L(\mathcal{M}) := \{w \in \Sigma^* \mid w$ is accepted by $\mathcal{M}\}$ is called the **language accepted by** $\mathcal{M}$.

(d) A TM $\mathcal{M}$ **recognizes** a language $L \subseteq \Sigma^*$ if for all $w \in \Sigma^*$ the following two conditions are satisfied.

(i) $w \in L$ if $q_0 w \vdash_A^* q_a a_1$, and

(ii) $w \notin L$ if $q_0 w \vdash_A^* q_a$.

Here a_1 is a fixed symbol from Σ.

Definition 1.3.10

(a) A language $L \subseteq \Sigma^*$ is **recursive** if there exists a TM that recognizes this language.

(b) A language $L \subseteq \Sigma^*$ is **recursively enumerable** if there exists a TM that accepts L.

There are many different definitions of recursive and recursively enumerable languages. However, one of the main results of recursion theory states that all these various definitions yield the same classes of languages, and therefore they are all equivalent. This observation supports Church's Thesis that there exists an algorithm to decide the membership problem of a language if and only if this language is recursive, and there exists an algorithm to enumerate the elements of a language if and only if this language is recursively enumerable.

We close this section by restating a fundamental result from recursion theory.

Theorem 1.3.11

(a) *There exists a language L_1 that is recursively enumerable, but not recursive.*

(b) *There exists a language L_2 that is not recursively enumerable.*

1.4   Some Turing Machine Constructions

For those readers not so well versed in automata theory, we present some constructions for Turing machines that we shall make use of in later chapters. Accordingly this section is not intended as an introduction to automata theory as such, it merely explains some particular constructions. Therefore, the reader may prefer to skip this section on first reading and return to it later once he encounters the applications of these constructions.

The Turing machine of Definition 1.3.9 is usually refered to as a **single-tape Turing machine**, since it has a single unbounded tape that it uses to store and to retrieve information. This type of Turing machine is already powerful enough to recognize all recursive languages and to accept all recursively enumerable languages. However, in many applications it is much more convenient to use a Turing machine that has more than one tape. We describe a type of Turing machine that has several tapes, and prove that these multi-tape Turing machines are only as powerful as the single-tape Turing machines.

Definition 1.4.1 *Let $k \geq 2$.*

(a) A **k-tape Turing machine** $\mathcal{M}$ is given through a 5-tuple $\mathcal{M} = (Q, \Sigma, \delta, q_0, q_a)$, where

Q is a finite set of states,

Σ is a finite alphabet,

$q_0 \in Q$ is the initial state,

$q_a \in Q$ is the halting state, and

$\delta : (Q - \{q_a\}) \times \Sigma_b^k \to Q \times (\Sigma_b \cup \{R, L\})^k$ is the transition function, where $b \notin \Sigma$ denotes the blank symbol, and $\Sigma_b = \Sigma \cup \{b\}$.

(b) A **configuration** of $\mathcal{M}$ consists of a state, the inscription of the k tapes, and the head positions on these tapes. It is written in the form of a k-tuple $(u_1 q v_1, u_2 q v_2, \ldots, u_k q v_k)$, where $u_i, v_i \in \Sigma_b^*$, $1 \le i \le k$, and $q \in Q$. The string $u_i v_i$ is the **tape inscription** of tape i with the head scanning the first letter of v_i, and q is the actual **state**. As in the case of single-tape Turing machines the single-step computation relation on the set of configurations that is induced by $\mathcal{M}$ will be denoted by $\vdash_{\mathcal{M}}$. The reflexive and transitive closure $\vdash_{\mathcal{M}}^*$ is the **computation relation** of $\mathcal{M}$. For $w \in \Sigma^*$, the configuration $(q_0 w, q_0 b, \ldots, q_0 b)$ is the **initial configuration** on input w, that is, tape 1 serves as input tape. A configuration $(u_1 q v_1, \ldots, u_k q v_k)$ is **halting** if q is q_a.

(c) A string $w \in \Sigma^*$ is accepted by $\mathcal{M}$ if $(q_0 w, q_0 b, \ldots, q_0 b) \vdash_{\mathcal{M}}^* (u_1 q_a v_1, \ldots, u_k q_a v_k)$ for some $u_i, v_i \in \Sigma_b^*$, $1 \le i \le k$. The language $L(\mathcal{M}) = \{w \in \Sigma^* \mid w$ is accepted by $\mathcal{M}\}$ is the **language accepted** by $\mathcal{M}$.

Obviously, if a language $L \subseteq \Sigma^*$ is accepted by a single-tape Turing machine, then it is also accepted by some k-tape Turing machine for each $k \ge 2$. Although not as obvious, the converse also holds.

Theorem 1.4.2 *A language is accepted by a single-tape Turing machine if and only if it is accepted by some k-tape Turing machine for some $k \ge 2$.*

The proof of this result can be found in almost any book dealing with Turing machines. Nevertheless we want to give a short outline of it, since we need the basic technique again with the next construction.

Proof of Theorem 1.4.2 Let $\mathcal{M} = (Q, \Sigma, \delta, q_0, q_a)$ be a k-tape Turing machine for some $k \ge 2$, and let $L = L(\mathcal{M})$. We will present a single-tape Turing machine $\mathcal{N}$ that accepts the same language L. Informally, the Turing machine $\mathcal{N}$ will have a single tape with $2k$ tracks, two tracks for each of $\mathcal{M}$'s tapes. One track will record the contents of the corresponding tape of $\mathcal{M}$, while the other track will contain markers that identify the relative position of the head of this tape. Hence, we need three markers: $<, \wedge, >$. The first one $<$ is used when the head is somewhere to the left. $\wedge$ marks the actual head position, and $>$ is used when the head is somewhere to the right. The finite control of $\mathcal{N}$ will store the actual state of $\mathcal{M}$ along with the contents of those cells of $\mathcal{M}$ that are currently being scanned by $\mathcal{M}$'s heads and that are to the left of $\mathcal{N}$'s head.

Each step of $\mathcal{M}$ is simulated by a sweep from left to right and then back from right to left by the tape head of $\mathcal{N}$. Initially, $\mathcal{N}$'s head is on

Simulation of two tapes by one

Tape 1	b	b	a_1	a_2	a_3	a_1	b	a_2	a_2	b		
Head 1	>	>	>	>	>	∧	<	<	<	<	b	...
Tape 2	a_1	b	a_2	a_3	a_1	b	a_2	b	b	b		
Head 2	>	>	∧	<	<	<	<	<	<	<		

the leftmost cell containing a head marker ∧. To simulate a single step of
$\mathcal{M}$, $\mathcal{N}$ sweeps right, visiting each of the cells containing a head marker ∧
and recording the symbols scanned by $\mathcal{M}$ in its finite control. After having
seen all head markers $\mathcal{N}$ "knows" the step $\mathcal{M}$ will perform next. Now $\mathcal{N}$
makes a pass left until it reaches the leftmost head marker ∧. As $\mathcal{N}$ passes
each head marker, it updates the tape symbol of $\mathcal{M}$ that is scanned by
the corresponding tape head, or it moves the head marker one symbol left
or right to simulate the move of $\mathcal{M}$. Finally, $\mathcal{N}$ changes the state of $\mathcal{M}$
recorded in its finite control to complete the simulation of one step of $\mathcal{M}$.
If the new state of $\mathcal{M}$ is the halting state of $\mathcal{M}$, then $\mathcal{N}$ also enters its
halting state.

Formally, the single-tape Turing machine $\mathcal{N}$ is obtained from $\mathcal{M}$ by
choosing the tape alphabet $\Gamma := \Sigma_b \cup (\Sigma_b \times \{>, \wedge, <\})^k$ and a sufficiently large set of states $Q(\mathcal{N})$ and by defining the transition function
$\delta(\mathcal{N})$ accordingly. We will not go into the technical details.   □1.4.2

Next consider the notion of "immortal" configurations of Turing machines.

Definition 1.4.3 *Let* $\mathcal{M} = (Q, \Sigma, \delta, q_0, q_a)$ *be a (single-tape) Turing machine. A configuration* uqv $(u, v \in \Sigma_b^*,\ q \in (Q - \{q_a\}))$ *is called* **immortal** *if there does not exist a halting configuration* $u_1 q_a v_1$ *such that*
$uqv \overset{*}{\vdash}_\mathcal{M} u_1 q_a v_1$, *that is, if the Turing machine* $\mathcal{M}$ *starting from the configuration* uqv *will not halt.*

If the language $L(\mathcal{M})$ is a proper subset of Σ^*, then there exist initial
configurations $q_0 w$ that are immortal, since $q_0 w$ is immortal if and only
if $w \notin L(\mathcal{M})$. However, even if $L(\mathcal{M})$ is all of Σ^*, that is, if $\mathcal{M}$ halts on
all inputs, there may exist immortal configurations for $\mathcal{M}$, which of course
cannot be initial. This means that in general we must distinguish between
the following two variants of the halting problem for Turing machines.

Definition 1.4.4

(a) *The* **(special) halting problem** *for* $\mathcal{M} = (Q, \Sigma, \delta, q_0, q_a)$ *is the
following:*

  Instance: *A string* $w \in \Sigma^*$.

  Question: *Does* $\mathcal{M}$ *halt on input* w, *that is, is the initial configuration* $q_0 w$ *mortal?*

Start:

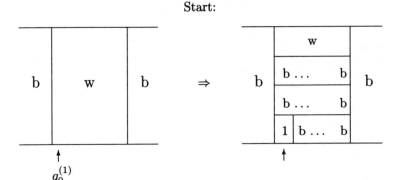

(b) *The **general halting problem** for M is the following:*

Instance: *Two strings $u, v \in \Sigma_b^*$ and a state $q \in Q$.*

Question: *Does M starting from the configuration uqv halt eventually, that is, is the configuration uqv mortal?*

In fact, one can construct examples of Turing machines for which the general halting problem is much more complex than the special halting problem. On the other hand there are situations in which it is desirable to consider Turing machines for which these two problems are equivalent. Since we will encounter one such situation in Section 2.5, we present a construction that transforms a given Turing machine M into a Turing machine N such that the two machines have the same input-output behavior, but for N the two variants of the halting problem are equivalent. We present a sketch.

Let $M = (\Sigma, Q, \delta, q_0, q_a)$ be a single-tape Turing machine, let $L := L(M)$ be the language accepted by M, and for $w \in L$, let $f(w)$ denote the tape inscription of the halting configuration that M reaches from the initial configuration $q_0 w$. The string $f(w)$ can be interpreted as the **result** or **output** that M generates on input w. We modify the Turing machine M to obtain the announced Turing machine $N = (\Sigma_1, Q_1, \delta_1, q_0^{(1)}, q_a^{(1)})$ with $\Sigma \subset \Sigma_1$.

The Turing machine N works as follows: starting from an initial configuration $q_0^{(1)} w$ ($w \in \Sigma^*$), N divides its tape into four tracks, copies the input w onto the first track, and prints the symbol "1" below the leftmost letter of w into track 4.

While doing so N checks whether $w \in \Sigma^*$. If a letter $s \in \Sigma_1 - \Sigma$ is encountered in w, then N prints a special symbol $\#$ and halts. Otherwise N enters the following loop.

Loop:

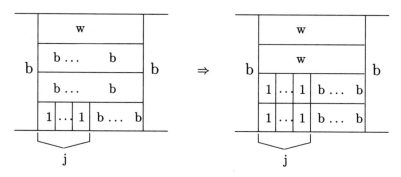

$\mathcal{N}$ simulates the Turing machine $\mathcal{M}$ starting from its initial configuration $q_0 w$ on its second track for as many steps as the inscription of track 4 contains symbols 1. To do so track 1 is copied onto track 2, and track 4 is copied onto track 3. The steps of the simulation are counted by erasing a symbol 1 from the right end of the inscription of track 3 for each step of $\mathcal{M}$ simulated. When $\mathcal{M}$ enters its halting state q_a, then $\mathcal{N}$ enters a special state q_e. If the inscription of track 3 is completely erased while the simulation of $\mathcal{M}$ is still going on, then $\mathcal{N}$ ends the simulation of $\mathcal{M}$, erases track 2, appends a symbol 1 to the right-hand side of the inscription of track 4, and starts the loop again. Furthermore, if $\mathcal{N}$ recognizes somehow during its computation that it has reached a configuration which is not accessible from a proper initial configuration, then it immediately enters state $q_a^{(1)}$. In state q_e, $\mathcal{N}$ performs the following action:

End:

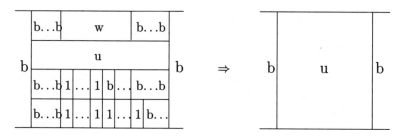

Tracks 1, 3 and 4 are erased, and only the contents of track 2, which is a string from Σ_b^*, is left on the tape. Then $\mathcal{N}$ enters its halting state $q_a^{(1)}$.

If all these steps of $\mathcal{N}$ are designed carefully, then $\mathcal{N}$ has the following properties:

(i) $\mathcal{N}$ accepts the language $L \cup (\Sigma_1^* - \Sigma^*)$, that is, $L(\mathcal{N}) \cap \Sigma^* = L(\mathcal{M})$.

(ii) For all $w \in L$, $\mathcal{M}$ halts with the tape inscription $f(w)$.

(iii) Starting from an arbitrary configuration uqv, $\mathcal{N}$ either halts within $O(|uv|^2)$ steps or it begins the simulation of $\mathcal{M}$ from an initial configuration $q_0 w$ for some $w \in \Sigma^*$ satisfying $|w| \leq |uv|$.

The first two statements express the fact that on Σ^*, $\mathcal{M}$ and $\mathcal{N}$ have the same input-output behavior. Statement (iii) implies that the general halting problem for $\mathcal{N}$ reduces to the special halting problem for $\mathcal{M}$. In particular, it shows that $\mathcal{N}$ has an immortal configuration if and only if it has an immortal initial configuration. We summarize the result of the above consideration as follows.

Theorem 1.4.5 *Given a Turing machine $\mathcal{M} = (Q, \Sigma, \delta, q_0, q_a)$, a Turing machine $\mathcal{N}$ can be constructed such that $\mathcal{M}$ and $\mathcal{N}$ have the same input-output behavior on Σ^*, and the general halting problem for $\mathcal{N}$ is equivalent to its special halting problem.*

This completes our consideration of the general Turing machine model. In the remainder of this section we will deal with certain restricted variants of the Turing machine. First we will state the definition of the linearly bounded automaton (LBA), which is a nondeterministic Turing machine satisfying a strict space bound. Then we will discuss a technicality regarding pushdown automata.

Definition 1.4.6 *A **linearly bounded automaton** (LBA) is a single-tape Turing machine $\mathcal{M} = (Q, \Sigma, \delta, q_0, q_a)$ satisfying the following conditions:*

(a) *The input alphabet Σ includes two special symbols $\$$ and $\pounds$, called **left** and **right endmarkers**, respectively.*

(b) *$\mathcal{M}$ cannot print another symbol over $\$$ or $\pounds$. Further, whenever $\mathcal{M}$ sees the symbol $\$$ ($\pounds$) on its tape, then it cannot move its tape head to the left (right).*

(c) *$\mathcal{M}$ is nondeterministic, that is, the transition function δ associates with each pair $(q, a) \in (Q - \{q_a\}) \times \Sigma_b$ a finite set of pairs from $Q \times (\Sigma_b \cup \{R, L\})$.*

Because of its nondeterminism $\mathcal{M}$ may have several possible moves that it can make from some configuration. The computation relation $\overset{*}{\vdash}_\mathcal{M}$ of $\mathcal{M}$ can easily be adopted to this situation.

Definition 1.4.7 *Let $\mathcal{M} = (Q, \Sigma, \delta, q_0, q_a)$ be an LBA.*

(a) *The **language** $L(\mathcal{M})$ **accepted by** $\mathcal{M}$ is defined to be $L(\mathcal{M}) :=$ $\{w \in (\Sigma - \{\$, \pounds\})^* \mid q_0 \$ w \pounds \overset{*}{\vdash}_\mathcal{M} uq_a v$ for some $u, v \in \Sigma_b^*\}$.*

(b) $\mathcal{M}$ is called a **deterministic LBA** if its transition function δ satisfies the following restriction:

$$|\delta(q, a)| \leq 1 \text{ for all } q \in Q - \{q_a\} \text{ and } a \in \Sigma_b.$$

Observe that an LBA $\mathcal{M}$ starting from the initial configuration $q_0\$w\pounds$ cannot move its tape head off the portion of the tape containing the inscription $\$w\pounds$, because of condition (b) of Definition 1.4.6. Thus, on input $w \in (\Sigma - \{\$, \pounds\})^*$, $\mathcal{M}$ only visits at most $|w| + 2$ tape squares; thus, the amount of tape it visits is **linearly bounded**.

Definition 1.4.8 A language $L \subseteq \Sigma^*$ is **context-sensitive** if there exists an LBA $\mathcal{M}$ that accepts exactly the language L.

The language $L = \{a^n b^n c^n \mid n \geq O\}$ is a typical example of a context-sensitive language that is not context-free. By simulating all possible computations of an LBA $\mathcal{M}$ on input w a (deterministic) Turing machine M can decide in polynomial space whether or not $\mathcal{M}$ accepts w. On the other hand there exists a deterministic LBA $\mathcal{M}$ such that the language $L(\mathcal{M})$ is **PSPACE**-complete. Thus, LBA's capture exactly the complexity class **PSPACE**. However, it is a famous open problem whether each context-sensitive language can be accepted by some deterministic LBA, that is, whether deterministic LBA's are as powerful as (non-deterministic) LBA's.

We conclude this section with a remark concerning pushdown automata. In Section 4.2 we shall construct nondeterministic and deterministic pushdown automata in order to prove that certain languages are context-free, respectively, deterministic context-free. In each case the pushdown automaton will be described in an informal way using certain procedures called READ, SEARCH, and DECIDE. It is straightforward to translate this informal description into a formal specification. However, there is one minor difficulty with the procedure READ which we wish to clarify in the following way.

The procedure READ describes the behavior of the (deterministic) pushdown automaton to be constructed on its input tape. It has the following form:

READ: Attempt to read an input symbol and push it onto the pushdown store. If the input is empty, then do something; otherwise, do something else.

The problem lies in the fact that technically speaking a pushdown automaton cannot decide whether its remaining input is empty. Either it can perform some internal computation without reading an input symbol, or it can perform some computation that depends on the actually scanned input symbol. To overcome this problem we can proceed as follows.

Assume that $L \subseteq \Sigma^*$ is the language to be accepted. We introduce an additional symbol $\$ \notin \Sigma$ that we use as an end marker, that is, we consider inputs of the form $w\$$ with $w \in \Sigma^*$. Then the test "Is the input empty?" is realized by the test "Is the actual input only the symbol $\$$?", which is easily incorporated into the transition function of a pushdown automaton. With this adjustment, our proof shows that the language $L \cdot \{\$\}$ is (deterministic) context-free. However, as it turns out we can even avoid this end marker.

Definition 1.4.9 *Let $L_1, L_2 \subseteq \Sigma^*$ be two languages. The* **quotient** *of L_1 with respect to L_2, denoted by L_1/L_2, is the language*

$$L_1/L_2 := \{x \in \Sigma^* \mid \text{ there exists } y \in L_2 \text{ such that } xy \in L_1\}.$$

Now the following result is of interest to us.

Proposition 1.4.10 *Both the class of context-free languages and also the class of deterministic context-free languages are closed under quotient with a regular set, that is, if L_1 is (deterministic) context-free and L_2 is a regular set, then the quotient L_1/L_2 is (deterministic) context-free.*

Since the set $L_2 := \{\$\}$ is regular, $L \cdot \{\$\}$ being (deterministic) context-free implies that the quotient $L \cdot \{\$\}/L_2$ is (deterministic) context-free, and this quotient is simply the language L itself. Thus, the informal descriptions of (deterministic) pushdown automata in Section 4.2 can indeed be translated into formal definitions.

1.5   Bibliographic Remarks

The use of notions such as "reduction" and "confluence" in the study of term-rewriting systems and equational reasoning is well illustrated by Huet [Hue80], Huet and Oppen [HuOp80], and by Dershowitz and Jouannaud [DeJo90]. Of course, the paper by Knuth and Bendix [KnBe70] played an extremely important role in the development of such ideas, as did some of the papers in the volume edited by Siekmann and Wrightson [SiWr83].

The development of abstract reduction systems and their properties given in Sections 1.1 and 1.2 essentially follow the initial part of an important paper by Huet [Hue80]. Theorem 1.1.13 is often referred to as the "Newman Lemma" since M.H.A. Newman [New43] used it quite successfully. As might be expected, the Church-Rosser property comes from the work of Church and Rosser [ChRo39] on the lambda calculus. The Church-Rosser property became known in computer science when the lambda calculus was recognized as being useful for the study of programming languages, but it became more widely appreciated when it was used in various other aspects (for example, see [Ros73]).

The material on strings, languages, automata, computability, and related notions can be found in many undergraduate textbooks. The book by Hopcroft and Ullman [HoUl79] is a suitable reference.

2

String-Rewriting Systems

In this chapter we introduce the string-rewriting systems and study their basic properties. Such systems are the primary subject of this work. We provide formal definitions of string-rewriting systems and their induced reduction relations and Thue congruences. Some of the basic ideas that occur in the study of term-rewriting systems are considered. We rely on Section 1.4 for basic definitions and notation for strings, and we rely on Section 1.1 for basic definitions and results on notions such as reduction, confluence, the Church-Rosser property, and so forth.

2.1 Rewriting Systems for Strings

We begin with the basic definitions.

Definition 2.1.1 *Let Σ be a finite alphabet.*

(a) *A **string-rewriting system** R on Σ is a subset of $\Sigma^* \times \Sigma^*$. Each element (ℓ, r) of R is a **(rewrite) rule**. The set $\{\ell \in \Sigma^* \mid$ for some $r \in \Sigma^*, (\ell, r) \in R\}$ is called the **domain** of R and is denoted $\mathrm{dom}(R)$. The set $\{r \in \Sigma^* \mid$ for some $\ell \in \Sigma^*, (\ell, r) \in R\}$ is called the **range** of R and is denoted $\mathrm{range}(R)$. If R is finite, then the **size** of R is defined to be $\sum_{(\ell,r) \in R}(|\ell| + |r|)$ and is denoted $\| R \|$.*

(b) *If R is a string-rewriting system on Σ, then the **single-step reduction relation** on Σ^* that is induced by R is defined as follows: for any $u, v \in \Sigma^*$, $u \to_R v$ if and only if there exists $(\ell, r) \in R$ such that for some $x, y \in \Sigma^*$, $u = x\ell y$ and $v = xry$. The **reduction relation** on Σ^* induced by R is the reflexive, transitive closure of $\to_R$ and is denoted by $\overset{*}{\to}_R$.*

If R is a string-rewriting system on Σ, then $(\Sigma^*, \to_R)$ is a reduction system, just as in Definition 1.1.2. When considering a string-rewriting system R, the set of objects is always the set Σ^* for some finite alphabet Σ and the binary relation on Σ^* is $\to_R$. Thus, it is sufficient to specify Σ and R, and often Σ is specified from the context. Thus, we will frequently use R, as opposed to $(\Sigma^*, \to_R)$, when a reduction system is considered.

Definition 2.1.1 (continued)

(c) *The* **Thue congruence** *generated by R is the relation $\longleftrightarrow^{*}_{R}$.*

(d) *Two strings u, $v \in \Sigma^{*}$ are* **congruent** *mod(R) if $u \longleftrightarrow^{*}_{R} v$. For each $w \in \Sigma^{*}$, $[w]_R$ is called the* **congruence class** *of $w(\mathrm{mod}(R))$.*

In the literature string-rewriting systems are also known as **semi-Thue systems**. A string-rewriting system R with the property that $(\ell, r) \in R$ implies $(r, \ell) \in R$ is also called a **Thue system**. For a Thue system R, the single-step reduction relation $\rightarrow_R$ is symmetric, so that the reduction relation $\rightarrow^{*}_R$ coincides with the Thue congruence $\longleftrightarrow^{*}_R$.

Notice that for any string-rewriting system R, if u and v are strings such that $u \rightarrow^{*}_R v$, then for all x, $y \in \Sigma^{*}$, $xuy \rightarrow^{*}_R xvy$, and if $u \longleftrightarrow^{*}_R v$, then for all x, $y \in \Sigma^{*}$, $xuy \longleftrightarrow^{*}_R xvy$. This is the reason that the relation $\longleftrightarrow^{*}_R$ is called a "congruence" relation: it is an equivalence relation that is compatible with respect to the concatenation of strings (which is the "multiplication" in the free monoid Σ^{*}).

As an example of a string-rewriting system, let $\Sigma = \{a, b\}$ and consider $R = \{(ab, e), (ba, e)\}$. Then the set $\nabla^{*}_R(e)$ of ancestors of the empty word e is $\{w \in \Sigma^{*} \mid |w|_a = |w|_b\}$, that is, it is the Dyck language D'^{*}_1. If $R' = \{(ab, e)\}$, then the set $\nabla^{*}_{R'}(e)$ of ancestors of e is the restricted Dyck language D'^{*}_1 of "matching parentheses," where a is interpreted as the left parenthesis symbol "(" and b is interpreted as the right parenthesis symbol ")".

Definition 2.1.2 *Let R be a string-rewriting system on alphabet Σ. The* **monoid** $\mathcal{M}_R$ *presented by the ordered pair (Σ, R) is defined as follows:*

(i) *the elements of $\mathcal{M}_R$ are the congruence classes $[x]_R$, $x \in \Sigma^{*}$;*

(ii) *the multiplication in $\mathcal{M}_R$ is $[x]_R \cdot [y]_R := [xy]_R$, for each x, $y \in \Sigma^{*}$;*

(iii) *the identity of $\mathcal{M}_R$ is $[e]_R$.*

The monoid $\mathcal{M}_R$ is the "factor monoid" or "quotient monoid" of the free monoid Σ^{*} by the Thue congruence $\longleftrightarrow^{*}_R$. For example, if $\Sigma = \{a, b\}$ and $R = \{(ab, e), (ba, e)\}$, then the monoid $\mathcal{M}_R$ presented by (Σ, R) is the free group F_1 on one generator.

Whenever the context prevents ambiguity from being introduced, the subscript R will be omitted from $\rightarrow_R, \leftrightarrow_R, \rightarrow^{*}_R, \longleftrightarrow^{*}_R, [w]_R$, etc.

In Definition 1.1.3 we introduced the word problem, the common descendant problem, and the common ancestor problem for a reduction system $(\mathbf{B}, \rightarrow)$. Here we extend these problems in that we take the rewriting system to be a part of the problem instance. We consider the following common problems for a class of combinatorial rewriting systems:

(a) the **uniform word problem**

   Instance: *A rewriting system R and two elements x, y.*

Question: *Are x and y congruent with respect to R?*

(b) the **uniform version of the common descendant problem:**

    Instance: *A rewriting system R and two elements x, y.*

    Question: *Do x and y have a common descendant with respect to R?*

(c) the **uniform version of the common ancestor problem:**

    Instance: *A rewriting system R and two elements x, y.*

    Question: *Do x and y have a common ancestor with respect to R?*

We will see that each of these problems is undecidable for finite string-rewriting systems.

Recall the notion of irreducible element (Definition 1.1.2). If R is a string-rewriting system, then it is clear that a string w is irreducible if and only if no string in $\mathrm{dom}(R)$ occurs as a substring of w. If R is finite, then from R one can construct a deterministic finite-state acceptor A such that $L(A) = IRR(R)$. This means that for a finite string-rewriting system R, $IRR(R)$ is a regular set. This fact will be used frequently in this work and so will be stated formally.

Lemma 2.1.3 *If R is a finite string-rewriting system on alphabet Σ, then the set $IRR(R)$ of irreducible strings with respect to R is a regular set; furthermore, a finite-state acceptor for $IRR(R)$ can be constructed in polynomial time from R.*

Proof. Let R be a finite string-rewriting system on Σ. Obviously, the set $IRR(R)$ only depends on the set $\mathrm{dom}(R)$ of the left-hand sides of the rules of R. In fact, we can delete all words ℓ from $\mathrm{dom}(R)$ such that ℓ contains a proper substring which belongs to $\mathrm{dom}(R)$ without affecting the set $IRR(R)$. Since this can be done in polynomial time, we may assume without loss of generality that no string from $\mathrm{dom}(R)$ contains another string from this set as a proper subword. Let $L = \{\ell_1, \ldots, \ell_n\} = \mathrm{dom}(R)$. If $e \in L$, then $IRR(R) = \emptyset$, and the result follows trivially. So assume that $e \notin L$. Then $e \in IRR(R)$.

A string $u \in \Sigma^*$ is called a **prefix** of L if there exists a string $v \in \Sigma^*$ such that $uv \in L$, it is called a **proper prefix** of L if $uv \in L$ for some $v \neq e$. Let Q denote the set of all proper prefixes of L. Then $Q \subseteq IRR(R)$. Now we define a *dfa* $\mathcal{A}$ as follows:

- $Q' := Q \cup \{w\}$ is the set of states, where w is a fixed string from $\Sigma^* - IRR(R)$,

- Σ is the input alphabet,

- e is the initial state,

- Q is the set of final states, that is, w is the only non-final state, and

- the transition function $\delta : Q' \times \Sigma \to Q'$ is defined by

$$\delta(u, a) := \begin{cases} ua & \text{if } ua \in Q, \\ u_2 & \text{if } ua \notin Q, \text{ but } ua \in IRR(R), \text{ and } u_2 \text{ is the} \\ & \text{largest suffix of } ua \text{ such that } u_2 \in Q, \\ w & \text{if } ua \notin IRR(R) \end{cases}$$

for all $u \in Q$ and $a \in \Sigma$, and $\delta(w, a) = w$ for all $a \in \Sigma$.

Obviously $\mathcal{A}$ can be constructed in polynomial time. Thus, it remains to show that $L(\mathcal{A}) = IRR(R)$.

Claim: Let $u \in \Sigma^*$. Then

$$\delta(e, u) = \begin{cases} w & \text{if } u \notin IRR(R), \\ u_2 & \text{where } u_2 \text{ is the largest suffix of } u \text{ such that } u_2 \in Q, \\ & \text{if } u \in IRR(R) \end{cases}$$

Proof by induction on $|u|$:

$\delta(e, e) = e$, which is correct since $e \in IRR(R)$.

Now assume that $\delta(e, u) = v$. If $v = w$, then $u \notin IRR(R)$, and so $ua \notin IRR(R)$. By construction $\delta(e, ua) = \delta(w, a) = w$. If $v = u_2 \in Q$, we must distinguish three cases.

(i) $u_2a \in Q$: Then $\delta(e, ua) = \delta(u_2, a) = u_2a \in Q$. Since u_2 is the largest suffix of u such that $u_2 \in Q$, u_2a is the largest suffix of ua such that $u_2a \in Q$.

(ii) $u_2a \notin Q$, but $u_2a \in IRR(R)$: Let x be the largest suffix of u_2a such that $x \in Q$. Then $\delta(e, ua) = \delta(u_2, a) = x \in Q$. Since u_2 is the largest suffix of u such that $u_2 \in Q$, and $u_za \notin Q_>$ x is the largest suffix of ua such that $x \in Q$.

(iii) $u_2a \notin IRR(R)$: Then $\delta(e, ua) = \delta(u_2, a) = w$, and $ua = u_1u_2a \notin IRR(R)$. This completes the proof of the claim.   □ Claim

From the claim we immediately see that $L(\mathcal{A}) = IRR(R)$.   □ 2.1.3

Suppose that a finite string-rewriting system R is convergent. Then every $w \in \Sigma^*$ has a unique normal form, that is, there is a unique irreducible string in $[w]$. Hence, from a finite-state acceptor for $IRR(R)$, one can effectively determine the cardinality of $IRR(R)$ and, hence, of $\mathcal{M}_R$. There are other important problems that are decidable for finite string-rewriting systems that are convergent, and some examples of this will be given later in this chapter. But at this point it is reasonable to show that a fundamental problem about rewriting sytems is undecidable, so that the reader will see some justification for the investigations of systems with restricted properties that will be studied in this and future chapters. Therefore we proceed to sketch a proof that the uniform word problem for finite string-rewriting systems is undecidable. To do so we rely on the well-known result of Post that the Correspondence Problem is undecidable.

The Correspondence Problem is the following. Given a finite alphabet Σ, consider a nonempty finite sequence $S = (x_1, y_1), (x_2, y_2), \ldots, (x_n, y_n)$ of ordered pairs of strings over Σ. A **solution to the Correspondence Problem** for S is a nonempty sequence $i_1, i_2, \ldots, i_k \in \{1, \ldots, n\}$ with the property that $x_{i_1} \ldots x_{i_k} = y_{i_1} \ldots y_{i_k}$.

The Modified Correspondence Problem is a variation on the Correspondence Problem. Given a nonempty finite sequence $S = (x_1, y_1), (x_2, y_2), \ldots, (x_n, y_n)$ of ordered pairs of strings over Σ, a **solution to the Modified Correspondence Problem** for S is a nonempty sequence $i_1, i_2, \ldots, i_k \in \{1, \ldots, n\}$ with the property that $x_1 x_{i_1} x_{i_2} \ldots x_{i_n} = y_1 y_{i_1} y_{i_2} \ldots y_{i_n}$.

Post proved that there is no algorithm that on input a finite sequence S of ordered pairs of strings will determine whether there is a solution to the Correspondence Problem for S. Thus, the Correspondence Problem is undecidable and so is the Modified Correspondence Problem. This result has been very useful in formal language theory where it has been used to show the undecidability of a number of different problems involving formal grammars.

We claim that the Correspondence Problem is reducible to the uniform word problem for finite string-rewriting systems, and, hence, the uniform word problem is undecidable. The idea is to show that from any given instance of the Correspondence Problem, one can construct a finite string-rewriting system with the property that two specific strings are congruent if and only if there is a solution to that instance of the Correspondence Problem.

Theorem 2.1.4 *There is no algorithm to solve the following problem:*

Instance: *A finite string-rewriting system R and two strings z_1, z_2 on the alphabet of R;*

Question: *Are z_1 and z_2 congruent modulo R?*

Proof. Let $S = (x_1, y_1), (x_2, y_2), \ldots, (x_n, y_n)$ be a sequence of ordered pairs of strings over Σ. Let $0, 1, A, B, C$ be five different symbols that are not in Σ. Let R_S be the string-rewriting system on the alphabet $\Sigma \cup \{0, 1, A, B, C\}$ with the following set $R_1 \cup R_2$ of rules where $R_1 = \{(A, x_i A 0^i 1), (x_i A 0^i 1, x_i C C 0^i 1) \mid 1 \leq i \leq n\}$ and $R_2 = \{(B, y_i B 0^i 1), (y_i B 0^i 1, y_i C C 0^i 1) \mid 1 \leq i \leq n\}$.

Consider the two strings (of length one) A and B. Suppose that $A \stackrel{*}{\longleftrightarrow} B$. Then it is clear that the only way this can happen is if there exist strings u, v such that $u \in \Sigma^*$ and $v \in \{0, 1\}^*$ where by using rules in R_1, $A \stackrel{*}{\longleftrightarrow}$

$uAv \longleftrightarrow uCCv$, and by using rules in R_2, $B \overset{*}{\longleftrightarrow} uBv \longleftrightarrow uCCv$. By factoring v it is clear that there must exist a sequence $i_1, i_2, \ldots, i_k \in \{1, \ldots, n\}$ such that $v = 0^{i_k} 1 \ldots 0^{i_1} 1$. This means that $uCC0^{i_k} 1 \ldots 0^{i_1} 1 \longleftrightarrow uAv \overset{*}{\longleftrightarrow} A$ so that $u = x_{i_1} \ldots x_{i_k}$. Since $B \overset{*}{\longleftrightarrow} uBv \longleftrightarrow uCCv$ by using the rules in R_2, we conclude that $x_{i_1} \ldots x_{i_k} = y_{i_1} \ldots y_{i_k}$. Hence, $i_1, i_2, \ldots, i_k$ is a solution to the Correspondence Problem for S.

In a similar way we see that if $i_1, i_2, \ldots, i_k$ is a solution to the Correspondence Problem for S, then there exist $u, v \in \Sigma^*$ and $w \in \{0, 1\}^*$ such that $A \overset{*}{\longleftrightarrow} uAw \longleftrightarrow uCCw$ and $B \overset{*}{\longleftrightarrow} vBw \longleftrightarrow vCCw$, where $w = 1^{i_k} 1 \ldots 0^{i_1} 1$. This means that $u = x_{i_1} \ldots x_{i_k}$ and $v = y_{i_1} \ldots y_{i_k}$. Since $i_1, i_2, \ldots, i_k$ is a solution to the Correspondence Problem for S, this means that $x_{i_1} \ldots x_{i_k} = y_{i_1} \ldots y_{i_k}$ so that $u = v$. Thus, $A \overset{*}{\longleftrightarrow} uAw \longleftrightarrow uCCw = vCCw \longleftrightarrow vBw \overset{*}{\longleftrightarrow} B$ so that $A \overset{*}{\longleftrightarrow} B$.

Hence, we see that $A \overset{*}{\longleftrightarrow} B$ if and only if there is a solution to the Correspondence Problem for S. If the problem (as given in the statement of the theorem) were decidable, then the Correspondence Problem would be decidable, contradicting the result of Post. □ 2.1.4

The proof of Theorem 2.1.4 yields two additional results. Notice that the strings A and B have a common descendant with respect to $R_1 \cup R_2$ if and only if there is a solution to the Correspondence Problem for S. When reversing the direction of the rewrite rules (that is, (u, v) becomes (v, u)), then the resulting rewriting system is such that the strings A and B have a common ancestor if and only if there is a solution to the Correspondence Problem for S.

Corollary 2.1.5 *Each of the following problems is undecidable:*

Instance: *A finite rewriting system R and two strings z_1, z_2 on the alphabet of R;*

Question 1: *Do z_1 and z_2 have a common ancestor?*

Question 2: *Do z_1 and z_2 have a common descendant?*

Hence, we see that the uniform word problem, common ancestor problem, and common descendant problem are undecidable for finite string-rewriting systems.

In fact, a stronger result can be obtained. Using the fact that the halting problem for Turing machines is undecidable, one can show that there is a specific finite string-rewriting system with the property that the word problem, the common descendant problem, and the common ancestor problem are undecidable (see Section 2.5).

Later in this chapter it will be shown that other simply stated questions are also undecidable for finite string-rewriting systems.

2.2   Computing Normal Forms

In Section 1.1, we observed that the word problem is decidable for a finite reduction system with the property that every element has a unique normal form as long as there exist algorithms that (i) allow one to compute for a given element that unique normal form and (ii) allow one to compare two objects to determine whether they are identical.

The property of having unique normal forms is guaranteed for any system that is confluent and noetherian. In the case of string-rewriting systems, the existence of a fast algorithm for (ii) is trivial since it is only a matter of comparing strings symbol by symbol and, thus, is a linear-time algorithm. The important content of this section is an algorithm that can be applied to string-rewriting systems whose reduction relation is noetherian. On input x, a string over the appropriate alphabet, the algorithm will compute an irreducible string $\bar{x}$ such that $x \xrightarrow{*} \bar{x}$. Since the property that the reduction relation is noetherian is crucial for this algorithm, we start with discussing a technique that allows us to verify that certain string-rewriting systems induce reduction relations that are noetherian. The general problem of deciding whether or not a finite string-rewriting system has this property will be considered in Section 2.5.

Definition 2.2.1 *Let $>$ be a binary relation on Σ^*.*

(a) *The relation $>$ is a **strict partial ordering** if it is irreflexive, anti-symmetric, and transitive.*

(b) *$>$ is a **linear ordering** if it is a strict partial ordering, and if, for all $x, y \in \Sigma^*$, either $x > y$, or $x = y$, or $y > x$ holds.*

(c) *The relation $>$ is **admissible**, if, for all $u, v, x, y \in \Sigma^*$, $u > v$ implies $xuy > xvy$.*

In the following we give some examples of admissible partial orderings on Σ^*.

Definition 2.2.2 *Let $\Sigma = \{a_1, \ldots, a_n\}$.*

(a) *Define $x > y$ as follows:*
$x > y$ *if $|x| > |y|$. $>$ is the **length ordering** on Σ^*.*

(b) *Let $w : \Sigma \to \mathbf{N}_+$ be a mapping that associates a positive integer (a **weight**) with each letter. Define the **weight ordering** $>_w$ induced by w as follows:*
$x >_w y$ *if $w(x) > w(y)$. Here w is extended to a mapping from Σ^* into $\mathbf{N}$ by taking $w(e) := 0$ and $w(xa) := w(x) + w(a)$ for all $x \in \Sigma^*$, $a \in \Sigma$.*

(c) *The* **lexicographical ordering** $>_{\text{lex}}$ *on Σ^* is defined as follows:* $x >_{\text{lex}} y$ *if there is a non-empty string z such that $x = yz$, or $x = ua_i v$ and $y = ua_j z$ for some $u, v, z \in \Sigma^*$, and $i, j \in \{1, \dots, n\}$ satisfying $i > j$.*

(d) *The* **length-lexicographical ordering** $>_{\ell\ell}$ *is a combination of the length ordering and the lexicographical ordering:* $x >_{\ell\ell} y$ *if $|x| > |y|$ or $(|x| = |y|$ and $x >_{\text{lex}} y)$.*

Analogously, the weight ordering $>_w$ and the lexicographical ordering can be combined to yield the **weight-lexicographical ordering** $>_{w\ell}$.

It is easily checked that indeed all the relations defined above are admissible partial orderings on Σ^*. In fact, the lexicographical ordering, the length-lexicographical ordering and the weight-lexicographical ordering are linear, while the length ordering and weight ordering are not linear.

Convergent systems that are in addition normalized have been called **canonical**. Thus, Theorem 2.2.14 shows that for each string-rewriting system T on Σ^* and each admissible well-founded partial ordering $>$ on Σ^* there exists at most one canonical string-rewriting system R that is equivalent to T and compatible with $>$.

Definition 2.2.3 *Let $>$ be a strict partial ordering on Σ^*. It is called* **well-founded** *if there is no infinite chain of the form $x_0 > x_1 > x_2 > \dots$. If $>$ is linear and well-founded, then it is called a* **well-ordering**.

The length ordering and the weight ordering are obviously well-founded. Since there are only finitely many strings of any given length or weight, the length-lexicographical ordering and the weight-lexicographical ordering are well-orderings. However, if $n > 1$ (that is, Σ contains more than one letter), then the lexicographical ordering $>_{\text{lex}}$ is not well-founded since we have the following infinite descending chain:

$$a_2 >_{\text{lex}} a_1 a_2 >_{\text{lex}} a_1 a_1 a_2 >_{\text{lex}} \dots >_{\text{lex}} a_1^i a_2 >_{\text{lex}} a_1^{i+1} a_2 >_{\text{lex}} \dots$$

Admissible well-founded partial orderings are of interest in the study of rewriting for the following reason.

Theorem 2.2.4 *Let R be a string-rewriting system on Σ. Then the following two statements are equivalent:*

(a) *the reduction relation $\to_R$ is noetherian;*

(b) *there exists an admissible well-founded partial ordering $>$ on Σ^* such that $\ell > r$ holds for each rule $(\ell, r) \in R$.*

Proof. Consider the binary relation $>_R$ defined by

$$x >_R y \quad \text{if} \quad x \xrightarrow{+}_R y.$$

This relation is obviously transitive and admissible, and it is irreflexive and well-founded if and only if $\to_R$ is noetherian. Further, since $\ell \to_R r$ for each $(\ell, r) \in R$, we have $\ell >_R r$ for each rule $(\ell, r) \in R$. Thus, (a) implies (b). Conversely, assume that $>$ is an admissible well-founded strict partial ordering such that $\ell > r$ holds for each rule $(\ell, r) \in R$. Since $>$ is admissible, we have $\to_R \subseteq >$, and so, since $>$ is transitive, we have $>_R \subseteq >$. Thus, $>$ being irreflexive and well-founded implies that $>_R$ has these properties, and hence, $\to_R$ is noetherian by the above observation.   □ 2.2.4

Thus, in order to verify that a string-rewriting system R on Σ is noetherian it suffices to construct an admissible well-founded strict partial ordering $>$ on Σ^* such that R is **compatible** with $>$, that is, $\ell > r$ holds for each rule $(\ell, r) \in R$. Easy as this seems at first glance, in general this is a difficult task; the reason for this will become clear in Section 2.5. In the context of term-rewriting systems, the problem of constructing appropriate well-founded strict partial orderings has received a good deal of attention.

Notice that if R is a finite string-rewriting system on Σ, then for each string $x \in \Sigma^*$ the set $\Delta(x)$ of immediate descendants of x is finite. Thus, if $\to_R$ is noetherian, then for every $x \in \Sigma^*$ the set $\Delta^*(x)$ of descendants of x is finite by König's Infinity Lemma.

Consider a finite string-rewriting system R such that $\to_R$ is noetherian. Define a function $g_R : \Sigma^* \to \mathbf{N}$ as follows: for each $x \in \Sigma^*$, let $g_R(x)$ be the maximum k such that there exists a sequence $x_0 \to_R x_1 \to_R \cdots \to_R x_k$ where $x_0 = x$. Then the **derivational complexity** of R is the function $f_R : \mathbf{N} \to \mathbf{N}$, which is defined as follows: for each $n \in \mathbf{N}$, $f_R(n) := \max\{g_R(x) \mid x \in \Sigma^n\}$.

It follows that if R is a finite string-rewriting system and $\to_R$ is noetherian, then g_R is a total recursive function and, hence, f_R is a total recursive function. In fact, the following result is now easily established.

Proposition 2.2.5 *If R is a finite string-rewriting system and $\to_R$ is noetherian, then there is a total recursive function f_R such that*

(a) *for every $x \in \Sigma^*$ there is no sequence of reductions that begins with x and has more that $f_R(|x|)$ steps, and*

(b) *if $t = \max\{|u|, |v| \mid (u, v) \in R\}$, then for every $y \in \Delta^*(x)$, $|y| \le |x| + t \cdot f_R(|x|)$.*

Now we turn to the task of computing irreducible descendants with respect to a finite noetherian string-rewriting system.

Definition 2.2.6 *Let R be a rewriting system on alphabet Σ. A reduction $w \to z$ is **leftmost**, denoted $w \xrightarrow{L} z$, if the following condition is satisfied: if $w = x_1 u_1 y_1$, $z = x_1 v_1 y_1$, and $(u_1, v_1) \in R$, and also $w = x_2 u_2 y_2$ and $(u_2, v_2) \in R$, then $x_1 u_1$ is a proper prefix of $x_2 u_2$, or $x_1 u_1 = x_2 u_2$ and x_1 is* *a proper prefix of x_2 or $x_1 = x_2$ and $u_1 = u_2$. Let $\xrightarrow{*L}$ denote the transitive reflexive closure of $\xrightarrow{L}$. For every w, $z \in \Sigma^*$, a sequence of reductions that begins with w and ends with z such that every step is leftmost is also called a **leftmost reduction** from w to z.*

The reader familiar with formal language theory will note that the definition of leftmost reduction is a straightforward generalization of that of "left to right derivation" in context-free grammars.

Let R be a rewriting system on alphabet Σ with the property that $\rightarrow$ is noetherian. Then for any $x \in \Sigma^*$, one can find an irreducible descendant of x by simply applying any appropriate reduction rule and continuing until an irreducible string results. It is useful to note that this can be done by restricting attention to leftmost reductions. We state this formally.

Lemma 2.2.7 *Let R be a rewriting system on alphabet Σ with the property that $\rightarrow$ is noetherian. For each $x \in \Sigma^*$ there is an irreducible $y \in \Sigma^*$ such that $x \xrightarrow{*L} y$.*

An efficient algorithm to implement Lemma 2.2.7 will be developed below. One additional fact will be very useful in developing that algorithm.

Lemma 2.2.8 *Let R be a rewriting system on alphabet Σ. Let R' be any subset of R with the property that $\mathrm{dom}(R') = \mathrm{dom}(R)$. Then*

(a) *$IRR(R') = IRR(R)$.*

(b) *for any x, $y \in \Sigma^*$, if $x \xrightarrow{*L}_{R'} y$, then $x \xrightarrow{*L}_R y$.*

The proofs of Lemmas 2.2.7 and 2.2.8 are left to the reader.
Now we can describe the algorithm implementing Lemma 2.2.7.

Theorem 2.2.9 *Let R be a finite rewriting system on alphabet Σ with the property that $\rightarrow$ is noetherian. There is an algorithm to solve the following problem:*

Input: *a string $w \in \Sigma^*$.*

Output: *an irreducible string $\overline{w}$ such that $w \xrightarrow{*L} \overline{w}$.*

Proof. Let R' be any subset of R with the properties that $\mathrm{dom}(R') = \mathrm{dom}(R)$ and for each $u \in \mathrm{dom}(R)$ there exists exactly one $v \in \mathrm{range}(R)$ with $(u, v) \in R'$. To be precise, construct R' by choosing the lexicographically smallest v' with $(u, v') \in R$. Then $IRR(R') = IRR(R)$ and for every $x \in \Sigma^*$ there is a unique irreducible $\overline{x}$ such that $x \xrightarrow{*L}_{R'} \overline{x}$. The choice of R' does not depend on w and so we will assume that R' has been determined by preprocessing. Let $t = \max\{|u|, |v| \mid (u, v) \in R'\}$; recall that R (hence,

R') is finite so that t exists. It is sufficient to describe an algorithm based on R'.

We describe our algorithm in terms of the Turing machine model. The machine $\mathcal{M}$ has two pushdown stores, Store 1 and Store 2, and a finite-state control. Initially, Store 1 is empty and Store 2 contains the input w with the leftmost symbol of w on the top of the store. When Store 2 is empty, Store 1 will contain the desired result. At any point between the initial and final steps, Stores 1 and 2 contain an intermediate string y such that $w \overset{*L}{\to}_{R'} y$ with a prefix of y stored on Store 1 and the corresponding suffix of y stored on Store 2. The step-by-step computation is described in terms of three operations, READ, SEARCH, and REWRITE.

(i) **READ.** $\mathcal{M}$ attempts to read a new symbol from Store 2, popping that symbol from Store 2 and pushing that symbol onto the top of Store 1. If $\mathcal{M}$ is able to read such a symbol, then it performs the SEARCH operation. If $\mathcal{M}$ is not able to read such a symbol, then $\mathcal{M}$ halts.

(ii) **SEARCH.** $\mathcal{M}$ reads the top t symbols from Store 1 and determines whether there exists a string u stored on the top $|u|$ squares of Store 1 such that there exists v, $(u, v) \in R'$. If at least one such u exists, then $\mathcal{M}$ chooses the longest such u, remembers (u, v), and performs the REWRITE operation; in this case, we say that SEARCH "succeeds." Otherwise, we say that SEARCH "fails;" in this case, $\mathcal{M}$ restores the top t symbols of Store 1 and performs the READ operation.

(iii) **REWRITE.** Having remembered the rewrite rule (u, v), $\mathcal{M}$ pops the string u from the top of Store 1 and pushes the string v onto the top $|v|$ squares of Store 2 so that the leftmost symbol of v is on the top of Store 2. Then $\mathcal{M}$ performs the READ operation.

From the construction of R' and $\mathcal{M}$, if an application of SEARCH succeeds, then both of the strings u and v are unique; hence, $\mathcal{M}$ is deterministic. Since $(u, v) \in R'$, then $u \overset{L}{\to}_{R'} v$; hence, it is easy to see that the computation of $\mathcal{M}$ on input w is a leftmost reduction using the rewrite rules of R'. By hypothesis, $\to_R$ is noetherian and so $\to_{R'}$ is noetherian since $R' \subseteq R$; thus, $\mathcal{M}$'s computation on w must halt; let z be the string contained on Store 1 when the computation halts, with the leftmost symbol of z being at the bottom of Store 1. Thus, the computation of $\mathcal{M}$ on input w that computes z simulates the unique leftmost reduction $w \overset{*L}{\to}_{R'} z$. It is clear that z is irreducible (mod R'). Hence, the desired string $\overline{w}$ is precisely z.   □2.2.9

Consider $\mathcal{M}$'s running time. The process of reading and writing up to t symbols takes an amount of time independent of the input string w (but it does depend on the system R'). Clearly, $\mathcal{M}$'s running time on w is proportional to the total number $r(w)$ of READ steps performed. The number

$r(w)$, in turn, is the number of symbols originally appearing on Store 2 plus the number of symbols written onto Store 2 when REWRITE is performed, so $r(w)$ is $|w|$ plus the sum of the lengths of the right-hand sides v of rules (u, v) found in SEARCH. Since $\to_R$ is noetherian there are at most $f_R(|w|)$ successful applications of SEARCH (Proposition 2.2.5); also, each right-hand side v has length at most t, so $r(w) \leq |w| + t \cdot f_R(|w|)$. Thus, the running time of $\mathcal{M}$'s computation on w is bounded above by $c \cdot (|w| + t \cdot f_R(|w|))$ for some constant c. In particular, if $f_R(n) \geq d \cdot n$ for some constant $d > 0$ and all $n \in \mathbf{N}$, we see that $\mathcal{M}$'s running time on w is $0(f_R(|w|))$.

The algorithm described in the proof of Theorem 2.2.9 will be used frequently in the sections that follow. Notice that this algorithm is uniform in R so that one may consider an algorithm that has the system R as part of the input. We refer to this algorithm as REDUCE and, once R is fixed, we write $z := \text{REDUCE}_R(w)$ where z is an irreducible string such that $w \xrightarrow{*L}_R z$. As a uniform algorithm that, on input a finite noetherian string-rewriting system R and a string w, computes an irreducible descendant of $w \bmod R$, this algorithm has running time $O(\| R \| \cdot (|w| + \| R \| \cdot f_R(|w|)))$, which is $O(\| R \|^2 \cdot f_R(|w|))$ if $f_R(n) \geq cn$ holds for some constant c and all $n \in \mathbf{N}$.

In the algorithm REDUCE the given string-rewriting system R is replaced by a subsystem R' such that $\text{dom}(R') = \text{dom}(R)$, but no two rules of R' have the same left-hand side. In fact, there is a stronger property of string-rewriting systems that is of interest.

Definition 2.2.10

(a) *A string-rewriting system R on Σ is called* **normalized** *if the following conditions hold for each rule $(\ell, r) \in R : \ell \in IRR(R - \{(\ell, r)\})$ and $r \in IRR(R)$, that is, the right-hand side r is irreducible, and the left-hand side ℓ can be reduced only by the rule (ℓ, r) itself.*

(b) *Two string-rewriting systems R and S on the same alphabet Σ are called* **equivalent** *if they generate the same Thue congruence, that is, if $\overset{*}{\leftrightarrow}_R = \overset{*}{\leftrightarrow}_S$.*

Let $>$ be an admissible well-founded partial ordering on Σ^*, and let R be a finite string-rewriting system on Σ that is compatible with this ordering. In general, there will not exist a normalized system R_1 that is equivalent to R, and that is compatible with the given ordering. For example, let $>$ be the length ordering, and let $R := \{a^2 \to b, a^2 \to c\}$. Obviously, no length-reducing system can both be normalized and equivalent to R, since the strings b and c are incomparable with respect to the ordering $>$. The situation is different when we deal with an admissible well-ordering $>$ on Σ^*. Given a finite string-rewriting system R compatible with $>$, we will construct a finite normalized system R_1 that is also compatible with $>$, and that is equivalent to R. For the first stage of this construction, we need the following lemma.

Lemma 2.2.11 *Let $>$ be an admissible well-ordering on Σ^*, and let R be a string-rewriting system on Σ that is compatible with $>$. For each $w \in \Sigma^*$, let $\hat{w}$ denote some irreducible descendant of w. Then the string-rewriting system $R_0 := \{\ell \to \hat{r} \mid (\ell \to r) \in R\}$ is equivalent to R, is compatible with $>$, and $\text{range}(R_0) \subseteq IRR(R_0)$. In addition, if R is confluent, then so is R_0.*

Proof. Obviously, R_0 is compatible with $>$, $\text{range}(R_0) \subseteq IRR(R) = IRR(R_0)$, and $\to_{R_0} \subseteq \overset{*}{\to}_R$. Thus, it remains to prove that $\ell \overset{*}{\leftrightarrow}_{R_0} r$ holds for all $(\ell \to r) \in R$. Assume to the contrary that there exists a rule $(\ell \to r) \in R$ such that $\ell \overset{*}{\not\leftrightarrow}_{R_0} r$. Since $>$ is a well-ordering on Σ^*, we may choose this rule among all rules having the property that r is minimum with respect to the ordering $>$. Since $\ell \overset{*}{\not\leftrightarrow}_{R_0} r$, we have $(\ell \to r) \notin R_0$, that is, $r \overset{+}{\to}_R \hat{r}$ and $(\ell \to \hat{r}) \in R_0$. However, for each rule $(\ell_1 \to r_1) \in R$ that is used in the reduction $r \overset{+}{\to}_R \hat{r}$, we have $r > r_1$. Thus, according to the choice of the rule $(\ell \to r) \in R$, we have $\ell_1 \overset{*}{\leftrightarrow}_{R_0} r_1$, and therefore, we can conclude that $r \overset{*}{\leftrightarrow}_{R_0} \hat{r} \leftrightarrow_{R_0} \ell$. Hence, R and R_0 are indeed equivalent.

Finally, assume that R is confluent. Then each congruence class $[w]_R$ contains a unique irreducible string w_0. Since $IRR(R) = IRR(R_0)$, and since R and R_0 are equivalent, this implies that R_0 is confluent too. $\square$2.2.11

Although $\text{range}(R_0) \subseteq IRR(R_0)$, the system R_0 will in general not be normalized, since a left-hand side of a rule of R_0 may contain another left-hand side as a factor. The second stage of the proposed construction now takes care of this situation. We now present the full construction in the form of an algorithm.

Algorithm 2.2.12 *Construction of an equivalent normalized system REDUCE-SYSTEM:*

> **Input:** An admissible well-ordering $>$ on Σ^*, and a finite string-rewriting system R on Σ compatible with $>$;

> **begin** $R_1 \leftarrow R;$
>   reduce the right-hand sides of the rules of R_1 by the algorithm REDUCE;
>   (Comment: By Lemma 2.2.11 the resulting system R_1 is equivalent to R, it is compatible with $>$, and $\text{range}(R_1) \subseteq IRR(R_1)$.)
>   **while** $\exists(\ell_1, r_1), (\ell_2, r_2) \in R_1 \exists x, y \in \Sigma^* : \ell_2 = x\ell_1 y$ **and** $(xy \neq e$ **or** $r_2 > r_1)$ **do**
>   **begin** $R_1 \leftarrow R_1 - \{\ell_2 \to r_2\};$

$$\textbf{if } r_2 \notin \Delta_{R_1}^*(xr_1y) \textbf{ then}$$
$$\textbf{begin if } xr_1y > r_2 \textbf{ then } R_1 \leftarrow R_1 \cup \{xr_1y \rightarrow r_2\}$$
$$\textbf{else } R_1 \leftarrow R_1 \cup \{r_2 \rightarrow xr_1y\};$$
$$\textit{reduce the right-hand sides of the rules}$$
$$\textit{of } R_1 \textit{ by the algorithm REDUCE}$$

end

end;

OUTPUT: R_1

end

Whenever a rule $\ell_2 \rightarrow r_2$ is deleted from R_1, then there exists another rule $(\ell_1 \rightarrow r_1) \in R_1$ such that $\ell_2 = x\ell_1 y$, that is, $r_2 \stackrel{*}{\longleftrightarrow}_{R_1} xr_1y$. If $xr_1y \stackrel{*}{\rightarrow}_{R_1} r_2$, then the deleted rule is not used in this reduction, and therefore, the system $R_1 - \{\ell_2 \rightarrow r_2\}$ is equivalent to R_1. If $xr_1y \stackrel{*}{\not\rightarrow}_{R_1} r_2$, then either the rule $xr_1y \rightarrow r_2$ or the rule $r_2 \rightarrow xr_1y$ is added to the system. Obviously, the resulting system $(R_1 - \{\ell_2 \rightarrow r_2\}) \cup \{xr_1y \rightarrow r_2\}$, respectively $(R_1 - \{\ell_2 \rightarrow r_2\}) \cup \{r_2 \rightarrow xr_1y\}$, is equivalent to R_1. Thus, we see that whenever we enter the **while**-loop, the actual system R_1 is equivalent to R, is compatible with $>$, and satisfies range$(R_1) \subseteq IRR(R_1)$. These statements together with the condition leading to the termination of the **while**-loop imply that whenever the above algorithm terminates, then it correctly computes a finite normalized string-rewriting system R_1 that is equivalent to the input system R, and that is compatible with the given ordering $>$. Thus, it remains to prove the termination of this algorithm.

Let $>$ be the admissible well-ordering on Σ^* that is used in the above algorithm. We extend this ordering to an ordering of finite sets of pairs of strings from Σ^* as follows.

Let $x_1, x_2, y_1, y_2 \in \Sigma^*$. We define an ordering $>_2$ on $\Sigma^* \times \Sigma^*$ by setting $(x_1, x_2) >_2 (y_1, y_2)$ if and only if $x_1 > y_1$ or $(x_1 = y_1$ and $x_2 > y_2)$. Obviously, $>_2$ is a well-ordering.

Now, for finite subsets $S_1, S_2 \subseteq \Sigma^* \times \Sigma^*$, we use the multi-set ordering $\gg_2$ induced by $>_2$, that is, $S_1 \gg_2 S_2$ if and only if there exist a non-empty subset $T_1 \subseteq S_1$ and a subset $T_2 \subseteq S_2$ such that $S_2 = (S_1 - T_1) \cup T_2$, and for each pair $(y_1, y_2) \in T_2$ there is a pair $(x_1, x_2) \in T_1$ satisfying $(x_1, x_2) >_2 (y_1, y_2)$.

Then $\gg_2$ is a well-ordering on the finite subsets of $\Sigma^* \times \Sigma^*$. Using this ordering we can now prove the following result.

Theorem 2.2.13 *On input an admissible well-ordering $>$ on Σ^*, and a finite string-rewriting system R on Σ compatible with $>$, algorithm REDUCE-SYSTEM computes a finite normalized string-rewriting system R_1 such that R_1 is equivalent to R and R_1 is compatible with $>$.*

Proof. Because of the preceding observations we only need to show that algorithm REDUCE-SYSTEM terminates on input $(>, R)$.

First, a system R_0 is computed that results from R by replacing every right-hand side by one of its irreducible descendants. Obviously, either $R_0 = R$ or $R \gg_2 R_0$.

Now for all $i \geq 1$, let R_{i-1} denote the string-rewriting system with which the i-th execution of the **while**-loop is entered.

Claim. For all $i \geq 1$, $R_{i-1} \gg_2 R_i$.

Proof. The **while**-loop is entered for the i-th time only if there exist rules $(\ell_1, r_1), (\ell_2, r_2) \in R_{i-1}$ and words $x, y \in \Sigma^*$ such that $\ell_2 = x\ell_1 y$ and $(xy \neq e$ or $r_2 > r_1)$. In this case rule $(\ell_2 \to r_2)$ is deleted from R_{i-1}. If $r_2 \in \Delta^*_{R_{i-1}-\{\ell_2 \to r_2\}}(xr_1y)$, then $R_i = R_{i-1} - \{\ell_2 \to r_2\}$, and hence, $R_{i-1} \gg_2 R_i$, otherwise a system R'_i is obtained from $R_{i-1} - \{\ell_2 \to r_2\}$ by introducing the rule $(xr_1y \to r_2)$ or the rule $(r_2 \to xr_1y)$. Since $\ell_2 > r_2$ and $\ell_1 > r_1$, and since $>$ is an admissible ordering, we can conclude that $\ell_2 = x\ell_1y > xr_1y$, that is, in either case $R_{i-1} \gg_2 R'_i$. Now, R_i is obtained from R'_i by replacing each right-hand side by one of its irreducible descendants, and hence $R_i = R'_i$ or $R'_i \gg_2 R_i$. Thus, $R_{i-1} \gg_2 R_i$.   □ Claim.

Since $\gg_2$ is a well-ordering, there does not exist an infinite sequence $(R_i)_{i \geq 0}$ of string-rewriting systems satisfying $R_{i-1} \gg_2 R_i$ for all $i \geq 1$. Thus, the **while**-loop is executed only a finite number of times, and hence, algorithm REDUCE-SYSTEM terminates.   □ 2.2.13

The complexity of algorithm REDUCE-SYSTEM depends on the following factors:

- the complexity of computing irreducible descendants,

- the complexity of the ordering $>$, that is, given two strings $x, y \in \Sigma^*$, how hard is it to verify whether $x > y$ holds,

- the order in which the rules $(\ell_1, r_1), (\ell_2, r_2) \in R_1$ are chosen in the **while**-loop, and

- on the choice of the factor ℓ_1 that is actually used in reducing ℓ_2, if ℓ_1 has several occurences as a factor of ℓ_2.

Recall that an upper bound for the complexity of computing an irreducible descendant is given through the length of the longest applicable sequence of reductions.

Observe that the normalized system R_1 is not uniquely determined by R and $>$. To see this let $>$ be the length-lexicographical ordering on Σ^*, where $\Sigma = \{a, b, c, d\}$, and let $R = \{ab \to c, ba \to d, aba \to d\}$. Depending on which of the first two rules we use to reduce the left-hand side of the third rule we obtain either the normalized system $R_1 = \{ab \to c, ba \to d, ca \to d\}$ or the normalized system $R_2 = \{ab \to c, ba \to d, ad \to d\}$.

Finally, notice that if the system R is confluent, then the normalized system R_1 is simply a subsystem of the system $R_0 := \{\ell \to \hat{r} \mid (\ell \to$

$r) \in R\}$ that we obtain from Lemma 2.2.11. Since $\to_{R_0} \subseteq \overset{*}{\to}_{R_1}$, R_1 is also confluent. In contrast to the general situation, normalized confluent systems are unique. This is the next result.

Theorem 2.2.14 *Let $>$ be an admissible well-founded partial ordering on Σ^*, and let R_1 and R_2 be two string-rewriting systems on Σ that are normalized, confluent, and compatible with $>$. If R_1 and R_2 are equivalent, then they are in fact identical.*

Proof. Assume that R_1 and R_2 are equivalent, but that they are not identical, and let $(\ell, r) \in (R_1 - R_2) \cup (R_2 - R_1)$. From all the rules in the symmetric difference of R_1 and R_2 let the rule (ℓ, r) be chosen in such a way that $|\ell|$ is minimum. We assume that $(\ell, r) \in R_1$, the other case being symmetric. Then $r \in IRR(R_1)$, since R_1 is normalized, and so $w > r$ for all $w \in [r]_{R_1}$, $w \ne r$, since R_1 is confluent and compatible with $>$. The systems R_1 and R_2 are equivalent. Thus $[r]_{R_1} = [r]_{R_2}$, and since R_2 is also confluent and compatible with $>$, this means that $w \overset{*}{\to}_{R_2} r$ for all $w \in [r]_{R_1}$. In particular, $\ell \overset{*}{\to}_{R_2} r$. Since $(\ell, r) \notin R_2$, we see that either $(\ell, r') \in R_2$ and $r' \overset{*}{\to}_{R_2} r$ contradicting the fact that R_2 is normalized, or $(\ell', r') \in R_2$ such that $\ell = x\ell'y$ for some $x, y \in \Sigma^*$, $xy \ne e$, and $xr'y \overset{*}{\to}_{R_2} r$. However, this means that $|\ell'| < |\ell|$, and so $(\ell', r') \in R_1$ as well, due to the choice of (ℓ, r). This contradicts the fact that R_1 is normalized.   □ 2.2.14

2.3   Testing for Local Confluence

In Theorem 1.1.13 it is shown that under the hypothesis that $\to$ is noetherian, a reduction system is confluent if and only if it is locally confluent. In this section we show that there is an algorithm that on input a finite string-rewriting system R such that $\to_R$ is noetherian will determine whether R is locally confluent, and, thus, confluent.

How can one determine whether R is locally confluent? On first glance it appears to be impossible to test for local confluence since it is a global property: for all w, x, y, if $w \to x$ and $w \to y$, then there must exist z such that $x \overset{*}{\to} z$ and $y \overset{*}{\to} z$. Thus, one must consider every $w \in \Sigma^*$ and every pair x, y such that $w \to x$ and $w \to y$ and try to determine if they "resolve," that is, if there exists z such that $x \overset{*}{\to} z$ and $y \overset{*}{\to} z$. This cannot be done algorithmically and so it is necessary to bound the set of strings w for which local confluence must be tested.

Suppose that $w \to x$ and $w \to y$. If (u_1, v_1), (u_2, v_2) are in R and $w = w_1 u_1 w_2 u_2 w_3$, then $w \to w_1 v_1 w_2 u_2 w_3 \to w_1 v_1 w_2 v_2 w_3$ by first rewriting u_1 as v_1 and then rewriting u_2 as v_2, and $w \to w_1 u_1 w_2 v_2 w_3 \to w_1 v_1 w_2 v_2 w_3$ by first rewriting u_2 as v_2 and then rewriting u_1 as v_1. The results are the same, that is, $w_1 v_1 w_2 v_2 w_3$. Thus, in this case we are not required to test anything. Hence, we can restrict attention to those cases where $w = w_1 u_1 w_2$ and $w = w_3 u_2 w_4$ with

(a) $|w_1 u_1| < |w_3 u_2|$ and $|w_2| < |u_2 w_4|$ or

(b) $|w_3 u_2| < |w_1 u_1|$ and $|w_4| < |u_1 w_2|$.

Cases (a) and (b) occur when for some $x, y \in \Sigma^*$, $xy \neq e$, either $u_1 x = y u_2$ and $|x| < |u_2|$, or $u_1 = x u_2 y$. (Of course, the roles of u_1 and u_2 can be interchanged but it is sufficient to consider only these cases.)

Hence, to determine whether R is locally confluent, it is sufficient to consider pairs of rewrite rules from R. For each pair of not necessarily distinct rewriting rules from R, say (u_1, v_1) and (u_2, v_2), let the set of **critical pairs** corresponding to this pair be $\{\langle x v_1, v_2 y \rangle \mid$ there are $x, y \in \Sigma^*$, $x u_1 = u_2 y$ and $|x| < |u_2|\} \cup \{\langle v_1, x v_2 y \rangle \mid$ there are $x, y \in \Sigma^*$, $u_1 = x u_2 y\}$. We will say that a critical pair $\langle z_1, z_2 \rangle$ **resolves** if z_1 and z_2 have a common descendant. Notice that if a critical pair $x v_1$ and $v_2 y$ has two different irreducible descendants, that is, one from $x v_1$ and one from $v_2 y$, then R is not confluent (hence, not locally confluent) since that would imply that the congruence class of $x u_1 = u_2 y$ has more than one irreducible element. A similar statement can be made for a pair v_1 and $x v_2 y$. On the other hand, if every critical pair resolves, then the argument above implies that R is locally confluent.

To check whether a given pair resolves, we can use the algorithm RE-DUCE (described in the proof of Theorem 2.2.9) to determine whether the two strings have a common irreducible leftmost descendant. Recall that the algorithm REDUCE has the property that on input x it computes an irreducible string z such that $x \xrightarrow{*L} z$, that is, $z = \mathrm{REDUCE}(x)$. Thus, R is locally confluent if and only if for every critical pair $\langle x, y \rangle$, $\mathrm{REDUCE}(x) = \mathrm{REDUCE}(y)$.

How many critical pairs can there be? For any choice of strings u_1 and u_2, with $|u_1| > |u_2|$, there can be at most $|u_2| - 1$ pairs x, y such that $x u_1 = u_2 y$ and $0 < |x| < |u_2|$, and there can be at most $|u_1| - |u_2| + 1$ pairs x, y such that $u_1 = x u_2 y$. Thus, for any pair (u_1, v_1), (u_2, v_2) of (not necessarily distinct) rewriting rules in R with $|u_1| \geq |u_2|$, there are at most $|u_1|$ critical pairs. Furthermore, for any such pair of rules, it is easy to see that the corresponding set of critical pairs can be obtained in $O(|u_1|^2)$ steps. Let CP_R be the union of the sets of critical pairs where the union is taken over the set of all pairs of not necessarily distinct rewrite rules of R. Then there are at most $\| R \|^2$ choices of pairs of rewrite rules in R and so CP_R has size $O(\| R \|^3)$ and CP_R can be constructed in time $O(\| R \|^4)$. (Recall that $\| R \|$ denotes the size of R).

What we need to do is view this procedure as an algorithm that takes a finite string-rewriting system R as input. The alphabet need not be fixed, but it is sufficient to let Σ be the set of letters that occur in the rules of R. Having done this we obtain the following result.

Theorem 2.3.1 *There is an algorithm to solve the following problem:*

Instance: *A finite rewriting system R such that $\to_R$ is noetherian;*

Question: *Is R locally confluent?*

Corollary 2.3.2 *There is an algorithm to solve the following problem:*

Instance: *A finite rewriting system R such that $\to_R$ is noetherian;*

Question: *Is R confluent?*

The running time of the algorithm described above depends on the complexity of the algorithm REDUCE, that is, on the function f_R. Notice that if $\langle u_1, u_2 \rangle$ is a critical pair, then $|u_1|, |u_2| \leq \parallel R \parallel$. Hence determining whether $\langle u_1, u_2 \rangle$ resolves takes time

$$c \parallel R \parallel (|u_1| + t \cdot f_R(|u_1|)) + c \parallel R \parallel (|u_2| + t \cdot f_R(|u_2|)) +$$

$$f_R(|u_1|) + f_R(|u_2|) \leq 2c(\parallel R \parallel^2 + \parallel R \parallel^2 \cdot f_R(\parallel R \parallel)) + 2f_R(\parallel R \parallel) \leq$$

$$+c'(\parallel R \parallel^2 + \parallel R \parallel^2 \cdot f_R(\parallel R \parallel)) \text{ for some } c'.$$

Since CP_R has size $O(\parallel R \parallel^3)$ and CP_R can be constructed in time $O(\parallel R \parallel^4)$, this means that the running time of the algorithm is bounded above by

$$O(\parallel R \parallel^4) + O(\parallel R \parallel^3 \cdot (\parallel R \parallel^2 + \parallel R \parallel^2 \cdot f_R(\parallel R \parallel))) =$$

$$O(\parallel R \parallel^5 \cdot f_R(\parallel R \parallel)).$$

2.4   The Knuth-Bendix Completion Procedure

Let R be a string-rewriting system on Σ, and let $>$ be an admissible well-ordering on Σ^* such that R is compatible with $>$, that is, $\ell > r$ for each rule $(\ell, r) \in R$.

Suppose that R is not confluent. Then there exists a critical pair $\langle z_1, z_2 \rangle$ of R such that z_1 and z_2 do not have a common descendant modulo R. Let $\hat{z}_1$ and $\hat{z}_2$ be irreducible descendants of z_1 and z_2, respectively. One way to resolve the critical pair $\langle z_1, z_2 \rangle$ consists of introducing a new rule $(\hat{z}_1, \hat{z}_2)$ or $(\hat{z}_2, \hat{z}_1)$. In order to preserve the property that the system under consideration is noetherian, we want to orient this new rule in accordance with the well-ordering $>$. By repeating this process we attempt to **complete** the system R. However, observe that when adding a new rule, additional critical pairs may arise. Thus, this process of adding rules may not terminate.

Procedure 2.4.1 (Knuth-Bendix Completion Procedure)

Input: A finite string-rewriting system R on Σ, and an admissible well-ordering $>$ on Σ^*;

begin $R_0 \leftarrow \{(\ell, r) \mid \ell > r \text{ and } (\ell, r) \in R \text{ or } (r, \ell) \in R\}$;
           (Comment: All rules of R are oriented with respect to $>$.)
           $i \leftarrow -1$;
   repeat
           $i \leftarrow i + 1$;
           $R_{i+1} \leftarrow \emptyset$;
           $CP \leftarrow$ *set of critical pairs of R_i*;
           while $CP \neq \emptyset$ **do**
           begin *choose* $\langle z_1, z_2 \rangle \in CP$;
                   compute normal forms $\hat{z}_1$ *and* $\hat{z}_2$ *of* z_1 *and* z_2,
                       respectively, modulo R_i;
                   if $\hat{z}_1 > \hat{z}_2$ **then** $R_{i+1} \leftarrow R_{i+1} \cup \{(\hat{z}_1, \hat{z}_2)\}$;
                   if $\hat{z}_2 > \hat{z}_1$ **then** $R_{i+1} \leftarrow R_{i+1} \cup \{(\hat{z}_2, \hat{z}_1)\}$;
                   $CP \leftarrow CP - \{(z_1, z_2)\}$
           end;
           (Comment: all critical pairs of R_i have been resolved.)
           if $R_{i+1} \neq \emptyset$ **then** $R_{i+1} \leftarrow R_i \cup R_{i+1}$
   until $R_{i+1} = \emptyset$;
   $R^* \leftarrow \bigcup_{i \geq 0} R_i$
end.

Procedure 2.4.1 computes a sequence $R_0, R_1, R_2, \ldots$ of string-rewriting systems on Σ. If $\langle z_1, z_2 \rangle$ is a critical pair of R_i, then $\hat{z}_1 \overset{*}{\longleftrightarrow}_{R_i} \hat{z}_2$. Hence, one can easily prove by induction on i that the string-rewriting systems $R_0, R_1, R_2, \ldots$ and R^* are all equivalent to R. Since R is finite, R_0 is finite, and so R_0 only has finitely many critical pairs. Thus, R_1 is finite, too. Inductively we obtain that each system $R_i (i \geq 0)$ is finite. If Procedure 2.4.1 terminates, then $R^* = R_i$ for some $i \geq 0$ and R^* has no unresolved critical pair. Since all R_i are noetherian, this implies that Procedure 2.4.1 terminates as soon as a system R_i that is confluent is reached. If Procedure 2.4.1 does not terminate, then it computes an infinite sequence $R_0, R_1, R_2, \ldots$ of finite string-rewriting systems on Σ, none of which is confluent. In this situation an infinite string-rewriting system R^* on Σ is being enumerated.

Theorem 2.4.2 *Let R be a finite string-rewriting system on Σ, and let $>$ be an admissible well-ordering on Σ^*. Further, let R^* be the string-rewriting system on Σ that Procedure 2.4.1 enumerates on input $(R, >)$. Then the following statements hold:*

(a) *R^* is noetherian and confluent.*

(b) *R and R^* are equivalent, and*

(c) *$IRR(R^*) = \{x \in \Sigma^* \mid \forall y \in \Sigma^* : \text{if } x \overset{*}{\longleftrightarrow}_R y, \text{ then } y = x \text{ or } y > x\}$.*

Proof. As remarked before, R and R^* are equivalent. Further, by construction, we have $\ell > r$ for all $(\ell, r) \in R_i$, all $i \geq 0$. Since $R^* = \bigcup_{i \geq 0} R_i$, this yields that $\ell > r$ for all $(\ell, r) \in R^*$, implying that R^* is noetherian. Let $\langle z_1, z_2 \rangle$ be a critical pair of R^*, generated by overlapping the rules $(\ell_1, r_1), (\ell_2, r_2) \in R^*$. Then there is an index $i \geq 0$ such that $(\ell_1, r_1), (\ell_2, r_2) \in R_i$, and hence, $\langle z_1, z_2 \rangle$ is resolved modulo R_{i+1}, that is, z_1 and z_2 have a common descendant modulo R_{i+1}. Hence, z_1 and z_2 have a common descendant modulo R^* implying that R^* is confluent. These observations imply (c). □ 2.4.2

Thus, for each input $(R, >)$, the Knuth-Bendix Completion Procedure "produces" a confluent string-rewriting system that is equivalent to R, and that is based on the well-ordering $>$. In particular, this shows the following.

Corollary 2.4.3 *For each string-rewriting system R on Σ, and each admissible well-ordering $>$ on Σ^*, there exists a, possibly infinite, confluent string-rewriting system R^* on Σ such that*

- *R and R^* are equivalent, and*

- *$\ell > r$ for each rule $(\ell, r) \in R^*$.*

If no finite confluent system exists that is equivalent to R, and that is based on $>$, then obviously, this procedure cannot terminate. On the other hand, we do have the following termination property for the Knuth-Bendix completion procedure.

Theorem 2.4.4 *Procedure 2.4.1 terminates on input $(R, >)$ if and only if there exists a finite confluent string-rewriting system R' on Σ such that R and R' are equivalent, and $\ell > r$ for each rule $(\ell, r) \in R'$.*

Proof. If Procedure 2.4.1 terminates on input $(R, >)$, then R^* has all the required properties according to Theorem 2.4.2.

Conversely, let us assume that there exists a finite confluent string-rewriting system R' on Σ such that

- R and R' are equivalent, and

- $\ell > r$ for each rule $(\ell, r) \in R'$.

Let $R^* = \bigcup_{i \geq 0} R_i$ be the string-rewriting system on Σ that Procedure 2.4.1 enumerates on input $(R, >)$. Then R and R^* are equivalent, R^* is confluent, and $\ell > r$ for each rule $(\ell, r) \in R^*$.

Let $(\ell, r) \in R'$. Then $\ell \overset{*}{\longleftrightarrow}_{R^*} r$. By the remark preceding Theorem 2.2.14, we may assume without loss of generality that R' is reduced. Then $r \in IRR(R')$, and since R' is based on $>$, this means that $u > r$ for each $u \in [r]_R$, $u \neq r$. Thus, we have $\ell \overset{*}{\to}_{R^*} r$. Hence, there exists a finite subset $T \subseteq R^*$ such that $\ell \overset{*}{\to}_T r$ for all $(\ell, r) \in R'$. Since $R^* = \bigcup_{i \geq 0} R_i$, this means that there is an index $i \geq 0$ such that $\ell \xrightarrow{*}_{R_i} r$ for all $(\ell, r) \in R'$, and so $\rightarrow_{R'} \subseteq \xrightarrow{*}_{R_i}$. Using R' each word $u \in \Sigma^*$ can be reduced to the minimal element in its class (with respect to $>$), and hence, using R_i each word u can be reduced to the minimal element in its class. Thus, R_i is confluent, and therefore Procedure 2.4.1 terminates on input $(R, >)$.   □ 2.4.4

Examples 2.4.5

(a) *Let* $\Sigma = \{a, b, c\}$, *and let* $R = \{a^2 \rightarrow e, b^2 \rightarrow e, ab \rightarrow c\}$.
  As well-ordering $>$ *we take the length-lexicographical ordering that is induced by the following linear ordering on* Σ : $a < b < c$. *Then Procedure 2.4.1 performs the following computations on input* $(R, >)$:

$$R_0 \leftarrow R;$$
$$CP_0 \leftarrow \{(b, ac), (cb, a)\}, \text{ since } b \leftarrow aab \rightarrow ac, \text{ and } cb \leftarrow abb \rightarrow a;$$
$$R_1 \leftarrow \{a^2 \rightarrow e, b^2 \rightarrow e, ab \rightarrow c, ac \rightarrow b, cb \rightarrow a\};$$
$$CP_1 = \emptyset, \text{ since all critical pairs of } R_1 \text{ resolve:}$$

$$
\begin{array}{ccc}
aac \rightarrow ab & acb \rightarrow aa & cbb \rightarrow c \\
\downarrow\;\; \checkmark & \downarrow\quad\downarrow & \downarrow\;\; \nearrow \\
c & bb \rightarrow e & ab
\end{array}
$$

  Thus, $R^* = R_1$.

(b) *Let* $\Sigma = \{a, \bar{a}, b, \bar{b}\}$, *and let*

$$
\begin{aligned}
R \;=\; &\{a\bar{a} \rightarrow e, \bar{a}a \rightarrow e, b\bar{b} \rightarrow e, \bar{b}b \rightarrow e, ba \rightarrow ab, b\bar{a} \rightarrow \bar{a}b, \\
&\;\bar{b}a \rightarrow a\bar{b}, \bar{b}\bar{a} \rightarrow \bar{a}\bar{b}\}.
\end{aligned}
$$

  (i) *Let* $>$ *be the length-lexicographical ordering induced by the linear ordering* $a < \bar{a} < b < \bar{b}$ *on* Σ. *Then* $R_0 = R$, R *is confluent, and hence,* $R^* = R$.

  (ii) *Let* $>$ *be the length-lexicographical ordering induced by the linear ordering* $\bar{b} < a < \bar{a} < b$. *Then Procedure 2.4.1 performs the following computations on input* $(R, >)$:

$$R_0 \quad = \{a\bar{a} \to e, \ \bar{a}a \to e, \ b\bar{b} \to e, \ \bar{b}b \to e, \ ba \to ab,$$
$$b\bar{a} \to \bar{a}b, \ a\bar{b} \to \bar{b}a, \ \bar{a}\bar{b} \to \bar{b}\bar{a}\};$$

$$CP_0 \quad = \{(a, \bar{b}ab), (\bar{a}, \bar{b}\bar{a}b)\}, \ since \ a \leftarrow \bar{b}ba \to \bar{b}ab \ and$$
$$\bar{a} \leftarrow \bar{b}b\bar{a} \to \bar{b}\bar{a}b;$$

$$R_1 \quad = R_0 \cup \{\bar{b}ab \to a, \bar{b}\bar{a}b \to \bar{a}\};$$

$$CP_1 \quad = \{(\bar{b}a^2b, a^2), (\bar{b}\bar{a}^2b, \bar{a}^2)\}, \ since \ \bar{b}aab \leftarrow a\bar{b}ab \to aa$$
$$and \ \bar{b}\bar{a}^2b \leftarrow \bar{a}\bar{b}ab \to \bar{a}^2;$$

$$R_2 \quad = R_1 \cup \{\bar{b}a^2b \to a^2, \bar{b}\bar{a}^2b \to \bar{a}^2\}.$$

Inductively, we obtain $R_i = R_0 \cup \{\bar{b}a^jb \to a^j, \bar{b}\bar{a}^jb \to \bar{a}^j \mid j = 1, 2, \ldots, i\}.$
Hence, $R^* = R_0 \cup \{\bar{b}a^jb \to a^j, \bar{b}\bar{a}^jb \to \bar{a}^j \mid j \geq 1\}.$

Thus, it very much depends on the chosen well-ordering whether or not Procedure 2.4.1 terminates for a given finite string-rewriting system R. Instead of using an admissible well-ordering, we could also use an admissible well-founded partial ordering $>$ on Σ^*. However, then it may happen that for a critical pair $\langle z_1, z_2 \rangle$ of R_i, $\hat{z}_1 \neq \hat{z}_2$, neither $\hat{z}_1 < \hat{z}_2$ nor $\hat{z}_2 < \hat{z}_1$ holds. In this situation the Procedure would terminate with "failure."

Procedure 2.4.1 is very inefficient in general.

(1) At each state i, all critical pairs are computed. However, all the pairs that result from overlapping rules from R_{i-1} with one another are resolved in R_i. Thus, it suffices to compute only those critical pairs that result from overlapping a rule of $R_i - R_{i-1}$ (a new rule) with a rule from R_i.

(2) We have $R_0 \subseteq R_1 \subseteq R_2 \subseteq \ldots$, that is, rules are only added, but no rule is ever deleted. Thus, in general the resulting confluent system will not be normalized. Instead of normalizing R^* we could try to avoid generating too large a system. In Section 2.2 we considered the algorithm REDUCE-SYSTEM. Using this algorithm we could normalize each system R_i before we compute its critical pairs.

(3) All critical pairs of R_i, that cannot be resolved, are made into new rules at the same stage. It might be better to only introduce one rule at a time, because each new rule can be used to reduce all waiting critical pairs, possibly resolving some of them.

2.5 Some Undecidable Properties

In Section 2.1 we have seen that the uniform variants of the word problem, the common ancestor problem, and the common descendant problem are undecidable for finite string-rewriting systems. In this section we shall see that many additional interesting problems about finite string-rewriting systems are undecidable, among them the termination problem and the confluence problem.

First we deal with the (non-uniform) word problem, which is shown to be undecidable by a reduction from the halting problem for Turing machines. This reduction and variants of it will be used several times throughout this monograph.

Definition 2.5.1 *Let R be a string-rewriting system on Σ.*
The **word problem for R** *is the following decision problem:*

Instance: *Two strings $u, v \in \Sigma^*$.*

Question: *Does $u \overset{*}{\leftrightarrow}_R v$ hold?*

Analogously, the **common ancestor problem for R** *and the* **common descendant problem for R** *are defined.*

Let $\mathcal{A} = (Q, \Sigma, \delta, q_0, q_a)$ be a Turing machine. Without loss of generality we may assume that $\Sigma_b \cap Q = \emptyset$. Let $h, p_1, p \notin \Sigma_b \cup Q$ be three additional symbols, and let $\Omega := \Sigma_b \cup Q \cup \{h, p_1, p\}$.

Define a finite string-rewriting system $S(\mathcal{A})$ on Ω as follows, where $a_k, a_\ell \in \Sigma_b$ and $q_i, q_j \in Q$:

(1)	$q_i a_k$	$\rightarrow$	$q_j a_\ell$	if	$\delta(q_i, a_k)$	$= (q_j, a_\ell)$
(2)	$q_i h$	$\rightarrow$	$q_j a_\ell h$	if	$\delta(q_i, b)$	$= (q_j, a_\ell)$
(3)	$q_i a_k$	$\rightarrow$	$a_k q_j$	if	$\delta(q_i, a_k)$	$= (q_j, R)$
(4)	$q_i h$	$\rightarrow$	$b q_j h$	if	$\delta(q_i, b)$	$= (q_j, R)$
(5)	$a_m q_i a_k$	$\rightarrow$	$q_j a_m a_k$	if	$\delta(q_i, a_k)$	$= (q_j, L)$
(6)	$a_m q_i h$	$\rightarrow$	$q_j a_m h$	if	$\delta(q_i, b)$	$= (q_j, L)$
(7)	$h q_i a_k$	$\rightarrow$	$h q_j b a_k$	if	$\delta(q_i, a_k)$	$= (q_j, L)$
(8)	$h q_i h$	$\rightarrow$	$h q_j b h$	if	$\delta(q_i, b)$	$= (q_j, L)$

for all $a_m \in \Sigma_b$ (braces spanning rules (5)–(8))

(9)	q_a	$\rightarrow$	p_1
(10)	$p_1 a_k$	$\rightarrow$	p_1
(11)	$a_\ell p_1 h$	$\rightarrow$	$p_1 h$
(12)	$h p_1 h$	$\rightarrow$	p

for all $a_k, a_\ell \in \Sigma_b$ (braces spanning rules (10)–(11))

A configuration $u q_i v$ of $\mathcal{A}$ is described by the strings in $\{h b^n u q_i v b^m h \mid n, m \in \mathcal{N}\}$. The symbol h serves as a **delimiter**. The rules of the form (1) to (8) enable the system $S(\mathcal{A})$ to simulate $\mathcal{A}$ step by step.

Lemma 2.5.2 *Let $u, v, u_1, v_1 \in \Sigma_b^*$ and $q, q_1 \in Q$ such that u_1 does not begin with a 'b', and v_1 does not end in a 'b'. Then the following two statements are equivalent:*

(a) $uqv \xleftrightarrow[A]{*} u_1 q_1 v_1$;

(b) $\exists n, m \in \mathbf{N} : huqvh \xrightarrow{*}_{S(\mathcal{A})} hb^n u_1 q_1 v_1 b^m h$.

Proof. For $w_1, w_2 \in \Omega^*$, if $w_1 \xrightarrow{*}_{S(\mathcal{A})} w_2$, then $|w_1|_p + |w_1|_{p_1} \leq |w_2|_p + |w_2|_{p_1}$. Since $|hb^n u_1 q_1 v_1 b^m h|_p + |hb^n u_1 q_1 v_1 b^m h|_{p_1} = 0$, we see that during the reduction sequence in (b) only rules of the form (1) to (8) are applied. Since these rules simulate the effect of the transition function δ, the above two statements are equivalent. $\qquad\square$ 2.5.2

Also from the definition of $S(\mathcal{A})$ the following lemma can be derived easily.

Lemma 2.5.3 Let $w \in \Omega^*$. Then $w \xrightarrow{*}_{S(\mathcal{A})} p$ if and only if one of the following three conditions is satisfied:

(i) $w = p$, or

(ii) $\exists u, v \in \Sigma_b^* : w = hup_1 vh$, or

(iii) $\exists u, v \in \Sigma_b^* \exists q \in Q : w = huqvh$, and $\mathcal{A}$ reaches a final configuration when it is started at configuration uqv.

Proof. Obviously, conditions (i) to (iii) are sufficient. On the other hand, if $w \xrightarrow{*}_{S(\mathcal{A})} p$, and $w \neq p$, then w is of the form $w = huqvh$ for some strings $u, v \in \Sigma_b^*$ and $q \in Q \cup \{p_1\}$. If $q \neq p_1$, then $huqvh$ describes the configuration uqv of $\mathcal{A}$. In order to reduce $w = huqvh$ to p, the rule $q_a \to p_1$ must be used, that is, there exist $u_1, v_1 \in \Sigma_b^*$ such that $huqvh \xrightarrow{*}_{S(\mathcal{A})} hu_1 q_a v_1 h$. Since $u_1 q_a v_1$ is a final configuration of $\mathcal{A}$, we see that $\mathcal{A}$ reaches a final configuration when it is started in configuration uqv. $\qquad\square$ 2.5.3

Lemma 2.5.3 immediately implies the following result.

Corollary 2.5.4 Let $w \in \Sigma^*$. Then $hq_0 wh \xrightarrow{*}_{S(\mathcal{A})} p$ if and only if $w \in L(\mathcal{A})$.

Observe that since $p \in IRR(S(\mathcal{A}))$, the strings $hq_0 wh$ and p have a common descendant modulo $S(\mathcal{A})$ if and only if $hq_0 wh \xrightarrow{*}_{S(\mathcal{A})} p$. Thus, if the Turing machine $\mathcal{A}$ is chosen such that the language $L(\mathcal{A})$ is non-recursive, then the common descendant problem for $S(\mathcal{A})$ is undecidable.

Corollary 2.5.5 There exists a finite string-rewriting system R such that the common descendant problem for R is undecidable.

Let p_0 be an additional symbol, let $\Gamma := \Omega \cup \{p_0\}$, and let $S_0(\mathcal{A}) := S(\mathcal{A}) \cup \{p_0 \to q_0\}$. Then, for each $w \in \Sigma^*$, $hp_0 wh \xrightarrow{*}_{S_0(\mathcal{A})} hq_0 wh$, but $hp_0 wh$ does not have any proper ancestors. Thus, $hp_0 wh$ and p have a common ancestor modulo $S_0(\mathcal{A})$ if and only if $hp_0 wh \xrightarrow{*}_{S_0(\mathcal{A})} p$, which in turn holds if and only if $w \in L(\mathcal{A})$. If $L(\mathcal{A})$ is non-recursive, this means that the common ancestor problem for $S_0(\mathcal{A})$ is undecidable.

Corollary 2.5.6 *There exists a finite string-rewriting system R such that the common ancestor problem for R is undecidable.*

Since the Turing machine $\mathcal{A}$ is deterministic, each string of the form $huqvh(u, v \in \Sigma_b^*, q \in Q)$ has a unique immediate descendant $hu_1q_1v_1h$ $(u_1, v_1 \in \Sigma_b^*, q_1 \in Q \cup \{p_1\})$ with respect to $S(\mathcal{A})$. Based on this observation we obtain the following lemma.

Lemma 2.5.7 *Let $w \in \Omega^*$. Then the following two statements are equivalent:*

(a) $w \xrightarrow{*}_{S(A)} p$, *and*

(b) $w \xleftrightarrow{*}_{S(A)} p$.

Proof. We must verify that (b) implies (a). So let $w \in \Omega^*$ such that $w \xleftrightarrow{*}_{S(A)} p$. From the form of the rules of $S(\mathcal{A})$, we conclude that either $w = p$ or that $w = huqvh$ for some $u, v \in \Sigma_b^*$ and $q \in Q \cup \{p_1\}$. If $w = p$, or if $w = huqvh$ for some u, $v \in \Sigma_b^*$ and $q \in \{q_a, p_1\}$, then obviously $w \xrightarrow{*}_{S(A)} p$. Therefore, let $w = huqvh$ for some u, $v \in \Sigma_b^*$ and $q \in Q - \{q_a\}$, and let $w = huqvh = w_0 \xleftrightarrow{}_{S(A)} w_1 \xleftrightarrow{}_{S(A)} w_2 \xleftrightarrow{}_{S(A)} \cdots \xleftrightarrow{}_{S(A)} w_k = p$ be a shortest transformation from w to p. Since $hp_1h \to p$ is the only rule of $S(\mathcal{A})$ containing an occurrence of the symbol p, we have $w_{k-1} = hp_1h$. Let i be the smallest index such that w_i contains an occurrence of p_1. Then $w_i = hu_ip_1v_ih$ and $w_{i-1} = hu_iq_av_ih$ for some $u_i, v_i \in \Sigma_b^*$. Obviously, $w_{i-1} \xrightarrow{*}_{S(A)} p$. Thus, it remains to show that $w \xrightarrow{*}_{S(A)} w_{i-1}$.

The system $S(\mathcal{A})$ has been constructed from the Turing machine $\mathcal{A}$, the final state of which is q_a. Thus, whenever $\mathcal{A}$ enters this state, it halts. Therefore, $q_a \to p_1$ is the only rule of $S(\mathcal{A})$ that contains an occurrence of q_a on its left-hand side. According to the choice of i the symbol p_1 does not occur in $w_0, w_1, w_2, \ldots, w_{i-1}$, and so $w_{i-2} \xrightarrow{}_{S(A)} w_{i-1}$.

Let j be the largest index such that $w \xleftrightarrow{*}_{S(A)} w_j \xleftarrow{}_{S(A)} w_{j+1} \xrightarrow{}_{S(A)}$ $w_{j+2} \xrightarrow{*}_{S(A)} w_{i-1}$. If no such index exists, then $w \xrightarrow{*}_{S(A)} w_{i-1}$, and we are done. So assume that $j \in \{0, 1, \ldots, i - 3\}$. The string w_{j+1} has the form $w_{j+1} = hu_{j+1}q_rv_{j+1}h$ for some $u_{j+1}, v_{j+1} \in \Sigma_b^*$ and $q_r \in Q - \{q_a\}$, that is, w_{j+1} encodes the configuration $u_{j+1}q_rv_{j+1}$ of $\mathcal{A}$. Hence, w_j and w_{j+2} both describe the unique successor configuration of $u_{j+1}q_rv_{j+1}$, and therefore, $w_j = w_{j+2}$. Deleting the steps $w_j \xleftarrow{}_{S(A)} w_{j+1} \xrightarrow{}_{S(A)} w_{j+2} = w_j$ we obtain a shorter transformation from w to p, thus contradicting our choice of $w \xleftrightarrow{}_{S(A)} w_1 \xleftrightarrow{}_{S(A)} \cdots \xleftrightarrow{}_{S(A)} w_k = p$. Hence, this sequence is actually a reduction sequence, that is, $w \xrightarrow{*}_{S(A)} p$.   □ 2.5.4

Thus Corollary 2.5.4 can be restated as follows.

Corollary 2.5.8 *Let $w \in \Sigma^*$. Then $hq_0wh \xleftrightarrow{*}_{S(A)} p$ if and only if $w \in L(\mathcal{A})$.*

Theorem 2.5.9 *There exists a finite string-rewriting system R such that the word problem for R is undecidable.*

On the other hand, we do have the following positive result.

Theorem 2.5.10 *If R is a finite string-rewriting system on alphabet $\Sigma = \{a\}$, then the word problem for R is decidable.*

Proof. Let $R = \{a^{n_i} \to a^{m_i} \mid i = 1, 2, \ldots, k\}$. Without loss of generality we may assume that $n_i > m_i \geq 0$ for $i = 1, 2, \ldots, k$. Let $m := \min\{m_i \mid i = 1, 2, \ldots, k\}$. Then $[a^n]_R = \{a^n\}$ for all $n \in \{0, 1, \ldots, m-1\}$. Further, let $t := \gcd(n_1 - m_1, \ldots, n_k - m_k)$. Then, for all integers ℓ and r such that $\ell \geq r \geq 0$, the following claim holds.

Claim. $a^\ell \overset{*}{\leftrightarrow}_R a^r$ if and only if $\ell = r$ or $[\ell, r \geq m$ and t divides $(\ell - r)]$.

Proof. It is easily seen that this condition is necessary for $a^\ell \overset{*}{\leftrightarrow}_R a^r$ to hold. To prove that it is also sufficient it is enough to observe that there exist integers $j_1, \ldots, j_k \in Z$ such that $\Sigma_{i=1,\ldots,k} \; j_i(n_i - m_i) = t$. □ Claim.

Since m and t can easily be obtained from R, the above condition is decidable. Therefore, the word problem for R is decidable.   □2.5.10

What is the least cardinality of an alphabet Σ such that a finite string-rewriting system R with an undecidable word problem exists on Σ? To answer this question we make use of the following construction.

Let $\Sigma = \{a_1, a_2, \ldots, a_n\}$ be a finite alphabet of cardinality $n \geq 2$, and let $\Gamma = \{s_1, s_2\}$ be an alphabet of cardinality 2. We define an encoding $\varphi : \Sigma^* \to \Gamma^*$ through $a_i \mapsto s_1 s_2^i s_1 s_2^{2n+1-i}$ for all $i = 1, 2, \ldots, n$. Then $|\varphi(a_i)| = 2n + 3$ for all i, and for $i, j \in \{1, 2, \ldots, n\}$, if $\varphi(a_i) = uv$ and $\varphi(a_j) = vw$ for some $v \neq e$, then $u = e = w$, and therefore $i = j$. This means that there are no non-trivial overlaps between the strings $\varphi(a_1), \ldots, \varphi(a_n)$. For a string-rewriting system R on Σ, let R_φ denote the following system on $\Gamma : R_\varphi := \{\varphi(\ell) \to \varphi(r) \mid (\ell \to r) \in R\}$. Now it is straightforward to check the following.

Lemma 2.5.11 *For all strings $u, v \in \Sigma^*, u \overset{*}{\leftrightarrow}_R v$ if and only if $\varphi(u) \overset{*}{\leftrightarrow}_{R_\varphi} \varphi(v)$.*

Theorem 2.5.9 thus implies the following result.

Theorem 2.5.12 *Let Σ be an alphabet of cardinality at least two. Then there exists a finite string-rewriting system R on Σ such that the word problem for R is undecidable.*

We conclude our collection of undecidable problems for string-rewriting systems with the following three decision problems.

Noetherian System:

Instance: *A finite string-rewriting system R on Σ.*

Question: *Is R noetherian?*

Local Confluence:

Instance: *A finite string-rewriting system R on Σ.*

Question: *Is R locally confluent?*

Confluence:

Instance: *A finite string-rewriting system R on Σ.*

Question: *Is R confluent?*

Theorem 2.5.13 *The problem "Noetherian system" is undecidable in general.*

Proof. (At this point the reader may wish to review Definitions 1.4.1 and 1.4.3). Let $\mathcal{M} = (Q, \Sigma, \delta, q_0, q_a)$ be a Turing machine on Σ. We may assume that $\mathcal{M}$ has an immortal configuration, that is, a configuration from which it cannot reach a final configuration, if and only if it has an immortal initial configuration. Now $\mathcal{M}$ is being simulated by a finite string-rewriting system. Let $\Sigma = \{s_0, s_1, \ldots, s_n\}$, where s_0 is the blank symbol, let $\Sigma' = \{s_0', s_1', \ldots, s_n'\}$ be an alphabet in 1-to-1 correspondence with Σ such that $\Sigma \cap \Sigma' = \emptyset$, and let h, h', q be three additional symbols. We define a string-rewriting system R on the alphabet $\Omega := \Sigma \cup \Sigma' \cup Q \cup \{h, h', q\}$ as follows:

(a) rules to simulate the Turing machine $\mathcal{M}$:

$$
\begin{array}{llll}
q_i s_p & \to & q_j s_\ell & \text{if } \delta(q_i, s_p) = (q_j, s_\ell), \\
q_i h & \to & q_j s_\ell h & \text{if } \delta(q_i, s_0) = (q_j, s_\ell), \\
q_i s_p & \to & s_p' q_j & \text{if } \delta(q_i, s_p) = (q_j, R), \\
q_i h & \to & s_0' q_j h & \text{if } \delta(q_i, s_0) = (q_j, R), \\
s_\ell' q_i s_p & \to & q_j s_\ell s_p & \text{if } \delta(q_i, s_p) = (q_j, L) \\
s_\ell' q_i h & \to & q_j s_\ell h & \text{if } \delta(q_i, s_0) = (q_j, L) \\
h' q_i s_p & \to & h' q_j s_0 s_p & \text{if } \delta(q_i, s_p) = (q_j, L), \\
h' q_i h & \to & h' q_j s_0 h & \text{if } \delta(q_i, s_0) = (q_j, L);
\end{array}
\quad \left. \right\} \text{ for } \ell = 0, 1, \ldots, n,
$$

(b) rules to deal with accepting configurations of $\mathcal{M}$:

$$
\begin{array}{lll}
q_a s_\ell & \to & q_a \\
s_\ell' q_a h & \to & q_a h \\
h' q_a h & \to & q.
\end{array}
\quad \left. \right\} \text{ for } \ell = 0, 1, \ldots, n,
$$

Claim. R is noetherian if and only if $\mathcal{M}$ halts on all inputs.

Proof. Since a computation of $\mathcal{M}$ can be simulated stepwise by a reduction modulo R, R being noetherian implies that $\mathcal{M}$ halts on all inputs.

To obtain the converse implication assume that $\mathcal{M}$ halts on all inputs. Then we can conclude that $\mathcal{M}$ has no immortal configurations at all, that is, no matter with which configuration $\mathcal{M}$ is being started, it will always halt eventually.

Let $w \in \Omega^*$, and let $Q_1 = Q \cup \{q\}$. Then w has a unique factorization $w = u_1 v_1 \ldots u_\ell v_\ell u_{\ell+1}$ such that

- $|u_j|_{Q_1} = 0$ for $j = 1, 2, \ldots, \ell+1$, and

- $v_j \in \{h', e\} \cdot \Sigma'^* \cdot Q_1 \cdot \Sigma^* \cdot \{h, e\}$, $j = 1, 2, \ldots, \ell$, is of maximum length.

The form of the rules of R implies that, if $w = u_1 v_1 \ldots u_\ell v_\ell u_{\ell+1} \overset{*}{\to}_R w'$, then $w' = u_1 v_1' u_2 \ldots u_\ell v_\ell' u_{\ell+1}$ with $v_j \overset{*}{\to}_R v_j'$ for $j = 1, 2, \ldots, \ell$.

Let $v \in \{h', e\} \cdot \Sigma'^* \cdot Q_1 \cdot \Sigma^* \cdot \{h, e\}$, that is, $v = t_1 x' q_i y t_2$ with $t_1 \in \{h', e\}$, $x' \in \Sigma'^*$, $q_i \in Q_1$, $y \in \Sigma^*$, and $t_2 \in \{h, e\}$. Since the TM $\mathcal{M}$ is deterministic, there is at most one rule in R that applies to v. If $q_i \in (Q - \{q_a\})$, then a reduction sequence starting with v simulates the stepwise behavior of $\mathcal{M}$ starting with the configuration $x q_i y$, where x and x' are related by the obvious homomorphism $' : \Sigma^* \to \Sigma'^*$. Such a reduction sequence can be continued until either the description of a halting configuration of $\mathcal{M}$ is reached, or until a string ending in a symbol from Q (if $t_2 = e$) or a string beginning with a symbol from Q (if $t_1 = e$) is obtained, where in the latter case, this string describes a configuration of $\mathcal{M}$ that would cause $\mathcal{M}$ to move its head to the left. The string obtained in this way is reducible if and only if it is the description of a halting configuration of $\mathcal{M}$, that is, if it is of the form $t_1 w' q_a z t_2$ with t_1 and t_2 as above, $w' \in \Sigma'^*$, and $z \in \Sigma^*$.

The rules of group (b) reduce this string within at most $|w'| + |z| + 1$ steps to an irreducible string. Since $\mathcal{M}$ has no immortal configuration, we conclude that each reduction sequence starting with v is of finite length. Hence, R is in fact noetherian.

Thus, R is noetherian if and only if $\mathcal{M}$ has no immortal initial configuration, which is true if and only if $\mathcal{M}$ halts on all inputs. Since in general it is undecidable whether or not a given Turing machine halts on all inputs, this proves our result. □ Claim.

□2.5.13

Based on the proof of Theorem 2.5.13 we can derive the following undecidability result.

Theorem 2.5.14 *The problems "Local confluence" and "Confluence" are undecidable in general.*

Proof. Let $\mathcal{M} = (Q, \Sigma, \delta, q_0, q_a)$ be a TM on Σ such that the language $L(\mathcal{M}) \subseteq \Sigma^*$ is non-recursive. In addition, we may assume without loss of generality that the initial state q_0 does not occur on the right-hand side of any transition, that is, after executing the first step in any computation $\mathcal{M}$ never gets back to state q_0. As before let $\Omega = \Sigma \cup \Sigma' \cup Q \cup \{h, h', q\}$, and let R be defined as in the proof of Theorem 2.5.13. Then the left-hand sides of the rules of R do not overlap. Finally, for $w \in \Sigma^*$, let $R_w := R \cup \{h'q_0wh \to q\}$. Then R_w is effectively constructible from w. R_w has a single critical pair only, which results from overlapping the rule $h'q_0wh \to q$ with the appropriate rule of R. This critical pair resolves if and only if $\mathcal{M}$ halts on input w. Thus, R_w is locally confluent if and only if $w \in L(\mathcal{M})$, and hence, the problem "Local confluence" is undecidable. Since $L(\mathcal{M})$ is non-recursive $\mathcal{M}$ does not halt on all inputs. Therefore, R_w is not noetherian for any $w \in \Sigma^*$.

If R_w is confluent, then it is locally confluent, and so $w \in L(\mathcal{M})$. On the other hand, if $w \in L(\mathcal{M})$, then R_w is locally confluent. Since R_w is not noetherian, Theorem 1.1.13 does not apply. However, from the form of the rules of R_w we can conclude nevertheless that R_w is confluent. The reason is that the only non-trivial situation of the form $u_1 \leftarrow_{R_w} v \to_{R_w} u_2$ involves an application of the rule $h'q_0wh \to q$. If $v = h'q_0wh$, then $u_1 = q$ is irreducible, and $u_2 \overset{*}{\to}_{R_w} q$. Since each word can be factored as detailed in the proof of Theorem 2.5.13, it suffices to look at strings that have a single syllable only. Thus, the problem "confluence" is undecidable.   □2.5.14

2.6 Bibliographic Remarks

String-rewriting as described in Section 2.1 has its roots in the work of Thue [Thu14]. Related work in combinatorial rewriting systems is briefly described by Davis [Dav58]; related work on formal grammars is described by Salomaa [Sal73] and to a lesser extent by Hopcroft and Ullman [HoUl79]. Properties of strings are studied in some depth by Lothaire [Lot83] and Chapter 1 is of some interest here.

The Correspondence Problem was shown to be undecidable by Post [Pos46], and proofs now appear in many textbooks on automata and formal language theory (for example, [HoUl79]).

Background on partial orders can be found in many algebra books. The problem of constucting appropriate partial orderings in the context of term-rewriting systems has been studied by Dershowitz [Der82, Der87] and by Dershowitz and Manna [DeMa79]. König's Infinity Lemma is shown in many elementary books on graph theory. Derivational complexity of formal grammars was studied by Book [Boo69], and derivational complexity of string-rewriting systems was studied by Madlener and Otto [MaOt85].

Theorem 2.2.9 is from [Boo92] and the algorithm given in the proof is a simple variation of a similar result in [Boo82a] where the notion of reduction depended on the strings becoming shorter. Theorem 2.2.13, and the material leading to it, is based on work by Kapur and Narendran [KaNa85b].

Theorem 2.3.1 is due to Book and C.O'Dúnlaing [BoÓ'Dú81b] but a more efficient version of the algorithm given in the proof of Theorem 2.3.1 is due to Kapur et al [KKMN85].

The idea of critical pairs arises in many parts of mathematics [Buc87] but it came to prominence in rewriting through the work of Knuth and Bendix [KnBe70]. Obviously, Section 2.4 is based on that work.

It is quite common to base a proof of the undecidability of the word problem on the undecidability of the halting problem for Turing machines, since the latter can be done from first principles. The reduction leading to Theorem 2.5.9 follows the outline of the presentation of the proof by Davis [Dav58]. Theorem 2.5.13 is due to Huet and Lankford [HuLa78].

We have occasionally mentioned infinite string-rewriting systems. There is always a difficulty when studying such systems: how can one develop algorithms for an infinite system unless it has a finite specification? Thus, attention has been restricted to monadic string-rewriting systems S with the property that for each symbol $a \in \Sigma \cup \{e\}$, the set $\{u \mid (u, a) \in S$ is regular or context-free. The properties of such systems have been studied by Book, Jantzen, and Wrathall [BJW82] and by Ó'Dúnlaing [Ó'Dú81, Ó'Dú83b]. Further study is left to the reader.

3

Length as the Basis for Reduction

In this section we consider the notion of the length of a string to obtain an orientation for the rules of a string-rewriting system. It appears that this approach was introduced by work of Nivat.

3.1 Basic Properties

For any string-rewriting system T we will assume in this chapter that $(u, v) \in T$ implies $|u| \geq |v|$. Since we want to use the length of a string as the basis for reduction, we decompose the system T into two subsystems, which are defined as follows:

(1) $R_T := \{(u, v) \in T \mid |u| > |v|\}$, and

(2) $S_T := \{(u, v) \in T \mid |u| = |v|\}$.

Thus R_T is the set of length-reducing rules of T, while S_T consists of the length-preserving rules of T. This means that the reduction relation $\to_{R_T}$ is noetherian. This will be the basis for much of the development presented in this and the next two chapters.

Now we apply the notion of the length of a string to develop restrictions of Thue congruences. We will be interested in the situation that the reduction relation $\to_{R_T}$ suffices to solve the word problem for T.

Definition 3.1.1 *Let Σ be an alphabet, let T be a string-rewriting system on Σ, and let R_T and S_T be the subsystems of T as defined above.*

(a) *By $\overset{*}{\vdash}_T$ we denote the relation $\overset{*}{\longleftrightarrow}_{S_T}$, that is, $\overset{*}{\vdash}_T$ is the reflexive and transitive closure of the relation $\vdash_T$ which is defined as follows: if $(u, v) \in T$ and $|u| = |v|$, then for all $x, y \in \Sigma^*$, $xuy \vdash_T xvy$ and $xvy \vdash_T xuy$.*

(b) *Let $\mapsto_T = \to_{R_T} \cup \vdash_T$, and let $\overset{*}{\mapsto}_T$ be the reflexive and transitive closure of $\mapsto_T$.*

Thus, in a reduction $u \mapsto_T v$ we can apply a length-reducing rule of T only from left to right, while we can apply a length-preserving rule of T in either direction. Since $\overset{*}{\longleftrightarrow}_T$ is an equivalence relation on Σ^*, this situation is an instance of the one discussed in Section 1.2, where the combined relation $(\longleftrightarrow_{R_T} \cup \overset{*}{\longleftrightarrow}_T)^*$ is simply the Thue congruence $\overset{*}{\longleftrightarrow}_T$.

If T has no length-preserving rules, that is, $T \cap \{(u,v) \in \Sigma^* \times \Sigma^* \mid |u| = |v|\} = \emptyset$, then $S_T = \emptyset$ and $R_T = T$. Hence, if the reduction relation $\to_{R_T}$ is confluent, then, for all $u, v \in \Sigma^*$, $u \overset{*}{\longleftrightarrow}_T v$ if and only if u and v have a common descendant mod $\to_{R_T}$, that is, in this situation the word problem for T can be solved by reduction mod R_T. If, however, T contains length-preserving rules, that is, $S_T \neq \emptyset$ and $R_T \subset T$, then it may happen that the word problem for T cannot be solved by reduction mod R_T, even though $\to_{R_T}$ is confluent. For example, consider the string-rewriting system $T = \{(aa, bb), (ac, b)\}$. Then $S_T = \{(aa, bb)\}$ and $R_T = \{(ac, b)\}$. Obviously, $\to_{R_T}$ is confluent, and $aa \overset{*}{\longleftrightarrow}_T bb$, but aa and bb do not have a common descendant mod $\to_{R_T}$. We are interested in conditions that guarantee that the word problem for T can be solved by reduction mod R_T.

Theorem 3.1.2 *Let T be a string-rewriting system on Σ, and let $R_T := \{(u,v) \in T \mid |u| > |v|\}$ and $S_T := \{(u,v) \in T \mid |u| = |v|\}$. Then the following two statements are equivalent:*

(1) *for all $x, y \in \Sigma^*$, $x \overset{*}{\longleftrightarrow}_T y$ implies that x and y have a common descendant mod $\to_{R_T}$, and*

(2) *R_T is confluent, and for every rule $(u,v) \in S_T$, u and v have a common descendant mod $\to_{R_T}$.*

Proof. Obviously (1) implies (2). To prove the converse we proceed by induction on the number of steps $\vdash_T$ in the sequence of steps that transform x into y. If no $\vdash_T$-step is used at all, then $x \overset{*}{\longleftrightarrow}_{R_T} y$. Since R_T is confluent, it is also Church-Rosser by Lemma 1.1.7. Hence, x and y have a common descendant mod $\to_{R_T}$. Now assume that $x \overset{*}{\longleftrightarrow}_T z_1 \vdash_T z_2 \overset{*}{\longleftrightarrow}_{R_T} y$, where m $\vdash_T$-steps occur in the transformation $x \overset{*}{\longleftrightarrow}_T z_1$. By the induction hypothesis x and z_1 have a common descendant mod $\to_{R_T}$, that is, there is a string $y_1 \in \Sigma^*$ such that $x \overset{*}{\to}_{R_T} y_1$ and $z_1 \overset{*}{\to}_{R_T} y_1$. Since $z_1 \vdash_T z_2$, we have $z_1 = w_1 u w_2$ and $z_2 = w_1 v w_2$ for some $w_1, w_2 \in \Sigma^*$ and some rule $(u,v) \in S_T$ or $(v,u) \in S_T$. By (2) there is a string $w_3 \in \Sigma^*$ such that $u \overset{*}{\to}_{R_T} w_3$ and $v \overset{*}{\to}_{R_T} w_3$, and hence, $z_1 = w_1 u w_2 \overset{*}{\to}_{R_T} w_1 w_3 w_2$ and $z_2 = w_1 v w_2 \overset{*}{\to}_{R_T} w_1 w_3 w_2$. Now R_T being confluent implies that y_1 and $w_1 w_3 w_2$ have a common descendant mod $\to_{R_T}$, say y_2, since $z_1 \overset{*}{\to}_{R_T} y_1$ and $z_1 \overset{*}{\to}_{R_T} w_1 w_3 w_2$. Thus, $x \overset{*}{\to}_{R_T} y_1 \overset{*}{\to}_{R_T} y_2$ and $y \overset{*}{\longleftrightarrow}_{R_T} z_2 \overset{*}{\to}_{R_T} w_1 w_3 w_2 \overset{*}{\to}_{R_T} y_2$, that is, $x \overset{*}{\longleftrightarrow}_{R_T} y$. Hence, the result follows as before. □3.1.2

Diagram for the proof of Theorem 3.1.2

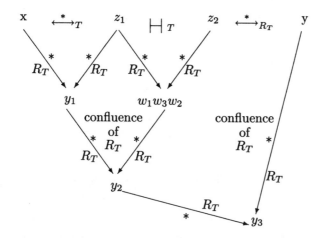

If T satisfies one (and therefore both) of the statements of Theorem 3.1.2 then the subsystem R_T is equivalent to T, that is, we can simply delete the length-preserving rules from T in this situation. Because of this fact, we restrict our attention for the rest of this section to finite string-rewriting systems T that only contain length-reducing rules, that is, we identify T with its subsystem R_T. We will show that if T is a finite string-rewriting system that is length-reducing and confluent, then there is a linear-time algorithm to solve the word problem for T. To accomplish this we turn to Theorem 2.2.9 and its proof.

Let T be a finite length-reducing string-rewriting system on Σ. Let $x \in \Sigma^*$ be taken arbitrarily. If x is not irreducible, then there is some sequence of descendants $x = x_0, x_1, \ldots, x_n$, where for each i, $1 \leq i \leq n$, $x_{i-1} \to_T x_i$, and x_n is irreducible. Since T contains length-reducing rules only, in any such sequence of applications of reduction steps, each application decreases the length of the actual string by at least one. Hence, it is the case that $n \leq |x|$.

We are especially interested in the case of leftmost reduction as implemented in the algorithm REDUCE described in the proof of Theorem 2.2.9. The fact that any chain of reduction steps applied to a string x has length at most $|x|$ implies that there can be at most $|x|$ steps where SEARCH finds the left-hand side u of a rule (u, v) on store 1, pops u from store 1, and pushes v onto the top of store 2. Each occurrence of SEARCH takes at most t_1 steps to search for u and, if successful, at most t_2 steps to push v onto store 2. Here $t_1 := \max\{|u| \mid u \in \mathrm{dom}(T)\}$ and $t_2 := \max\{|v| \mid v \in \mathrm{range}(T)\}$. Since T is length-reducing, we have $t_2 < t_1$, so that $2 \cdot t_1$ steps are sufficient. An occurrence of READ takes unit time. Thus, at most $|x| + t_2|x| \leq t_1 \cdot |x|$ iterations of the READ-SEARCH-cycle take place, where SEARCH is at most $|x|$ times successful, and unsuccessful in all other iterations. Hence, even a naive implementation will only have running time at most $t_1 \cdot |x| \cdot t_1 + |x| \cdot t_2 = (t_1^2 + t_2) \cdot |x|$ on input x.

This argument shows that for any finite length-reducing string-rewriting system T there is a constant k such that the algorithm REDUCE takes at most $k \cdot |x|$ steps on any input x. The reader should keep in mind that this analysis is based on the notion of length as the basis for reduction.

We will use this fact several times and so we state it formally.

Lemma 3.1.3 *Let T be a finite length-reducing string-rewriting system on alphabet Σ. There is a linear-time algorithm that on input $x \in \Sigma^*$ will compute an irreducible string $\overline{x}$ such that $x \xrightarrow{*L}_T \overline{x}$.*

Now we can prove the result stated above regarding a linear-time algorithm to solve the word problem for a finite string-rewriting system that is length-reducing and confluent.

Theorem 3.1.4 *Let T be a finite length-reducing string-rewriting system. If T is confluent, then there is a linear-time algorithm for the word problem for T.*

Proof. The argument is essentially that given in Section 2.2 that results in Theorem 2.2.9. Given x and y, use REDUCE to compute the unique irreducible strings $\overline{x}$ and $\overline{y}$ such that $x \xrightarrow{*} \overline{x}$ and $y \xrightarrow{*} \overline{y}$; by Lemma 3.1.3 only $O(|xy|)$ are needed. Compare $\overline{x}$ and $\overline{y}$ to determine whether $\overline{x}$ and $\overline{y}$ are equal; this can be done in $O(|xy|)$ steps. Since $x \xleftrightarrow{*} y$ if and only if $\overline{x} = \overline{y}$, only $O(|xy|)$ steps are needed to determine whether $x \xleftrightarrow{*} y$. □3.1.4

Let T be a finite string-rewriting system that contains length-reducing as well as length-preserving rules. Theorems 3.1.2 and 3.1.4 show that there is a linear-time algorithm for the word problem for T, if the subsystem R_T is confluent, and if, for every length-preserving rule $(u, v) \in T$, u and v have a common descendant mod $\rightarrow_{R_T}$.

3.2   Testing for Confluence

Consider the property of local confluence. In Theorem 2.3.1 we showed that local confluence is decidable for any finite string-rewriting system whose reduction relation is noetherian. Thus, we see that local confluence is decidable for finite string-rewriting systems that contain only length-reducing rules. Applying Lemma 3.1.3 to the proof of Theorem 2.3.1, we see that the problem of deciding whether a finite length-reducing string-rewriting system is locally confluent is a tractable problem.

Theorem 3.2.1 *There is a polynomial-time algorithm to solve the following problem:*

Instance: *A finite string-rewriting system T containing only length-reducing rules.*

Question: *Is T locally confluent?*

Since a length-reducing system T is noetherian, Theorem 1.1.13 shows that T is confluent if and only if it is locally confluent. Thus, we have the following.

Corollary 3.2.2 *There is a polynomial-time algorithm to solve the following problem:*

Instance: *A finite string-rewriting system T containing only length-reducing rules.*

Question: *Is T confluent?*

Let T be a string-rewriting system on Σ, and let R_T denote the subsystem of T containing all the length-reducing rules of T. Recall that we say that the word problem for T can be **solved by reduction mod R_T**, if, for all $x, y \in \Sigma^*$, $x \xleftrightarrow{*}_T y$ implies that x and y have a common descendant mod $\to_{R_T}$. By Theorem 3.1.2 this is equivalent to the facts that R_T is confluent, and that, for each length-preserving rule $(u, v) \in T$, u and v have a common descendant mod $\to_{R_T}$. The subsystem R_T is easily obtained from T, and its confluence is decidable in polynomial time by Corollary 3.2.2. Further, if $(u, v) \in T$ is a length-preserving rule, u and v have a common descendant mod $\to_{R_T}$ if REDUCE(u) = REDUCE(v), and given the system R_T and the strings u and v, this can be checked in time $O(\| R_T \|^2 \cdot |uv|)$. Since $(u, v) \in T$, we see that time $O(\| T \|^3)$ is sufficient for this test. Thus, since this test must be performed for all length-preserving rules of T, this observation yields the following.

Theorem 3.2.3 *There is a polynomial-time algorithm to solve the following problem:*

Instance: *A finite string-rewriting system T.*

Question: *Can the word problem for T be solved by reduction mod R_T, where R_T consists of the length-reducing rules of T?*

An example of a string-rewriting system that is confluent is the natural presentation of the free group F_n on n generators as a monoid. Let $\{a_1, \ldots, a_n\}$ be a set of n different symbols representing the generators of a group, let $\{\bar{a}_1, \ldots, \bar{a}_n\}$ be a set of n different symbols that is disjoint from $\{a_1, \ldots, a_n\}$, let $\Sigma = \{a_1, \ldots, a_n\} \cup \{\bar{a}_1, \ldots, \bar{a}_n\}$, and let $T = \{(a_i \bar{a}_i, e),$ $(\bar{a}_i a_i, e) \mid 1 \leq i \leq n\}$. Then the monoid $\mathcal{M}_T$ is the free group F_n on

n generators. In fact, define a mapping $^{-1} : \Sigma^* \to \Sigma^*$ through $e^{-1} := e$, $(wa_i)^{-1} := \bar{a}_i(w^{-1})$ and $(w\bar{a}_i)^{-1} := a_i(w^{-1})$ for $1 \leq i \leq n$ and $w \in \Sigma^*$. Then, for all $w \in \Sigma^*$, $ww^{-1} \stackrel{*}{\longleftrightarrow}_T e \stackrel{*}{\longleftrightarrow}_T w^{-1}w$, that is, w^{-1} is a **formal inverse** of w. It is easy to see that T is confluent since $a_i\bar{a}_ia_i \to a_i$ and $\bar{a}_ia_i\bar{a}_i \to \bar{a}_i$ for each i. Thus, we see that for a finitely generated free group, there is a linear-time algorithm to solve the word problem. In addition, for each $w \in \Sigma^*$ there is a unique irreducible string $w_0 \in [w]_T$, that is, w_0 contains neither a factor of the form $a_i\bar{a}_i$ nor a factor of the form $\bar{a}_ia_i$. In combinatorial group theory these irreducible strings are called "freely reduced." We will return to this example in later sections and note various facts; for example, we will show that for each $w \in \Sigma^*$, $[w]_T$ is a deterministic context-free language, and that for each regular subset A of Σ^*, $[A]_T = \{x \in \Sigma^* \mid \text{there exists } y \in A \text{ such that } y \stackrel{*}{\longleftrightarrow}_T x\}$ is a deterministic context-free language.

3.3   Confluence on a Single Class

The definition of confluence of a rewriting system is a global property since it applies to all strings over the underlying alphabet. There are occasions when it is sufficient to consider a local property. We will briefly discuss one such property here.

Definition 3.3.1 *Let R be a string-rewriting system on alphabet Σ, and let $w \in \Sigma^*$ be a given string. If for all $x, y, z \in [w]_R$, $x \stackrel{*}{\to} y$ and $x \stackrel{*}{\to} z$ imply that y and z have a common descendant, then R is **confluent on** $[w]_R$.*

Notice that R is confluent if and only if for every $w \in \Sigma^*$, R is confluent on $[w]_R$. If R is noetherian and R is confluent on $[w]_R$ for some $w \in \Sigma^*$, then $[w]_R$ contains exactly one irreducible element and the membership problem for $[w]_R$ is decidable; if the reduction $\to_R$ is based on length, then Lemma 3.1.3 can be applied to show that there is a linear-time algorithm to determine membership in $[w]_R$.

In general it is undecidable whether a finite noetherian string-rewriting system R is confluent on $[w]_R$ for a given w; this is true even if reduction is based on length. We will not prove this fact here but we will illustrate one of the uses of this concept.

In the early part of the twentieth century, Dehn considered presentations of fundamental groups of closed orientable surfaces and showed that the appropriate word problems are decidable. From the standpoint of rewriting systems, Dehn's strategy may be described in the following way.

(i) Let a group G be given through a presentation of the form $(\Sigma; R)$, where $\Sigma = \{a_1, \dots, a_n\} \cup \{\bar{a}_1, \dots, \bar{a}_n\}$ and $R = \{(a_i\bar{a}_i, e), (\bar{a}_ia_i, e) \mid 1 \leq i \leq n\} \cup \{(r_i, e) \mid 1 \leq i \leq m_R\}$ for some $n \geq 1$ and strings

$r_1, \ldots, r_{m_R} \in \Sigma^*$. Suppose that this presentation has the following property: every freely reduced non-empty string w (that is, $w \neq e$ and w contains no factor $a_i \bar{a}_i$ or $\bar{a}_i a_i$) that is equal to the identity e in G has a factorization xyz where for some $i \in \{1, \ldots, m_R\}$, r_i has a factorization yt with $|y| > |t|$. Now, let us form a string-rewriting system R_1 by adding certain rules:

$$R_1 := R \cup \{(y, t^{-1}) \mid \exists i \in \{1, \ldots, m_R\} : r_i = yt \text{ and } |y| > |t|\}.$$

Then R_1 contains length-reducing rules only, and R_1 is equivalent to R. Thus, $(\Sigma; R_1)$ is another presentation of the group G so that to solve the word problem for G, it is sufficient to solve the word problem for the presentation $(\Sigma; R_1)$.

(ii) Consider the reduction relation $\rightarrow_{R_1}$ induced by R_1. When w is a freely reduced non-empty string that is equal to the identity e in G, then $w = xyz$ where for some $i \in \{1, \ldots, m_R\}$, $r_i = yt$ and $|y| > |t|$. Thus, $w = xyz \rightarrow_{R_1} xt^{-1}z$, and $|w| > |xt^{-1}z|$. Using the "free reductions" $a_i \bar{a}_i \rightarrow e$ and $\bar{a}_i a_i \rightarrow e (1 \leq i \leq n)$, we reduce $xt^{-1}z$ to some freely reduced string w_1. Obviously, $w_1 \xleftrightarrow{*}_{R_1} w \xleftrightarrow{*}_{R_1} e$, that is, either $w_1 = e$, or again w_1 has a factorization $x_1 y_1 z_1$ where for some $j \in \{1, \ldots, m_R\}$, $r_j = y_1 t_1$ and $|y_1| > |t_1|$. Hence, continuing in this way we will eventually reduce w to e. What is known as "Dehn's Algorithm" is the notion of applying the non-trivial reduction rules in R_1 and the free reductions until no such rule is applicable. For the appropriate group presentations, it is the case that for any w equal to e in G, one can apply these rules arbitrarily until no rule is applicable any more, and **regardless of the order of application of these rules** the final result is e. Thus, to determine whether w_1 is equal to w_2 in G, it is sufficient to determine whether $w_1 w_2^{-1}$ reduces to e by applying **some** finite sequence of reduction steps.

Thus the string-rewriting system R_1 is confluent on the congruence class of the identity e. Since R_1 is length-reducing, we can conclude that the word problem for G can be decided in linear time by using the presentation $(\Sigma; R_1)$.

3.4 Equivalent Systems

Suppose that a noetherian string-rewriting system T is not confluent. Does there exist another string-rewriting system T' such that T' is noetherian and confluent, and T' is equivalent to T? In Section 2.4 we considered the Knuth-Bendix completion procedure that, given a string-rewriting system T on Σ and an admissible well-ordering $>$ on Σ^*, tries to construct such a system T'. In particular we did prove that this procedure terminates on input $(T, >)$ if and only if there exists a finite confluent system T' that is equivalent to T, and that is compatible with $>$. However, we did not discuss the question of whether, given T and $>$, it is decidable that such a system T' exists.

Here we will prove that in general this problem is undecidable. In fact, we will present an undecidability result which will imply the undecidability of the above problem as well as many additional undecidability results for finite string-rewriting systems. Before establishing these results we develop a decidability result for some restricted string-rewriting systems.

Definition 3.4.1 *A string-rewriting system T is* **special** *if $(u, v) \in T$ implies $v = e$. A special system T is* **homogenous of degree k**, $k > 1$ *an integer, if $(u, e) \in T$ implies $|u| = k$, and is* **homogenous** *if it is homogenous of degree k for some k.*

Theorem 3.4.2 *Let T be a string-rewriting system that is homogeneous. There is a length-reducing and confluent string-rewriting system that is equivalent to T if and only if T itself is confluent.*

Proof. Let T be homogeneous of degree k. If T is not confluent, then the proof of Theorem 2.3.1 shows that there exist (u_1, e), $(u_2, e) \in T$ and strings x, y such that $x \neq e \neq y$, $u_1 x = y u_2$, $|x| < |u_2|$, and there is no z such that $x \xrightarrow{*} z$ and $y \xrightarrow{*} z$. Since $|u_1| = |u_2| = k$ and $|x| < |u_2|, |y| = |x| < k$. Also, $x \xleftrightarrow{*} y$ since $u_1 \longleftrightarrow e \longleftrightarrow u_2$. This means that x and y are congruent, irreducible, and unequal.

Let T' be any length-reducing string-rewriting system that is equivalent to T. Since T is homogeneous of degree k, applications of rules in T' need to change length by a multiple of k, that is, $(u, v) \in T'$ implies that $|u| - |v|$ is a positive multiple of k. Since T' is equivalent to T and x and y are congruent $(\mathrm{mod}\,T)$, x and y are congruent $(\mathrm{mod}\,T')$ but $|x| = |y| < k$ so that there is no z such that $x \xrightarrow{*} z$ and $y \xrightarrow{*} z$ $(\mathrm{mod}\,T')$. Thus, T' cannot be confluent. $\square$3.4.2

The proof of Theorem 3.4.2 establishes the following.

Corollary 3.4.3 *Let T be a string-rewriting system that is homogeneous. Then the congruence $\xleftrightarrow{*}_T$ is generated by a length-reducing and confluent string-rewriting system if and only if T itself is confluent.*

We will now proceed to develop the announced undecidability result.

Definition 3.4.4 *Let T_i be a string-rewriting system on alphabet Σ_i, $i = 1, 2$. A homomorphism $h : \Sigma_1^* \to \Sigma_2^*$* **defines a homomorphism from T_1 to T_2** *if, for all $x, y \in \Sigma_1^*$, $x \xleftrightarrow{*}_{T_1} y$ implies that $h(x) \xleftrightarrow{*}_{T_2} h(y)$. This homomorphism is an* **embedding** *if in addition, for all $x, y \in \Sigma_1^*, h(x) \xleftrightarrow{*}_{T_2}$*

$h(y)$ implies that $x \xleftrightarrow{*}_{T_1} y$. A homomorphism h from T_1 to T_2 is an **iso-morphism** if it is an embedding and for every $z \in \Sigma_2^*$ there exists $x \in \Sigma_1^*$ such that $z \xleftrightarrow{*}_{T_2} h(x)$.

In algebraic terms this definition means the following. Let $\mathcal{M}_i$ denote the monoid $\Sigma_i^*/\xleftrightarrow{*}_{T_i}$, $i = 1, 2$. Then the homomorphism $h : \Sigma_1^* \to \Sigma_2^*$ defines a homomorphism from T_1 to T_2 if the mapping $[x]_{T_1} \mapsto [h(x)]_{T_2}$ is a monoid-homomorphism from $\mathcal{M}_1$ into $\mathcal{M}_2$. It is called an embedding if this monoid-homomorphism is injective, and it is an isomorphism if this monoid-homomorphism is bijective. In Chapter 7 we will discuss these notions in more detail.

Definition 3.4.5 A string-rewriting system R on Σ is called **trivial**, if $R = \{(a, e) \mid a \in \Sigma\}$. A Thue congruence $\xleftrightarrow{*}$ is **trivial** if it satisfies $u \xleftrightarrow{*} e$ for all $u \in \Sigma^*$.

The next technical result is a useful tool.

Lemma 3.4.6 Let Σ be a finite alphabet, let $c, d \notin \Sigma$ be two additional symbols, and let $\Gamma := \Sigma \cup \{c, d\}$. Given a finite string-rewriting system R on Σ and two strings $u, v \in \Sigma^*$, a finite string-rewriting system $R_{u,v}$ on Γ and a homomorphism h from R to $R_{u,v}$ can be constructed effectively such that either

(i) $u \xleftrightarrow{*}_R v$, and the congruence $\xleftrightarrow{*}_{R_{u,v}}$ on Γ^* is trivial, or

(ii) $u \not\xleftrightarrow{*}_R v$, and h is an embedding from R into $R_{u,v}$, that is, for all $x, y \in \Sigma^*$, $x \xleftrightarrow{*}_R y$ if and only if $h(x) \xleftrightarrow{*}_{R_{u,v}} h(y)$.

Proof. Let R be a finite string-rewriting system on Σ, and let $u, v \in \Sigma^*$. Define a string-rewriting system $R_{u,v}$ on Γ as follows:

$$R_{u,v} := R \cup \{(cud, e)\} \cup \{(acvd, cvd) \mid a \in \Gamma\}.$$

Further, let $h : \Sigma^* \to \Gamma^*$ be defined by $a \longmapsto a$ for all $a \in \Sigma$. Since $R \subseteq R_{u,v}, h(\ell) = \ell \xleftrightarrow{*}_{R_{u,v}} r = h(r)$ for all rules (ℓ, r) of R. Thus, h is a homomorphism from R to $R_{u,v}$. Obviously, $R_{u,v}$ and h can be constructed effectively from R, u and v. It remains to verify conditions (i) and (ii).

Assume that $u \xleftrightarrow{*}_R v$. Then, for each symbol $a \in \Gamma$, $a \longleftrightarrow_{R_{u,v}}$ $acud \xleftrightarrow{*}_{R_{u,v}} acvd \longleftrightarrow_{R_{u,v}} cvd \xleftrightarrow{*}_{R_{u,v}} cud \longleftrightarrow_{R_{u,v}} e$, that is, the Thue congruence $\xleftrightarrow{*}_{R_{u,v}}$ is indeed trivial.

Conversely assume that $u \not\xleftrightarrow{*}_R v$. We must verify that the homomorphism h is an embedding. To this end it suffices to show that, for all strings $x, y \in \Sigma^*$, $x \xleftrightarrow{*}_{R_{u,v}} y$ implies $x \xleftrightarrow{*}_R y$, since $h(x) = x$ and $h(y) = y$.

Let $R_1 := R \cup \{(cud, e)\}$. As an intermediate step we prove the following claim.

Claim 1. For all $x, y \in \Sigma^*$, if $x \stackrel{*}{\longleftrightarrow}_{R_1} y$, then $x \stackrel{*}{\longleftrightarrow}_R y$.

Proof. If $z \in \Gamma^*$ satisfies $z \stackrel{*}{\longleftrightarrow}_{R_1} x$, then occurrences of c and d in z function as left and right parentheses, respectively, and the occurrences of c and d are correctly balanced, that is, $|z|_c = |z|_d$, and whenever $z = z_1 z_2$, then $|z_1|_c \geq |z_1|_d$.

Let $x = x_0 \longleftrightarrow_{R_1} x_1 \longleftrightarrow_{R_1} \cdots \longleftrightarrow_{R_1} x_n = y$ be a derivation of minimum length of y from x in R_1. If $x_i \in \Sigma^*$ holds for all i, then this derivation is actually an R-derivation implying that $x \stackrel{*}{\longleftrightarrow}_R y$. So assume that for some $i \in \{1, 2, \ldots, n-1\}$, $|x_i|_c = |x_i|_d > 0$. Then there exists an index $p \in \{1, 2, \ldots, n-1\}$ such that $0 = |x_0|_c \leq |x_1|_c \leq \cdots \leq |x_p|_c = |x_{p+1}|_c + 1$, that is, x_p is the first string in the above derivation to which the rule $cud \to e$ is applied. Thus, $x_p = wcudz \longleftrightarrow_{R_1} wz = x_{p+1}$ for some strings $w, z \in \Gamma^*$. Since $x = x_0 \in \Sigma^*$, and since the rules of R do not contain any occurrences of the letters c and d, the particular occurrences of c and d that are cancelled in the step from x_p to x_{p+1} must have been introduced together at some earlier step $q \in \{0, 1, \ldots, p-1\}$, that is, there exist an index $q \in \{0, 1, \ldots, p-1\}$ and strings $w_1, z_1 \in \Gamma^*$ such that $x_q = w_1 z_1 \longleftrightarrow_{R_1} w_1 cudz_1 = x_{q+1}$, $w_1 \stackrel{*}{\longleftrightarrow}_{R_1} w$, and $z_1 \stackrel{*}{\longleftrightarrow}_{R_1} z$. Hence, the above derivation has the following form:

$$x = x_0 \longleftrightarrow_{R_1} \cdots \longleftrightarrow_{R_1} x_q = w_1 cudz_1 = x_{q+1} \stackrel{*}{\longleftrightarrow}_{R_1}$$

$$x_p = wcudz \longleftrightarrow_{R_1} wz = x_{p+1} \longleftrightarrow_{R_1} \cdots \longleftrightarrow_{R_1} x_n = y.$$

Thus, we obtain a shorter derivation of y from x as follows: $x = x_0 \longleftrightarrow_{R_1} \cdots \longleftrightarrow_{R_1} x_q = w_1 z_1 \stackrel{*}{\longleftrightarrow}_{R_1} wz = x_{p+1} \longleftrightarrow_{R_1} \cdots \longleftrightarrow_{R_1} x_n = y$, which contradicts the choice of the original derivation. Therefore, we conclude that $x_i \in \Sigma^*$ holds for all $i \in \{1, 2, \ldots, n\}$. $\square$ Claim 1.

Now the proof of Lemma 3.4.6 is completed by proving the following claim.

Claim 2. For all $x, y \in \Sigma^*$, if $x \stackrel{*}{\longleftrightarrow}_{R_{u,v}} y$, then $x \stackrel{*}{\longleftrightarrow}_{R_1} y$.

Proof. Let $x = x_0 \longleftrightarrow_{R_{u,v}} x_1 \longleftrightarrow_{R_{u,v}} \cdots \longleftrightarrow_{R_{u,v}} x_n = y$ be a derivation of minimum length of y from x in $R_{u,v}$. If this derivation consists of applications of rules of R_1 only, then it witnesses that $x \stackrel{*}{\longleftrightarrow}_{R_1} y$, and we are done.

So assume that rules from $R_{u,v} - R_1 = \{(acvd, cvd) \mid a \in \Gamma\}$ are used as well, and let $p \in \{1, 2, \ldots, n-1\}$ be the smallest index such that x_p contains cvd as a factor. The form of the rules in $R_{u,v} - R_1$ implies that the initial segment of length p of the above derivation is of the form $x = x_0 \longleftrightarrow_{R_1} x_1 \longleftrightarrow_{R_1} \cdots \longleftrightarrow_{R_1} x_p = wcvdz$, where $w, z \in \Gamma^*$, that is, it is an R_1-derivation of x_p from x. According to the choice of the derivation of y from x given above, also this R_1-derivation is of minimum length. Hence, we can conclude from the proof of Claim 1, that the rule $cud \to$

e is not applied during this derivation. Since $x \in \Sigma^*$, this means that there exist an index $q \in \{0, 1 \ldots, p-1\}$ and strings $w_1, z_1 \in \Gamma^*$ such that $x_q = w_1 z_1 \longleftrightarrow_{R_1} w_1 c u d z_1 = x_{q+1}$, $w_1 \overset{*}{\longleftrightarrow}_{R_1} w$, $u \overset{*}{\longleftrightarrow}_{R_1} v$, and $z_1 \overset{*}{\longleftrightarrow}_{R_1} z$. Since $u, v \in \Sigma^*$, Claim 1 induces $u \overset{*}{\longleftrightarrow}_R v$, thus contradicting our assumption $u \overset{*}{\not\longleftrightarrow}_R v$. Hence, each derivation of minimum length of y from x in $R_{u,v}$ only contains applications of rules of R_1.   □ Claim 2.
  □3.4.6

Lemma 3.4.6 is the technical tool needed to establish a "meta-theorem" regarding undecidable properties of finite string-rewriting systems.

Theorem 3.4.7 *Let P be a property that finite string-rewriting systems may or may not have, such that P satisfies the following three conditions:*

(1) *If R_1 and R_2 are finite string-rewriting systems that are equivalent, then $P(R_1)$ implies $P(R_2)$.*

(2) *Each trivial string-rewriting system R has property P.*

(3) *Each finite string-rewriting system R with property P has a decidable word problem.*

Then the following problem is undecidable in general:

Instance: *A finite string-rewriting system R.*

Question: *Does R have property P?*

Proof. Let P be a property of finite string-rewriting systems that satisfies conditions (1) to (3), and let R be a finite string-rewriting system on Σ that has an undecidable word problem. We shall prove the undecidability of property P by effectively reducing the word problem for R to the problem of deciding P.

Let $u, v \in \Sigma^*$. By Lemma 3.4.6 we can effectively construct a finite string-rewriting system $R_{u,v}$ on $\Gamma := \Sigma \cup \{c, d\}$ and a homomorphism $h : \Sigma^* \to \Gamma^*$ such that either

(a) $u \overset{*}{\longleftrightarrow}_R v$, and the congruence $\overset{*}{\longleftrightarrow}_{R_{u,v}}$ on Γ^* is trivial, or

(b) $u \overset{*}{\not\longleftrightarrow}_R v$, and h induces an embedding from R into $R_{u,v}$.

Assume first that $u \overset{*}{\longleftrightarrow}_R v$. Then $R_{u,v}$ is equivalent to the trivial string-rewriting system $R_t := \{(a, e) \mid a \in \Gamma\}$. By conditions (1) and (2) this yields $P(R_{u,v})$. Conversely, if $u \overset{*}{\not\longleftrightarrow}_R v$, then R is embedded in $R_{u,v}$ by h, and hence, the word problem for $R_{u,v}$ is undecidable. By condition (3) this means that $R_{u,v}$ does not have property P. Thus, $R_{u,v}$ has property P if and only if $u \overset{*}{\longleftrightarrow}_R v$. Since $R_{u,v}$ can effectively be constructed from

R, u and v, we can conclude that it is undecidable whether or not a finite string-rewriting system has property P.   □3.4.7

Observe that because of property (1), Theorem 3.4.7 essentially deals with properties of Thue congruences induced by finite string-rewriting systems.

We conclude this section with some applications of the above theorem.

Corollary 3.4.8 *It is undecidable whether a finite string-rewriting system generates the trivial Thue congruence.*

Proof. Let P be the following property of finite string-rewriting systems: R has property P if and only if the Thue congruence $\overset{*}{\longleftrightarrow}_R$ is trivial. Clearly, P satisfies conditions (1) to (3) of Theorem 3.4.7.   □3.4.8

We have seen that there are finite string-rewriting systems that have an undecidable word problem. We will see that in general it is undecidable whether a finite string-rewriting system has a decidable word problem. For doing so let P be the following property of finite string-rewriting systems: R has property P if and only if R has a decidable word problem. Clearly, P satisfies the conditions of Theorem 3.4.7. Hence, we have the following result.

Corollary 3.4.9 *It is undecidable whether a finite string-rewriting system has a decidable word problem.*

From the discussion in Chapter 1 we know that a finite, noetherian, and confluent string-rewriting system has a decidable word problem. Thus, the following property P also satisfies the conditions of Theorem 3.4.7: R has property P if and only if there exists a finite, noetherian, and confluent string-rewriting system that is equivalent to R.

Hence, Theorem 3.4.7 yields the following.

Corollary 3.4.10 *It is undecidable whether there is some finite, noetherian, and confluent system that is equivalent to a given finite string-rewriting system.*

In fact, Corollary 3.4.10 remains valid even if we fix an admissible well-founded partial ordering $>$ in advance, provided $a > e$ holds for all $a \in \Sigma$. This holds in particular for the ordering by length: $x > y$ if and only if $|x| > |y|$.

Thus, we also have the following result.

Corollary 3.4.11 *The following problem is undecidable.*

Instance: *A finite string-rewriting system T.*

Question: *Does there exist a finite length-reducing string-rewriting system that is confluent and is equivalent to T?*

In particular, we see that in general the termination of the Knuth-Bendix completion procedure is undecidable.

3.5   Church-Rosser Congruences

Corollary 3.4.3 shows that there exists a length-reducing and confluent string-rewriting system that is equivalent to a given homogeneous string-rewriting system T if and only if T itself is confluent. We will see in the following that in general this is not true for finite length-reducing systems T. In fact, given a finite length-reducing system T it is in general undecidable whether there exists a (finite or infinite) system that is length-reducing, confluent, and equivalent to T. Observe that Theorem 3.4.7 does not apply in this situation, since the word problem for an infinite length-reducing and confluent string-rewriting system may well be undecidable. To simplify the notation we introduce the following notion.

Definition 3.5.1 *A congruence relation $\sim$ on Σ^* is called a* **Church-Rosser congruence** *if there exists a (finite or infinite) length-reducing and confluent string-rewriting system T on Σ such that $\sim$ coincides with the Thue congruence $\xleftrightarrow{*}_T$.*

We are interested in the problem of deciding whether or not the Thue congruence generated by a given finite string-rewriting system T is a Church-Rosser congruence. A slight modification of Lemma 3.4.6 will produce the undecidability of this property.

Definition 3.5.2 *Let $\sim$ be a congruence relation on Σ^*. A string $x \in \Sigma^*$ is* **minimal with respect to** $\sim$ *if there is no $y \in \Sigma^*$ such that $|y| < |x|$ and $x \sim y$.*

Clearly, if T is a length-reducing string-rewriting system on Σ, then every string that is minimal with respect to $\xleftrightarrow{*}_T$ is irreducible, and if T is also confluent, then every irreducible string is minimal. For an arbitrary length-reducing finite system it is undecidable if a string is minimal. However, it is only the notion of minimality itself that is relevant to the current discussion so that we leave the proof of this fact to an appendix to this section.

Lemma 3.5.3 *Let $\sim$ be a congruence relation on Σ^*. Then $\sim$ is a Church-Rosser congruence if and only if there do not exist two strings x, $y \in \Sigma^*$ such that $x \neq y$, $x \sim y$, and both x and y are minimal with respect to $\sim$.*

Proof. Let $S = \{(u,v) \mid u, v \in \Sigma^*, |u| \geq |v|, \text{ and } u \sim v\}$, and let $R = \{(u,v) \in S \mid |u| > |v|\}$. If R is confluent and if R and S are equivalent, then $\sim$ is obviously a Church-Rosser congruence, since it is easily seen that $\sim = \xleftrightarrow{*}_S$ holds.

Assume now that $\sim$ is a Church-Rosser congruence. Then there exists a (finite or infinite) length-reducing and confluent string-rewriting system T on Σ such that the congruences $\sim$ and $\longleftrightarrow_T$ coincide. Thus, if $(\ell, r) \in T$, then $|\ell| > |r|$ and $\ell \sim r$, that is, T is a subsystem of R. Hence, $\sim = \overset{*}{\longleftrightarrow}_T \subseteq \overset{*}{\longleftrightarrow}_R \subseteq \overset{*}{\longleftrightarrow}_S = \sim$ implying that R and S are equivalent, and that R is confluent, too.

It remains to prove that R is confluent and equivalent to S if and only if there do not exist two strings $x, y \in \Sigma^*$ such that $x \neq y$, $x \sim y$, and both x and y are minimal with respect to $\sim$.

First suppose that R is confluent and equivalent to S, and let $x, y \in \Sigma^*$ be distinct and minimal with respect to $\sim$. Since R is equivalent to S, $\overset{*}{\longleftrightarrow}_R = \sim$, and hence, x and y are minimal with respect to $\overset{*}{\longleftrightarrow}_R$. Thus, x and y are irreducible (mod R), which means that they have no common descendant with respect to R, and so are not congruent mod R.

Conversely, suppose that there do not exist two strings $x, y \in \Sigma^*$ such that $x \neq y$, $x \sim y$, and both x and y are minimal with respect to $\sim$. Let u and v be distinct and congruent modulo $\sim$, that is, $u \overset{*}{\longleftrightarrow}_S v$. The congruence class $[u]$ has at least one minimal element, say $\bar{u}$, and has at most one minimal element by assumption. Then $\bar{u} \overset{*}{\longleftrightarrow}_S u \overset{*}{\longleftrightarrow}_S v$, so that $\bar{u}$ minimal implies that $u \overset{*}{\rightarrow}_R \bar{u}$ and $v \overset{*}{\rightarrow}_R \bar{u}$ by the definition of R. Hence, u and v have a common descendant modulo R. This means that R is confluent and equivalent to S.   □3.5.3

Consider the construction in the proof of Lemma 3.4.6. Let T be a finite string-rewriting system on Σ, let $c, d, f, g \notin \Sigma$ be four additional symbols, and let $\Gamma := \Sigma \cup \{c, d, f, g\}$. For $u, v \in \Sigma^*$, let $T_0(u, v)$ be the string-rewriting system $T_0(u, v) := T \cup \{(cud, e)\} \cup \{(acvd, cvd) \mid a \in \Sigma \cup \{c, d\}\} \cup \{(cvd, f), (cvd, g)\}$, and let $h : \Sigma^* \to \Gamma^*$ be again defined by $a \mapsto a$ for all $a \in \Sigma$. The system $T_0(u, v)$ is sufficiently similar to the system $T_{u,v}$ to allow the following conclusions:

(i) if $u \overset{*}{\longleftrightarrow}_T v$, then $T_0(u, v)$ generates the trivial congruence on Γ^*;

(ii) if $u \overset{*}{\not\longleftrightarrow}_T v$, then h is an embedding from T into $T_0(u, v)$ and cvd is not congruent to e (mod $T_0(u, v)$), so that f and g are congruent (mod $T_0(u, v)$) but are not congruent to e (mod $T_0(u, v)$) and so are minimal with respect to $T_0(u, v)$.

Thus, by Lemma 3.5.3 the congruence generated by $T_0(u, v)$ is a Church-Rosser congruence if and only if $u \overset{*}{\longleftrightarrow}_T v$. From this observation the argument in the proof of Theorem 3.4.7 yields the following result.

Corollary 3.5.4 *The following problem is undecidable:*

Instance: *A finite string-rewriting system T.*

Question: *Does T generate a Church-Rosser congruence?*

The reader may question whether any applications of Corollary 3.5.4 exist, that is, if a finite length-reducing system is not confluent and there is no finite length-reducing and confluent system equivalent to it, then it is conceivable that the congruence cannot be Church-Rosser. However, this is not the case.

Consider the system $T_1 = \{(aba, ab)\}$ on the alphabet $\{a, b\}$. This system is not confluent since $abba$ and abb are congruent and irreducible. Let $T_2 = \{(ab^n a, ab^n) \mid n \geq 1\}$ so that $T_1 \subset T_2$.

Claim 1. T_2 is equivalent to T_1.

Proof. Since $T_1 \subset T_2$, it is sufficient to show that for all $n > 0$, $ab^n a \overset{*}{\longleftrightarrow} ab^n \pmod{T_1}$. This is trivial for $n = 1$ so assume it is true for some $m \geq 1$. Then $ab^{m+1} a = (ab^m) ba \overset{*}{\longleftrightarrow} (ab^m a) ba = (ab^m)(aba) \longleftrightarrow (ab^m a) b \overset{*}{\longleftrightarrow} (ab^m) b = ab^{m+1} \pmod{T_1}$. $\square$ Claim 1.

Claim 2. T_2 is confluent.

Proof. Referring to the proof of Theorem 2.3.1 it is clear that the only critical pairs which must be checked are generated from strings of the form $ab^i ab^j a$. The pair $\langle ab^i b^j a, ab^i ab^j \rangle$ has common descendant ab^{i+j}. $\square$ Claim 2.

Thus, T_2 is an infinite length-reducing and confluent system that is equivalent to T_1. It is clear that T_2 is normalized. Hence, from Theorem 2.3.1 one concludes that T_2, hence T_1, is equivalent to no finite length-reducing and confluent system. $\square$3.5.4

APPENDIX TO SECTION 3.5

A string that is minimal is also irreducible, but for some systems there are irreducible strings that are not minimal. However, determining whether a string is minimal is sometimes difficult.

Theorem 3.5.5 *The following question is undecidable: for a finite string-rewriting system T on alphabet Σ and $x \in \Sigma^*$, is x minimal with respect to $\overset{*}{\longleftrightarrow}_T$?*

Proof. Our proof depends on the well-known fact that there is a finitely presented group with an undecidable word problem. We will show that for every finitely presented group G, one can effectively construct from a finite presentation of G a finite system T such that the word problem for G is effectively reducible to the question of minimality with respect to $\overset{*}{\longleftrightarrow}_T$. The construction of T from a finite presentation of G is just the standard construction of a string-rewriting system T to present G as a quotient monoid. Let G be given through the **group-presentation** $\langle \Gamma; L \rangle$, that is, Γ is a finite alphabet, $\overline{\Gamma}$ is another alphabet disjoint from Γ but in one-to-one correspondence with Γ, and $L \subseteq (\Gamma \cup \overline{\Gamma})^*$. We take $\Sigma = \Gamma \cup \overline{\Gamma}$ and $T = \{(w, e) \mid w \in L\} \cup \{(a\overline{a}, e), (\overline{a}a, e) \mid a \in \Gamma\}$. Then G is isomorphic to the factor monoid $\Sigma^* /\!\!\overset{*}{\leftrightarrow}_T$. Let $^{-1} : \Sigma^* \to \Sigma^*$ denote a function that associates with each string $w \in \Sigma^*$ a formal inverse w^{-1}, that is, $ww^{-1} \overset{*}{\longleftrightarrow}_T e \overset{*}{\longleftrightarrow}_T w^{-1}w$.

For any $x, y \in \Sigma^*$, $x \overset{*}{\longleftrightarrow}_T y$ if and only if $xy^{-1} \overset{*}{\longleftrightarrow}_T e$. Thus, it is sufficient to reduce the question "for $w \in \Sigma^*$, is $w \overset{*}{\longleftrightarrow}_T e$?" to the question "for $w \in \Sigma^*$, is w minimal?" Given $w \in \Sigma^*$, $w \neq e$, if w is minimal, then w is not congruent to e since $|e| < |w|$; otherwise, in a finite number of steps one can effectively find $w_1 \in \Sigma^*$ such that $w_1 \overset{*}{\longleftrightarrow}_T w$ and $|w_1| < |w|$. If $w_1 = e$, then $w \overset{*}{\longleftrightarrow}_T e$. If $w_1 \neq e$ and w_1 is minimal, then w_1 is not congruent to e since $|e| < |w_1|$. If $w_1 \neq e$ and w_1 is not minimal, then in a finite number of steps one can effectively find $w_2 \in \Sigma^*$ such that $w_2 \overset{*}{\longleftrightarrow}_T w_1$ and $|w_2| < |w_1|$. This process can continue for at most $|w|$ applications of the procedure.

Thus, if the question "for $x \in \Sigma^*$, is x minimal?" is decidable, then the question "for $y \in \Sigma^*$, is y congruent to e?" is decidable. Since there is a finitely presented group with an undecidable word problem, minimality is undecidable. □3.5.5

3.6 Other Systems Based on Length

For a string-rewriting system T satisfying $|u| \geq |v|$, for each rule $(u, v) \in T$ we have defined the following two subsystems:
$R_T = \{(u, v) \in T \mid |u| > |v|\}$ of length-reducing rules, and
$S_T = \{(u, v) \in T \mid |u| = |v|\}$ of length-preserving rules.

If the subsystem R_T is confluent, and if, for every rule $(u, v) \in S_T$, u and v have a common descendant mod $\rightarrow_{R_T}$, then for all $x, y \in \Sigma^*$, $x \overset{*}{\longleftrightarrow}_T y$ implies that x and y have a common descendant mod $\rightarrow_{R_T}$. Thus, in this case the length-preserving rules are superfluous, and the word problem for T can simply be solved by reduction mod $\rightarrow_{R_T}$. If there are length-preserving rules $(u, v) \in S_T$ such that u and v do not have a common descendant mod $\rightarrow_{R_T}$, then we cannot simply discard these rules. Of course, now we could use an admissible well-ordering $>$ compatible with length to enforce an orientation of the length-preserving rules such that the system $T_1 := R_T \cup \{(u, v) \mid (u, v) \in S_T \text{ or } (v, u) \in S_T, \text{ and } u > v\}$ would be noetherian. If, in addition, T_1 were confluent, then the word problem for T could be solved by reduction mod T_1. However, in the following we present a different approach that is motivated by the discussion in Section 1.2. We describe two classes of string-rewriting systems. Both these classes are specified by conditions that involve the length as the basis for reduction.

Recall that in this chapter we assume that for any string-rewriting system T considered, $|u| \geq |v|$ for each rule $(u, v) \in T$.

Let Σ be an alphabet, and let T be a string-rewriting system on Σ. Recall Definition 3.1.1.

Notice that the relation $\vdash\!\!\dashv_T$ is symmetric, and that $\vdash\!\!\dashv^*_T$ is the equivalence relation induced by $\vdash\!\!\dashv_T$. Further, the relation $\mapsto_T$ allows application of the length-reducing rules of T only from left to right, while the length-preserving rules may be applied in either direction. Finally, a string is called **irreducible** if it is irreducible $\bmod R_T$.

The first type of system that we consider is defined in the following way.

Definition 3.6.1 *Let Σ be an alphabet. A string-rewriting system T on Σ is* **almost-confluent** *if for all x, $y \in \Sigma^*$, $x \longleftrightarrow^*_T y$ if and only if there exist u, $v \in \Sigma^*$ such that $x \to^*_{R_T} u$, $y \to^*_{R_T} v$, and $u \vdash\!\!\dashv^*_T v$.*

We leave the proof of the following fact for the reader.

Lemma 3.6.2 *Let T be a string-rewriting system on alphabet Σ. Then T is almost-confluent if and only if each of the following conditions holds:*

(a) *for all x, $y \in \Sigma^*$, $x \longleftrightarrow^*_T y$ if and only if there exist irreducible u, $v \in \Sigma^*$ such that $x \to^*_{R_T} u$, $y \to^*_{R_T} v$, and $u \vdash\!\!\dashv^*_T v$.*

(b) *for all x, $y \in \Sigma^*$, $x \longleftrightarrow^*_T y$ if and only if for all irreducible u, $v \in \Sigma^*$ such that $x \to^*_{R_T} u$, and $y \to^*_{R_T} v$, it is the case that $u \vdash\!\!\dashv^*_T v$.*

The notion of being almost-confluent is a specific instance of being confluent modulo an equivalence relation as described in Definition 1.2.1. The string-rewriting system T specifies a reduction system $(\Sigma^*, \Rightarrow)$ where the definition of reduction is based on length and so is noetherian. The relation $\vdash\!\!\dashv$ is such that the composition $\vdash\!\!\dashv \circ \Rightarrow$ is also noetherian.

Consider the word problem for a finite string-rewriting system T that is almost-confluent. Given x and y one can apply the algorithm REDUCE to obtain irreducible strings $\bar{x}$ and $\bar{y}$ such that $x \to^*_{R_T} \bar{x}$ and $y \to^*_{R_T} \bar{y}$. If $\bar{x}$ is not congruent to $\bar{y}$ by using only length-preserving rules, then since T is almost-confluent, Lemma 3.6.2(b) applies and one can conclude that $\bar{x}$ is not congruent to $\bar{y}$ and, hence, that x is not congruent to y. If $\bar{x}$ is congruent to $\bar{y}$ by using only length-preserving rules, that is, $\bar{x} \vdash\!\!\dashv^*_T \bar{y}$, then $\bar{x} \longleftrightarrow^*_T \bar{y}$ so that $x \longleftrightarrow^*_T y$. Thus, the word problem for T is decidable.

We want to expand on the argument given in the last paragraph in order to classify the complexity of the word problem for finite almost-confluent systems.

Theorem 3.6.3 *The word problem for finite almost-confluent string-rewriting systems is complete for* **PSPACE**.

Proof. Combining Lemma 3.6.2 and the argument given above, it is easy to see that the word problem for a finite almost-confluent system T can be reduced to the word problem for irreducible strings of the same length where only length-preserving rules are used, that is, the word problem for strings in IRR(R_T) using the relation $\overset{*}{\longleftrightarrow}$. This reduction is carried out by applying the algorithm REDUCE and so can be performed in linear time and, hence, linear space. Using the correspondence between string-rewriting systems having only length-preserving rules and LBA's described in the Appendix to this section, it is clear that this problem can be solved by a nondeterministic LBA, and, hence, is solvable in polynomial space.

Notice that any string-rewriting system that has only length-preserving rules is almost-confluent. As described in the Appendix, for any LBA there is a string-rewriting system with only length-preserving rules such that the membership problem for the LBA can be reduced in a trivial way that preserves the space complexity to the word problem for the string-rewriting system. Since there is an LBA with a membership problem that is **PSPACE**-complete, the word problem for the corresponding string-rewriting system is **PSPACE**-complete.   □3.6.3

While the word problem for an almost-confluent system is not guaranteed to be tractable, it is decidable; there are cases where it is very easily decidable and we will describe one of these. Thus, there is the question of whether the property of being almost-confluent is decidable. We will show that this property is decidable for finite string-rewriting systems and provide an upper bound for the complexity of this problem.

To determine whether a noetherian reduction system is confluent, it is sufficient to determine if it is locally confluent; we showed this in Theorem 1.1.13. To determine whether a finite string-rewriting system is confluent (Corollary 2.3.2), we used this result as well as the fact that it was sufficient to consider only the finite number of critical pairs obtained by considering "overlaps" of left-hand sides of pairs of rewriting rules. To determine whether a noetherian reduction system is confluent modulo an equivalence relation, it is sufficient to determine if it is locally confluent modulo that relation; we showed this in Lemma 1.2.4. Applying this notion to a string-rewriting system T, we see that there are two conditions which must be considered:

(α) for every $x, y, z \in \Sigma^*$, if $x \to_{R_T} y$ and $x \to_{R_T} z$, then there exist u, v such that $y \overset{*}{\to}_{R_T} u$, $z \overset{*}{\to}_{R_T} v$, and $u \overset{*}{\longleftrightarrow} v$;

(β) for every $x, y, z \in \Sigma^*$, if $x \overset{*}{\longleftrightarrow} y$ and $x \to_{R_T} z$, then there exist u, v such that $y \overset{*}{\to}_{R_T} u$, $z \overset{*}{\to}_{R_T} v$, and $u \overset{*}{\longleftrightarrow} v$.

Testing condition (α) is not difficult. Just as in the proof of Theorem 2.3.1, it is sufficient to consider the finite set of critical pairs obtained by considering only the pairs of length-reducing rules where overlap between the left-hand sides occurs. By applying REDUCE one can compute the leftmost irreducible descendants, check whether they have the same length, and, if so, check whether they are congruent by using only the length-preserving rules (that is, the rules generating the congruence $\overset{*}{\longleftrightarrow}$). Just as in the proof of Theorem 2.3.1, the number of critical pairs to be checked in order to test that condition (α) is satisfied is $O(\parallel T \parallel^3)$ and the set of critical pairs can be constructed in time $O(\parallel T \parallel^4)$. Given a critical pair $\langle x, y \rangle$ the algorithm REDUCE will produce leftmost irreducible descendants $\bar{x}, \bar{y}$ in time $O(\parallel T \parallel^2)$ and determining whether $|\bar{x}| = |\bar{y}|$ can be done trivally. If $|\bar{x}| = |\bar{y}|$, then determining whether $\bar{x} \overset{*}{\longleftrightarrow} \bar{y}$ can be done nondeterministically in linear space. Thus, testing whether condition (α) holds can be done in space that is (at worst) polynomial in $\parallel T \parallel$.

Testing condition (β) is another matter. Consider the hypothesis of the condition: for every $x, y, z \in \Sigma^*$, if $x \overset{*}{\longleftrightarrow} y$ and $x \rightarrow_{R_T} z$. This means that for every $x \in \Sigma^*$, one must consider every $y, z \in \Sigma^*$ such that $x \overset{*}{\longleftrightarrow} y$ and $x \rightarrow_{R_T} z$; while for each such x there are only finitely many y and z to be considered, there are infinitely many choices for x. Thus, there is no hope of obtaining a direct test for condition (β).

This situation takes us to Lemma 1.2.5 where instead of an equivalence relation one considers a finite symmetric relation, say $\approx$, that generates an equivalence relation, say $\cong$. Lemma 1.2.5 asserts that if $\rightarrow \circ \approx$ is noetherian, then to prove local confluence it is sufficient to establish property (α) and property (γ) which is defined as follows:

(γ) for all w, x, y, if $w \approx x$ and $w \rightarrow y$, then there exist u, v such that $x \overset{*}{\rightarrow} u$, $y \overset{*}{\rightarrow} v$, and $u \cong v$.

In the present context the symmetric relation is $\longleftrightarrow$ and the equivalence relation is $\overset{*}{\longleftrightarrow}$. Consider the problem of testing condition γ.

If $(u_1, v_1), (u_2, v_2)$ are in T, $|u_1| = |v_1|$, $|u_2| > |v_2|$, and $w = w_1 u_1 w_2 u_2 w_3$, then $w \longleftrightarrow w_1 v_1 w_2 u_2 w_3 \rightarrow_{R_T} w_1 v_1 w_2 v_2 w_3$ by first rewriting u_1 as v_1 and then rewriting u_2 as v_2, and $w \rightarrow_{R_T} w_1 u_1 w_2 v_2 w_3 \longleftrightarrow w_1 v_1 w_2 v_2 w_3$ by first rewriting u_2 as v_2 and then rewriting u_1 as v_1. Thus, condition (γ) is satisfied. This means that we are not required to test anything in this case, and so we can restrict attention to those cases where $w = w_1 u_1 w_2$ and $w = w_3 u_2 w_4$ with

(a) $|w_1 u_1| \leq |w_3 u_2|$ and $|w_2| < |u_2 w_4|$ or

(b) $|w_3 u_2| \leq |w_1 u_1|$ and $|w_4| < |u_1 w_2|$.

Cases (a) and (b) occur when either for some $x, y, u_1 x = y u_2$ and $|x| < |u_2|$, or for some $x, y, u_1 = x u_2 y$. (Of course, the roles of u_1 and u_2 can be interchanged but it is sufficient to consider only these cases). That is, overlap between u_1 and u_2 occurs.

Once again we have the notion of a critical pair. But now the context is such that one rule is length-preserving, say $|u_1| = |v_1|$, and one rule is length-reducing, say $|u_2| > |v_2|$. First, the set of critical pairs must be generated. Then for each critical pair $\langle x, y \rangle$, the leftmost irreducible descendants $\bar{x}, \bar{y}$ must be generated and it must be determined whether $\bar{x} \xmapsto{*} \bar{y}$. Just as in the argument concerning condition (α), it is clear that this procedure allows one to determine whether condition (γ) holds using space that is (at most) polynomial in $\| T \|$.

The reader should notice that in testing either condition (α) or condition (γ), the entire process can be carried out in polynomial time except for the problem of determining whether two strings are congruent by using only the length-preserving rules, that is, whether $\bar{x} \xmapsto{*} \bar{y}$.

From the preceding argument we have the following result.

Theorem 3.6.4 *There is an algorithm to solve the following problem which uses polynomial work space:*

Instance: *A finite string-rewriting system T.*

Question: *Is T almost-confluent?*

As an example of almost-confluent systems, we consider rewriting in a "free partially commutative monoid." Recently several problems of concurrency control in data-base systems and in parallel computation have been modeled by considering properties of strings and the algebra of string-rewriting. In this framework, the "alphabet" represents a set of functions, and concatenation of symbols over the alphabet resulting in strings represents the composition of the functions represented by the symbols. In this context partial commutativity plays an interesting role. This has provided motivation for the more abstract study of words in partially commutative monoids, particularly in free partially commutative monoids.

Definition 3.6.5 *Let Σ be a finite alphabet. Let Θ be a binary relation on Σ that is irreflexive and symmetric. Let $\equiv_\Theta$ be the congruence relation on Σ^* determined by defining $xaby \equiv_\Theta xbay$ for every $x, y \in \Sigma^*$ and every $(a, b) \in \Theta$. It will be useful to write $u \equiv v (\mathrm{mod}\ \Theta)$ when $u \equiv_\Theta v$, and we say that "u and v are congruent ($\mathrm{mod}\ \Theta$)." The **free partially commutative monoid** generated by Σ with respect to the relation Θ is defined to be the quotient of Σ^* by $\equiv_\Theta$. Usually its elements, which are the congruence classes mod $\equiv_\Theta$, are called **traces**.*

A free partially commutative monoid may be viewed as the monoid M_T specified by a string-rewriting system T_Θ: given Σ and Θ, let $T_\Theta = \{(ab, ba) \mid (a, b) \in \Theta\}$; then the free partially commutative monoid generated by Σ with respect to Θ is precisely M_{T_Θ}.

It is clear that the word problem for a free partially commutative monoid is decidable. What we describe here is a linear-time algorithm for that problem.

Theorem 3.6.6 *Let Σ be a finite alphabet and let Θ be a binary relation on Σ that is irreflexive and symmetric. There is a linear-time algorithm to solve the following problem:*

Instance: *x and y in Σ^*.*

Question: *Are x and y congruent $(\mathrm{mod}\ \Theta)$?*

Sketch of the Proof. For every $w \in \Sigma^*$ and every $a \in \Sigma$, let $|w|_a$ denote the number of occurrences of a in w. For a subset $\Delta \subseteq \Sigma$ and every $w \in \Sigma^*$, let $\Pi_\Delta(w)$ denote the string obtained by erasing from w all occurrences of every symbol **not** in Δ; $\Pi_\Delta(w)$ is the **projection** of w on Δ^*. It is not difficult to show that for every two strings $x, y \in \Sigma^*$, $x \equiv_\Theta y$ if and only if both (i) for every $a \in \Sigma$, $|x|_a = |y|_a$, and (ii) for each pair (a, b) of symbols not in Θ, $\Pi_{\{a,b\}}(x) = \Pi_{\{a,b\}}(y)$. (Notice that (i) is subsumed by (ii) if pairs of the form (a, a) are allowed.) It is clear that both of these conditions can be tested in time $O(\|\Sigma\|^2 (|x| + |y|))$. Thus, for given Σ and Θ, the time is $O(|xy|)$, that is, it is linear in the lengths of x and y.   □3.6.6

Consider rewriting in a free partially commutative monoid. We will restrict attention to the case where a string-rewriting system T on alphabet Σ has only rewriting rules that are length-reducing. If Θ is a binary relation on Σ that is irreflexive and symmetric, then we consider the combined system $T \cup T_\Theta$. While one might consider various properties for such a system to have, we consider only the property that $T \cup T_\Theta$ is almost-confluent, which in this case is better referred to as "T is confluent modulo Θ."

From Theorem 3.6.3 we see that the word problem for a length-reducing string-rewriting system that is confluent modulo Θ is solvable in polynomial space. But the fact that the word problem for a free partially commutative monoid is solvable in linear time (Theorem 3.6.6) allows us to show that the complexity of the word problem in this case is much lower.

Theorem 3.6.7 *Let Σ be a finite alphabet and let Θ be a binary relation on Σ that is irreflexive and symmetric. If T is a finite length-reducing string-rewriting system on Σ that is confluent modulo Θ, then there is a linear time algorithm to solve the following problem:*

Instance: *x and y in Σ^*.*

Question: *Are x and y congruent mod $(T \cup T_\Theta)$?*

Proof. For any x, y, if $x \equiv_\Theta y$, then the result follows from Theorem 3.6.6. Otherwise, one can use REDUCE to compute irreducible $\overline{x}$ and $\overline{y}$ such that $x \xrightarrow{*}_T \overline{x}$ and $y \xrightarrow{*}_T \overline{y}$, and this can be done in time $O(|xy|)$. Since

T is confluent modulo Θ and both $\bar{x}$ and $\bar{y}$ are irreducible, $\bar{x} \overset{*}{\longleftrightarrow}_{T \cup T_\Theta} \bar{y}$ implies $|\bar{x}| = |\bar{y}|$ so that $\bar{x} \overset{*}{\longleftrightarrow}_{T \cup T_\Theta} \bar{y}$ if and only if $\bar{x} \equiv_\Theta \bar{y}$. Hence, $x \overset{*}{\longleftrightarrow}_{T \cup T_\Theta} y$ if and only if $\bar{x} \equiv_\Theta \bar{y}$. By Theorem 3.6.6 one can test whether it is the case that $\bar{x} \equiv_\Theta \bar{y}$ in time $O(|\bar{x}| + |\bar{y}|) = O(|xy|)$.   □3.6.7

Theorem 3.6.7 shows that being confluent modulo Θ is a desirable property for finite length-reducing string-rewriting systems since in that case there is a very fast algorithm for the word problem. Hence, it is of interest to find the complexity of determining when a finite length-reducing system has this property. Theorem 3.6.4 shows that this can be done by using at most polynomial work space since this property is a special case of being almost-confluent, but a considerable improvement to that bound can be made due to the fact that the word problem for a free partially commutative monoid is decidable in linear time.

Theorem 3.6.8 *Let Σ be a finite alphabet and let Θ be a binary relation on Σ that is irreflexive and symmetric. Then there is a polynomial time algorithm to decide the following:*

Instance: *A finite length-reducing string-rewriting system T on Σ.*

Question: *Is T confluent modulo Θ?*

Proof. Since $\rightarrow_{T \circ \Theta}$ is noetherian, the argument is just like the proof of Theorem 3.6.4 except that the bound can be improved. The problem of determining whether two irreducible strings are congruent while using only length-preserving rules, that is, $\bar{x} \overset{*}{\longmapsto} \bar{y}$, is much simpler from an algorithmic standpoint since Theorem 3.6.6 shows that it can be determined in time $O(|\bar{x}| + |\bar{y}|)$. Since the algorithm given in Theorem 3.6.4 involves answering this question for at most $O(\| T \|^3)$ such pairs of irreducible strings resulting from critical pairs, and the set of all such pairs of irreducible strings can be generated in time $O(\| T \|^6)$, the running time of the algorithm is $O(\| T \|^6)$.   □3.6.8

Thus, we conclude that if the length-preserving rules of a string-rewriting system are just those induced by an irreflexive and symmetric binary relation on the alphabet, then the standard questions about the string-rewriting system are much easier to solve than in the general case.

There is another class of string-rewriting systems with decidable word problems where the fact that the word problem is decidable follows immediately from considerations of length.

Definition 3.6.9 *A string-rewriting system T on alphabet Σ is **preperfect** if for all $x, y \in \Sigma^*$, $x \overset{*}{\longleftrightarrow} y$ if and only if there exists $z \in \Sigma^*$ such that $x \overset{*}{\longmapsto} z$ and $y \overset{*}{\longmapsto} z$.*

It is clear that the word problem for finite preperfect systems is decidable since it is sufficient to consider only strings whose length is at most that of the longer of the given strings. Since there are only finitely many strings of each length, the result follows trivially. In addition, this argument shows that the word problem for a finite preperfect system is decidable nondeterministically using linear space. Hence, following the same argument as that used to prove Theorem 3.6.3, we see that the word problem for finite preperfect systems is **PSPACE**-complete.

While the word problem for a preperfect system is decidable, it is undecidable whether a finite string-rewriting system is preperfect. In fact, preperfectness remains undecidable even if the length-preserving rules are restricted to be induced by an irreflexive and symmetric binary relation Θ on the alphabet, that is, if only systems of the form $T = R_T \cup T_\Theta$ are considered, where R_T contains length-reducing rules only.

APPENDIX TO SECTION 3.6

In this appendix we describe the correspondence between string-rewriting systems having only length-preserving rules and linearly bounded automata (LBA's) on which our proof of Theorem 3.6.3 rests. Recall from Section 1.4 the definition of LBA's and the remark on their accepted languages.

Lemma 3.6.10 *Let T be a string-rewriting system on Σ that only contains length-preserving rules. Then there exists an LBA $A(T) = (Q, \Sigma \cup \{\$, \pounds\}, \delta, q_0, q_a)$ such that for all $u, v \in \Sigma^*$ with $|u| = |v|$, the following two statements are equivalent:*

(i) $u \overset{*}{\longleftrightarrow}_T v$, *and*

(ii) $q_0 \$ u \pounds \overset{*}{\vdash}_{A(T)} q_a \$ v \pounds$.

Proof. We do not define the LBA $A(T)$ in detail; rather we describe its behavior informally. On input $u \in \Sigma^*$ the LBA $A(T)$ repeatedly performs the following action:

(1) Either enter the accepting state q_a or go to (2).

(2) Move the tape head to the right scanning the current tape inscription. If the left-hand side ℓ or the right-hand side r of a rule of T is discovered, then either replace this string by the other side of the corresponding rule of T and go to (3), or continue to move the tape head to the right. This is repeated until either some string is being replaced or the symbol $\pounds$ is encountered, in which case step (3) is performed.

(3) Move the tape head back to the left until the symbol $\$$ is found, and then go to (1).

From this description it is easily seen that on input $u \in \Sigma^*$, $A(T)$ computes a sequence $u = w_0 \leftrightarrow_T w_1 \leftrightarrow_T \ldots \leftrightarrow_T w_n$. Thus, if $q_0\$u\pounds \vdash^*_{A(T)} q_a\$v\pounds$, then $u \xleftrightarrow{*}_T v$. On the other hand, if $u \xleftrightarrow{*}_T v$, then there is a sequence of moves that $A(T)$ can make such that $q_0\$u\pounds$ is transformed into $q_a\$v\pounds$. This completes the proof of Lemma 3.6.10.   □3.6.10

Conversely, each LBA A can be simulated by a string-rewriting system containing only length-preserving rules.

Lemma 3.6.11 *Let $A = (Q, \Sigma, \delta, q_0, q_a)$ be an LBA. Then there exists a string-rewriting system $T(A)$ containing only length-preserving rules such that, for all configurations uqv and $u_1q_1v_1$ of A, the following two statements are equivalent:*

(i) $uqv \vdash^*_A u_1q_1v_1$, *and*

(ii) $uqv \xrightarrow{*}_{T(A)} u_1q_1v_1$.

Proof. Let $A = (Q, \Sigma, \delta, q_0, q_a)$ be an LBA. We define a string rewriting system $T(A)$ on the alphabet $\Gamma := Q \cup \Sigma$ as follows:

1.	qa	$\rightarrow$	$q'c$	if $(q', c) \in \delta(q, a)$,
2.	qa	$\rightarrow$	aq'	if $(q', R) \in \delta(q, a)$,
3.	cqa	$\rightarrow$	$q'ca$	if $(q', L) \in \delta(q, a), c \in \Sigma$.

Then $T(A)$ contains length-preserving rules only. In addition, the single-step reduction relation $\rightarrow_{T(A)}$ induced by $T(A)$ simulates the single-step computation relation $\vdash_A$. Thus, if uqv and $u_1q_1v_1$ describe proper configurations of A, then $uqv \vdash^*_A u_1q_1v_1$ if and only if $uqv \xrightarrow{*}_{T(A)} u_1q_1v_1$.
□3.6.11

3.7   Bibliographic Remarks

The use of reduction of the length of a string as the basis for the notion of reduction in string-rewriting systems was probably first introduced by Nivat and pursued by his students and colleagues. The best source for this work is the survey paper by Berstel [Ber77]. Theorem 3.1.2 is based on Lemma 1.1.7, while Lemma 3.1.3 and Theorem 3.1.4 are due to Book [Boo82a]. Theorem 3.2.1 is due to Book and Ó'Dúnlaing [BoÓ'Dú81b] but the idea of the proof was studied earlier by Nivat and Benois [NiBe72] who were not concerned with an algorithmic solution or with the computational complexity of the task. Later, Kapur et al [KKMN85] offered an algorithm which has running time $O(\| T^3 \|)$.

String-rewriting systems that are only confluent on a single class were studied by Otto [Ott87]. A detailed presentation of Dehn's algorithm for the word problem can be found in [LySc77].

Homogeneous systems were studied in [Boo84] where Theorem 3.4.2 appears. The remaining material in Section 3.4, and particularly Theorem 3.4.7, is due to Ó'Dúnlaing [Ó'Dú81, Ó'Dú83a] who followed the presentation of Markov [Mar51]. We will return to this topic in Chapter 7.

Corollary 3.5.4 is from [Ó'Dú83a], while Theorem 3.5.5 first appeared in [BoÓ'Dú81a].

The study of other systems based on length reduction appears in [Ber77] and [Boo82a] as well as others. (Before reading far in this section, the reader may wish to review Section 1.2 as well as Section 1.4). Theorem 3.6.3 is due to Jantzen and Monien and is reported in [BJMO'DW81].

There are very different approaches to partially commutative monoids, also called "trace monoids." Cartier and Foata [CaFo69] developed some of the fundamental results and established a normal form that can be used to prove Theorem 3.6.6. Book and Liu [BoLi87] gave a very different proof of Theorem 3.6.6 based on ideas in Sections 1.1 and 3.1. Diekert [Die86] studied complete string-rewriting systems for abelian groups, while Wrathall [Wra88] showed the word problem for free partially commutative groups to be decidable in linear time. Observations leading to Theorems 3.6.7 and 3.6.8 were made by Book and Liu based on results of Huet [Hue80]. Narendran and McNaughton [NaMc84] showed that the property of being preperfect is undecidable for finite string-rewriting systems. That this property remains undecidable even for systems of the form $T = R_T \cup T_\Theta$, where Θ is an irreflexive and symmetric binary relation on Σ and R_T contains only length-reducing rules, was established by Narendran and Otto [NaOt88b].

4
Monadic String-Rewriting Systems

Certain restrictions on the form of the rules of string-rewriting systems have yielded some extremely interesting results. Any finitely presented group can be presented by a finite special string-rewriting system (with no restriction to the notion of reduction). But special systems have a few undesirable limitations. Thus we turn to the study of "monadic" string-rewriting systems which extend the power of special string-rewriting systems in useful ways.

4.1   Basic Properties

Monadic string-rewriting systems are defined in such a way that reduction depends on length. Thus, the results of Chapter 3 are applicable here.

Definition 4.1.1 *A string-rewriting system T is* **monadic** *if $(u, v) \in T$ implies that $|u| > |v|$ and $|v| = 1$ or $|v| = 0$.*

Notice that every special string-rewriting system is monadic but the converse is not true.

The first result illustrates the usefulness of this restriction.

Theorem 4.1.2 *There is a polynomial-time algorithm that on input a non-deterministic finite-state acceptor $\mathcal{A}$ with input alphabet Σ and a finite monadic string-rewriting system T on Σ will compute a nondeterministic finite state acceptor $\mathcal{B}$ that accepts the set $\Delta_T^*(R)$ of descendants of R modulo T, where R is the regular subset of Σ^* accepted by $\mathcal{A}$.*

Proof.   Let T be a finite monadic string-rewriting system on Σ. For $r \in \Sigma \cup \{e\}$, let $D(r) = \{\ell \in \Sigma^* \mid (\ell, r) \in T\}$, that is, $D(r)$ is the set of all left-hand sides of rules of T that have right-hand side r. Further, let R be the regular subset of Σ^* that is accepted by the nondeterministic finite state acceptor $\mathcal{A} = (Q, \Sigma, \delta, q_0, F\}$, where $Q = \{q_0, q_1, \ldots, q_{n-1}\}$ is the finite set of states, $\delta : Q \times \Sigma \to 2^Q$ is the transition relation, $q_0 \in Q$ is the initial state, and $F \subseteq Q$ is the set of accepting states of $\mathcal{A}$. The transition relation $\delta : Q \times \Sigma \to 2^Q$ is extended to $Q \times \Sigma^* \to 2^Q$ as usual.

The algorithm constructs the desired acceptor $\mathcal{B}$ by modifying $\mathcal{A}$. This modification involves changing the transition relation δ and the set F of accepting states by adding certain transitions and by turning certain non-accepting states into accepting ones. The idea of adding transitions is as follows: suppose that for some letter $a \in \Sigma$, some string $\ell \in D(a)$, and some states $q_i, q_j \in Q, q_j \in \delta(q_i, \ell)$. Then we must add a transition from q_i to q_j with label a, if $q_j \notin \delta(q_i, a)$. The intent of adding this transition is to capture the notion that since $\ell \rightarrow_T a$, a transition from q_i to q_j with label a is equivalent to a sequence of transitions from q_i to q_j with label ℓ. Further, suppose that for some string $\ell \in D(e)$, and some states $q_i, q_j \in Q, q_j \in \delta(q_i, \ell)$. Then for each $a \in \Sigma$ and each $q_k \in Q$, if $q_k \in \delta(q_j, a)$ then we must add a transition from q_i to q_k with label a, if $q_k \notin \delta(q_i, a)$. The intent of adding this transition is to capture the notion that since $\ell a \rightarrow_T a$, a transition from q_i to q_k with label a is equivalent to a sequence of transitions from q_i to q_k with label ℓa. In addition, if this situation occurs and q_j is a final state, then q_i also becomes a final state. This process must be iterated until no further transitions can be added, which means that at most $|\Sigma| \cdot n^2$ iterations take place.

It is clear that this basic construction will lead to an acceptor for a subset of $\Delta_T^*(R)$. On the other hand, since the process of adding transitions is iterated until no further transitions can be added, it is not difficult to see that the resulting nondeterministic finite state acceptor actually accepts the set $\Delta_T^*(R)$. To prove that this construction can be performed in polynomial time, we consider the following formal description of it.

ALGORITHM:

Input: A nondeterministic finite state acceptor $\mathcal{A} = (Q, \Sigma, \delta, q_0, F)$ and a finite monadic string-rewriting system T on Σ;

    begin

(1) $z \leftarrow 1$;

(2)   **while** $z \leq |\Sigma| \cdot |Q|^2$ **do**

(3)   **begin for all** $q_i, q_j \in Q$ **and all** $r \in \Sigma \cup \{e\}$ **do**

(4)   **if** $q_j \in \bigcup_{\ell \in D(r)} \delta(q_i, \ell)$ **then**

(5)   **begin if** $r = e$ **then**

(6)   **for all** $a \in \Sigma$ **and all** $q_k \in Q$ **do**

(7)   **begin if** $q_k \in \delta(q_j, a)$ **and** $q_k \notin \delta(q_i, a)$ **then**

(8) $\delta(q_i, a) \leftarrow \delta(q_i, a) \cup \{q_k\}$;

(9)   **if** $q_j \in F$ **and** $q_i \notin F$ **then** $F \leftarrow F \cup \{q_i\}$

        end

(10)   **else if** $q_j \notin \delta(q_i, r)$ **then** $\delta(q_i, r) \leftarrow \delta(q_i, r) \cup \{q_j\}$

    end,

(11) $z \leftarrow z + 1$

  end

 end.

Since T is a finite string-rewriting system, the set $D(r)$ is finite for each $r \in \Sigma \cup \{e\}$. Hence, the test in line (4) can be performed in time bounded above by a polynomial in $|\Sigma|$, $|Q|$, and $\| T \|$. All the other statements can be performed in time bounded above by a polynomial in $|\Sigma|$ and $|Q|$. Thus, from $\mathcal{A}$ and T we obtain a non-deterministic finite state acceptor $\mathcal{B}$ for $\Delta_T^*(R)$ in polynomial time.   □ 4.1.2

Corollary 4.1.3 *Let T be a finite string-rewriting system on alphabet Σ. If T is monadic, then for every regular set $R \subseteq \Sigma^*$, the set $\Delta_T^*(R)$ is regular.*

Consider the common descendant problem for finite monadic string-rewriting systems. If T is finite and monadic, then for every x, y, the question "do x and y have a common descendant?" is equivalent to the question "is $\Delta_T^*(x) \cap \Delta_T^*(y) \neq \emptyset$?" Since $\Delta_T^*(x)$ and $\Delta_T^*(y)$ are regular, this question is decidable. A generalization of this problem is also decidable: "given regular sets R_1 and R_2, is $\Delta_T^*(R_1) \cap \Delta_T^*(R_2) \neq \emptyset$?" Using Theorem 4.1.2 and standard techniques for searching graphs, for example, breadth-first search, we have the following fact.

Corollary 4.1.4 *Let T be a finite monadic string-rewriting system on alphabet Σ. The following problem can be solved in polynomial time:*

  Instance: *Regular sets $R_1, R_2 \subseteq \Sigma^*$ specified by nondeterministic finite-state acceptors.*

  Question: *Is $\Delta_T^*(R_1) \cap \Delta_T^*(R_2)$ nonempty?*

In particular, the common descendant problem for T is decidable in polynomial time.

These results lead to the decidability of the "extended word problem" that is described in the next corollary.

Corollary 4.1.5 *Let T be a finite monadic string-rewriting system on alphabet Σ that is confluent. The following problem can be solved in polynomial time:*

  Instance: *Regular sets $R_1, R_2 \subseteq \Sigma^*$ specified by nondeterministic finite-state acceptors.*

  Question: *Do there exist $x \in R_1$ and $y \in R_2$ such that $x \xleftrightarrow{*}_T y$?*

4.2   Specification of Formal Languages

Here we turn to the study of formal languages. As noted in the Introduction, one motivation for studying confluent string-rewriting systems is the fact that in some cases, congruence classes are context-free languages. The French school initiated research in this area, and their choice of topics was influenced by the interface between algebra and formal language theory. We will develop some of the main results.

Definition 4.2.1 *A language L is* **congruential** *if there is a finite string-rewriting system T such that L is the union of finitely many of T's congruence classes.*

Theorem 4.2.2 *There is a context-free language that is not congruential.*

Proof. For each $L \subseteq \Sigma^*$ the syntactic congruence $\sim_L$ on Σ^* specified by L is defined by $u \sim_L v$ if and only if for every $x, y \in \Sigma^*$ $[xuy \in L$ if and only if $xvy \in L]$.

Suppose that L is congruential. Let T be a string-rewriting system such that for some $z_1, \ldots, z_n$, $L = \cup_{i=1}^{n} [z_i]_T$. Now consider any $u, v \in \Sigma^*$ such that $u \xleftrightarrow{*}_T v$. Then for all $x, y \in \Sigma^*$, $xuy \xleftrightarrow{*}_T xvy$, so for all i, $1 \leq i \leq n$, $xuy \in [z_i]_T$ if and only if $xvy \in [z_i]_T$, that is, $xuy \in L$ if and only if $xvy \in L$. Hence, $u \sim_L v$. Thus, the congruence $\xleftrightarrow{*}_T$ refines the syntactic congruence $\sim_L$.

Consider the linear context-free language $L = \{w \in \{a, b\}^* \mid w = w^R\}$, where for every string z, z^R is the reversal of z. We claim that L is not congruential. To prove this, assume to the contrary that T is a finite system and $z_1, \ldots, z_n \in \{a, b\}^*$ are such that $L = \cup_{i=1}^{n} [z_i]_T$. Since L is infinite, there exists j such that $[z_j]_T$ is infinite. Choose $w_1, w_2 \in [z_j]_T$ such that $|w_1| < |w_2|$. Since $w_1 \in [z_j]_T \subseteq L$, $w_1 = w_1^R$ so that $w_1 aaw_1 = w_1 aaw_1^R \in L$ and $w_1 bbw_1 = w_1 bbw_1^R \in L$. Since $w_1, w_2 \in [z_j]_T$, $w_1 \xleftrightarrow{*}_T w_2$ and so $w_1 \sim_L w_2$. Thus, $w_2(aaw_1) \in L$ and $w_2(bbw_1) \in L$. Since $w_2 aaw_1 \in L$, $w_2 aaw_1 = (w_2 aaw_1)^R = w_1 aaw_2$ so that $|w_1| < |w_2|$ implies that $w_1 a$ is a prefix of w_2. Similarly, since $w_2 bbw_1 \in L$, $w_1 b$ is a prefix of w_2. Since $a \neq b$, this is a contradiction.   □4.2.2

The reader will have noticed the obvious resemblance between a monadic string-rewriting system and a context-free grammar. To make this relationship more explicit we need the following technical lemma.

Lemma 4.2.3 *Let T be a monadic string-rewriting system on Σ, and let $x, y \in \Sigma^*$. Then $\nabla_T^*(xy) = \nabla_T^*(x) \cdot \nabla_T^*(y)$.*

Proof. Obviously $\nabla_T^*(x) \cdot \nabla_T^*(y) \subseteq \nabla_T^*(xy)$. Thus, it suffices to prove the following claim.

Claim. Let $u \in \nabla_T^*(xy)$. Then there are $u_1, u_2 \in \Sigma^*$ such that $u = u_1 u_2$, $u_1 \rightarrow_T^* x$ and $u_2 \rightarrow_T^* y$.

Proof. Let $u \in \nabla_T^*(xy)$. Then $u \rightarrow_T^* xy$, that is, there exist an integer $n > 0$ and strings $w_0, w_1, \ldots, w_n \in \Sigma^*$ with $u = w_0 \rightarrow_T w_1 \rightarrow_T \ldots \rightarrow_T w_n = xy$. We proceed by induction on n.

If $n = 0$, then we are done. If $u \rightarrow_T w \xrightarrow{n}_T xy$, then there are strings $z_1, z_2 \in \Sigma^*$ and a rule $(\ell, r) \in T$ such that $u = z_1 \ell z_2$ and $w = z_1 r z_2$. By induction hypothesis $w = w_1 w_2$ with $w_1 \xrightarrow{*}_T x$ and $w_2 \xrightarrow{*}_T y$, thus implying $z_1 r z_2 = w_1 w_2$.

If $|w_1| > |z_1|$, then $w_1 = z_1 r s$ and $z_2 = s w_2$ for some $s \in \Sigma^*$, since $|r| \leq 1$. Hence, with $u_1 = z_1 \ell s$ and $u_2 = w_2$ we have $u = z_1 \ell z_2 = z_1 \ell s w_2 = u_1 u_2$, $u_1 = z_1 \ell s \rightarrow_T z_1 r s = w_1 \xrightarrow{*}_T x$, and $u_2 = w_2 \xrightarrow{*}_T y$.

If $|w_1| \leq |z_1|$, then $z_1 = w_1 t$ and $w_2 = t r z_2$ for some $t \in \Sigma^*$. Hence, with $u_1 = w_1$ and $u_2 = t \ell z_2$ we have $u = z_1 \ell z_2 = w_1 t \ell z_2 = u_1 u_2$, $u_1 = w_1 \xrightarrow{*}_T x$, and $u_2 = t \ell z_2 \xrightarrow{*}_T t r z_2 = w_2 \xrightarrow{*}_T y$. $\square$4.2.3

Thus, for $z = a_1 a_2 \ldots a_m (a_i \in \Sigma)$ and $w \in \nabla_T^*(z)$, we can factor w as $w = w_1 w_2 \ldots w_m$ such that $w_i \xrightarrow{*}_T a_i$, $i = 1, \ldots, m$. Hence, if $w \xrightarrow{*}_T z$ is a sequence of reduction steps, then this sequence can be rearranged so as to "proceed from left to right," that is, $w = w_1 w_2 \ldots w_m \xrightarrow{*}_T a_1 w_2 \ldots w_m \xrightarrow{*}_T a_1 a_2 w_3 \ldots w_m \xrightarrow{*}_T \ldots \xrightarrow{*}_T a_1 a_2 \ldots a_{m-1} w_m \xrightarrow{*}_T a_1 a_2 \ldots a_{m-1} a_m = z$. Of course, this new sequence of reduction steps need not be a leftmost reduction (see Definition 2.2.6).

Theorem 4.2.4 *Let T be a finite monadic string-rewriting system on alphabet Σ. For every context-free language L, the set of ancestors of strings in L is a context-free language, that is, $\nabla_T^*(L) = \{y \mid$ for some $x \in L$, $y \xrightarrow{*}_T x\}$ is context-free.*

Proof. First we prove a weaker result: for every $z \in \Sigma^*$, $\nabla_T^*(z)$ is context-free. The proof of this fact is similar to that of Theorem 2.2.9. Consider a pushdown automaton that operates nondeterministically. Each computation may use any of three procedures, READ, SEARCH, and DECIDE. Initally, a READ operation is attempted.

READ: Attempt to read an input symbol and push it onto the pushdown store. If the input tape is empty, then go to DECIDE; otherwise, nondeterministically decide to go to SEARCH or continue to READ.

SEARCH: Pop from the pushdown store any string u that occurs as the left-hand side of a rule (u, a) or (u, e) in T; if no such u exists, halt. If u is popped and there is just one rule in T with u as its left-hand side, then push the right-hand side onto the pushdown store. If u is popped and there are more than one rule in T with u on the left-hand side, then nondeterministically choose one such rule (u, v) and push v

onto the pushdown store. Nondeterministically decide to go to READ or continue to search.

DECIDE: Compare the contents of the pushdown store with z where the symbol on the top of the store is compared with the rightmost symbol of z. If the contents is equal to z, then halt and accept; otherwise, halt.

The nondeterministic pushdown automaton scans the input string from left to right and nondeterministically guesses when to perform reductions. It is clear that if an input string x is accepted, then $x \xrightarrow{*}_T z$. Conversely, if $x \xrightarrow{*}_T z$, then there is a sequence of reduction steps that reduces x to z and that proceeds from left to right. Thus, an input string x is accepted if and only if $x \xrightarrow{*}_T z$ if and only if $x \in \nabla^*_T(z)$. This means that $\nabla^*_T(z)$ is context-free since a set of strings is accepted by a nondeterministic pushdown automaton if and only if it is context-free.

Consider the context-free substitution τ on Σ^* determined by defining $\tau(a) = \nabla^*_T(a)$ for $a \in \Sigma$ and $\tau(e) = \nabla^*_T(e)$. Then for any $a_1, \ldots, a_n \in \Sigma, \tau(a_1 \ldots a_n) = \tau(a_1) \ldots \tau(a_n) = \nabla^*_T(a_1) \ldots \nabla^*_T(a_n) = \nabla^*_T(a_1 \ldots a_n)$ by Lemma 4.2.3. Hence, for any $L \subseteq \Sigma^*$, $\tau(L) = \cup\{\tau(z) \mid z \in L\} = \cup\{\nabla^*_T(z) \mid z \in L\} = \nabla^*_T(L)$. Since the class of context-free languages is closed under substitution, if L is context-free, then so is $\nabla^*_T(L) = \tau(L)$.   □ 4.2.4

Corollary 4.2.5 *Let T be a finite monadic string-rewriting system on alphabet Σ. The following question is decidable: for $x \in \Sigma^*$, does x have infinitely many ancestors, that is, is $\nabla^*_T(x)$ infinite?*

Consider a finite string-rewriting system T that is confluent. For any x, consider $\nabla^*_T(\overline{x})$ where $\overline{x}$ is the unique irreducible string congruent to x. If y is congruent to x, then $y \xrightarrow{*}_T \overline{x}$ since T is confluent. Thus, $[x]_T \subseteq \nabla^*_T(\overline{x})$ and, clearly, $\nabla^*_T(\overline{x}) \subseteq [x]_T$. If T is also monadic, then $[x]_T$ is context-free since $[x]_T = \nabla^*_T(\overline{x})$ and $\nabla^*_T(\overline{x})$ is context-free by Theorem 4.2.4. The proof of Theorem 4.2.4 shows that if L is context-free and $L \subseteq IRR(T)$, then $[L]_T \ (= \cup\{[x]_T \mid x \in L\})$ is context-free, since $[L]_T = \nabla^*_T(L)$ and T is confluent.

Corollary 4.2.6 *Let T be a finite monadic string-rewriting system on alphabet Σ. If T is confluent, then for any context-free language L such that $L \subseteq IRR(T)$, $[L]_T$ is context-free.*

The condition that $L \subseteq IRR(T)$ cannot be omitted from Corollary 4.2.6. However, if attention is restricted to regular sets, then this condition can be omitted and the conclusion is even stronger.

Theorem 4.2.7 *Let T be a finite monadic string-rewriting system on alphabet Σ. Suppose that T is confluent. If $A \subseteq \Sigma^*$ is a regular set, then $[A]_T$ is a deterministic context-free language.*

Proof. Since T is confluent, $[A]_T = \nabla_T^*(\Delta_T^*(A) \cap IRR(T))$. Since T is monadic, $\Delta_T^*(A)$ is a regular set (Theorem 4.1.2), and since T is finite, $IRR(T)$ is regular; hence, $\Delta_T^*(A) \cap IRR(T)$ is regular, and so we lose no generality by assuming that $A \subseteq IRR(T)$ yielding $[A]_T = \nabla_T^*(A)$.

We assume that the "pre-processing" of T as described in the proof of Theorem 2.2.9 has been performed.

To obtain a deterministic pushdown automaton for $\nabla_T^*(A)$, we combine the arguments of the proof of Theorem 2.2.9 and the proof of Theorem 4.2.4. There are three procedures: READ, SEARCH, and DECIDE. Initially a READ operation is attempted.

READ: Attempt to read an input symbol and push it onto the pushdown store. If the input tape is empty, then go to DECIDE; otherwise, go to SEARCH.

SEARCH: Pop from the pushdown store the longest string u (if any) that occurs as a left-hand side of a rule (u, v) in T. If no such u is detected, then restore the pushdown store to its previous condition and go to READ. If such a u is detected, then push the corresponding v onto the pushdown store. Go to SEARCH.

DECIDE: Since A is regular, the reversal of A, $A^R = \{z^R \mid z \in A\}$, is regular. Thus there is a deterministic finite-state acceptor D that specifies A^R. A copy of D can be constructed as part of the pushdown automaton's finite-state control. The automaton can pop the store one symbol per step to determine whether the content of the pushdown store is in A^R. If so, halt and accept; if not, halt and reject.

Just as in the proof of Theorem 2.2.9, we see that for any input string w, the automaton's computation on w produces a string z on its pushdown store such that $w \xrightarrow{*L} z$ and z is irreducible. Since T is confluent, z is the unique irreducible descendant of w. By assumption $A \subseteq IRR(T)$ so that w is congruent to an element of A if and only if z^R belongs to A^R. Thus the deterministic pushdown automaton accepts precisely the strings in $\nabla_T^*(A)$. □ 4.2.7

Recall that the collection of regular subsets of a regular set forms a Boolean algebra.

Corollary 4.2.8 *Let T be a finite monadic string-rewriting system on alphabet Σ. Let $\mathcal{R} = \{[R]_T \mid R \subseteq \Sigma^* \text{ and } R \text{ is regular}\}$. If T is confluent, then $\mathcal{R}$ is a Boolean algebra of deterministic context-free languages.*

The last fact leads to some interesting questions. Does there exist a uniform way of specifying the languages in the class $\mathcal{R}$ in terms of grammars or automata or any other standard way of specifying context-free languages? That is, does there exist a uniform construction such that given T satisfying the hypotheses of Corollary 4.2.8, one can specify for each regular set R the deterministic context-free language $[R]_T$? Recall that the class of all deterministic context-free languages does not form a Boolean algebra. Berstel has suggested that these questions really depend on a characterization of the class of regular sets that can be the sets of irreducible strings of a finite string-rewriting system. Consider a finite string-rewriting system T on alphabet Σ. Notice that if $y \in \Sigma^*$ is reducible, then for every $x, z \in \Sigma^*$, the string xyz is reducible; hence, the set of reducible strings is an ideal of Σ^* and so the set $IRR(T)$ of irreducible strings forms a co-ideal. Further, if w is in $IRR(T)$, then so is every factor of w, that is, every string y such that for some $x, z \in \Sigma^*$, $w = xyz$. Can one characterize the sets of the form $IRR(T)$ in some way related to the structure of the monoid Σ^* or in some way related to the usual specifications of the class of regular sets?

Let T be a finite string-rewriting system that is confluent but not monadic. Is it the case that the conclusions of Theorems 4.2.4 and 4.2.7 still hold? The answer is "no" as seen by the following example.

Consider $T = \{(abc, ab), (bbc, cb)\}$, where $\Sigma = \{a, b, c\}$. It is easy to see that T is confluent. The string abb is irreducible, and $[abb]_T \cap \{a\}^*\{b\}^*\{c\}^* = \{ab^{2^n+1}c^n \mid n \geq 0\}$ which is not context-free. Since $\{a\}^*\{b\}^*\{c\}^*$ is a regular set, this means that $[abb]_T$ is not context-free.

4.3   A Decision Procedure

In Corollary 4.1.5 we noted that a certain "extended word problem" is decidable for finite monadic string-rewriting systems that are confluent. In this section we consider certain decision problems. By generalizing on the idea of the proof of Corollary 4.1.5, we will obtain a decision procedure that is applicable to a variety of properties of the monoid presented by a finite monadic string-rewriting system that is confluent.

Recall that if T is a string-rewriting system on alphabet Σ, then the set of congruence classes of the congruence $\overset{*}{\longleftrightarrow}_T$ forms a monoid $\mathcal{M}_T$. The multiplication in $\mathcal{M}_T$ is given by $[x] \circ [y] = [xy]$; the identity is $[e]$.

We will define a restricted class of sentences of the language of first-order predicate calculus without equality, where the set of nonlogical symbols consists of a binary predicate symbol $\equiv$, a binary function symbol $\cdot$, for each letter a from a fixed finite alphabet Σ, a constant symbol a, and a constant symbol 1. Let T be a string-rewriting system on alphabet Σ. By interpreting the function symbol $\cdot$ as the monoid-multiplication in $\mathcal{M}_T$, by interpreting each constant a as the monoid element $[a]$ and the constant 1 as the monoid element $[e]$, and by interpreting the predicate symbol $\equiv$ as equality in $\mathcal{M}_T$ (or equivalently, the congruence $\overset{*}{\longleftrightarrow}_T$), we obtain an interpretation for these sentences expressing some property of $\mathcal{M}_T$. If T is finite, monadic, and confluent, then the decision procedure described below provides an algorithm to determine whether this property holds for $\mathcal{M}_T$.

Thus, for a suitable sentence, the decision procedure allows one to determine whether with this interpretation of the nonlogical symbols, the specific monoid $\mathcal{M}_T$ satisfies the sentence (that is, is a model for the sentence); this means that a very specific restriction of the satisfiability problem for such sentences is decidable. But the interest in this decision procedure is not one of determining the satisfiability of certain sentences but rather that it allows one to determine whether the monoid $\mathcal{M}_T$ has certain properties. This follows from the fact that in many cases, this interpretation of the sentence represents an interesting property of $\mathcal{M}_T$ such as commutativity.

We proceed to describe the class of sentences and the decision procedure. Then we consider applications.

Let Σ be a finite alphabet.

(i) **Variables.** Let V_E and V_U be two disjoint countable sets of symbols such that $(V_E \cup V_U) \cap \Sigma = \emptyset$. The symbols of V_E are **existential variables**, while those of V_U are **universal variables**.

(ii) **Terms.** A **constant term** is a string in Σ^*. A **universal term** is a nonempty string in $(\Sigma \cup V_U)^*$. An **existential term** is a nonempty string in $(\Sigma \cup V_E)^*$.

(iii) **Atomic formulas.** If x and y are constant terms, then $x \equiv y$ is a **constant atomic formula**. If x and y are two existential terms or one existential term and one constant term, then $x \equiv y$ is an **existential atomic formula**. If x and y are two universal terms or one universal term and one constant term, then $x \equiv y$ is a **universal atomic formula**. If x is an existential term and y is a universal term, then $x \equiv y$ and $y \equiv x$ are **mixed atomic formulas**.

(iv) **Formulas.** An atomic formula is a **formula**. If F_1 and F_2 are formulas such that no existential variable occurs in both F_1 and F_2, then $(F_1 \wedge F_2)$ is a **formula**. If F_1 and F_2 are formulas such that no universal variable occurs in both F_1 and F_2, then $(F_1 \vee F_2)$ is a **formula**. A formula is **linear** if no variable occurs twice in that formula.

(v) **Sentences.** If F is a formula with existential variables $v_1, \ldots, v_q$ and universal variables $u_1, \ldots, u_p$, then

$$\forall u_1 \forall u_2 \ldots \forall u_p \exists v_1 \exists v_2 \ldots \exists v_q F$$

and

$$\exists v_1 \exists v_2 \ldots \exists v_q \forall u_1 \forall u_2 \ldots \forall u_p F$$

are sentences. Let $SEN(\Sigma)$ be the set of all sentences over the alphabet Σ and let $LINSEN(\Sigma)$ be the set of all sentences over Σ that contain only linear formulas.

The partition of the set of variables as "existential" and "universal" is a matter of convenience since it permits one to have a simple way of capturing the notion that a term may contain existential variables or universal variables but not both.

Let T be a string-rewriting system on Σ. If φ is a sentence over Σ containing the variables $v_1, \ldots, v_p \in (V_E \cup V_U)$, and if $S_1, \ldots, S_p$ are subsets of Σ^*, then define the following interpretation of φ:

(i) for each i, $1 \le i \le p$, the variable v_i takes values in the set S_i;

(ii) the symbol $\equiv$ is interpreted as the congruence $\overset{*}{\longleftrightarrow}_T$;

(iii) the symbol $\wedge$ is interpreted as conjunction and the symbol $\vee$ is interpreted as disjunction.

Under this interpretation the sentence φ is either true or false as a statement about the congruence $\overset{*}{\longleftrightarrow}_T$ and the sets $S_1, \ldots, S_p \subseteq \Sigma^*$, and hence about the monoid $\mathcal{M}_T$.

Observe that the binary function symbol $\cdot$ is used as concatenation to form the terms. Then it is interpreted as the multiplication operation in the monoid $\mathcal{M}_T$ and so we could write these terms simply as strings (in other words, without parentheses). We will restrict the subsets of Σ^* that are taken as the domains for the variables occuring in a (linear) sentence to be regular sets over Σ. Thus, for a string-rewriting system T on Σ we consider the following **decision problem for sentences:**

Instance: *A sentence $\varphi \in SEN(\Sigma)$ containing the variables $v_1, \ldots, v_m \in V_E \cup V_U$, and regular sets $S_1, \ldots, S_m \subseteq \Sigma^*$ specified through regular expressions.*

Question: *Is φ true under the interpretation induced by T and $S_1, \ldots, S_m$?*

Before stating the main result, we consider an example. Let T be a monadic string-rewriting system on the alphabet Σ and let $\mathcal{M}_T$ be the monoid presented by T. The **generalized word problem** for $\mathcal{M}_T$ is the following: given a subset A of Σ^* and a string $w \in \Sigma^*$, is $[w]$ in the submonoid of $\mathcal{M}_T$ generated by A, that is, does there exist a string y in A^* such that $w \overset{*}{\longleftrightarrow}_T y$?

For a regular set A and a string w, we can construct a linear sentence φ that expresses this problem instance. If we let v be an existential variable, then the sentence φ is $\exists v (v \equiv w)$. This sentence is true under the interpretation induced by the system T and the regular set A^* if and only if there exists a string y in A^* such that $w \overset{*}{\longleftrightarrow}_T y$. From Theorem 4.3.1 below we will see that if T is finite, monadic and confluent, then the decision procedure allows us to determine whether this linear sentence φ is true under this special interpretation. This example illustrates the usefulness of allowing each variable to have a domain that is a specific regular subset of Σ^* instead of every variable having the same domain Σ^*.

We wish to make use of the sets $[R]$ and $\Delta^*(R)$ for various regular sets R. To do so it will be useful to refer to the set $IRR(T)$ of irreducible strings of a string-rewriting system T. If a finite string-rewriting system is monadic and confluent, then for any regular set R, certain questions about $[R] = \bigcup_{x \in R}[x]$ can be answered by considering the corresponding questions about $\Delta^*(R) \cap IRR(T)$. Since T is finite, $IRR(T)$ is regular, and since T is monadic, $\Delta^*(R)$ is regular. Thus, a question about $[R]$ may be decidable if it can be interpreted as a question about $\Delta^*(R) \cap IRR(T)$ since many questions about regular sets are decidable. This is the basis for a decision procedure that applies to the class of linear sentences and finite monadic string-rewriting systems that are confluent.

Theorem 4.3.1 *Let T be a string-rewriting system on Σ. Suppose that T is finite, monadic, and confluent. Then the following problem for linear sentences is decidable in polynomial space:*

Instance: *A sentence $\varphi \in LINSEN(\Sigma)$ containing variables $v_1, v_2, \ldots,$ v_m, and regular sets $S_1, \ldots, S_m \subseteq \Sigma^*$ that are specified by regular expressions.*

Question: *Is φ true under the interpretation induced by T and $S_1, \ldots,$ S_m?*

Proof. Since φ is in $LINSEN(\Sigma)$, no term in φ has both existential and universal variables and every term is linear. If $(F_1 \wedge F_2)$ is a formula, then no existential variable occurs in both F_1 and F_2, and if $(F_1 \vee F_2)$ is a formula, then no universal variable occurs in both F_1 and F_2. Thus, one can distribute the quantifiers over $\wedge$ and $\vee$ so that any sentence in $LINSEN(\Sigma)$ is equivalent to a positive (that is, using only conjunctions and disjunctions) combination of sentences in $LINSEN(\Sigma)$ where each sentence has only a single atomic formula. This means that it is sufficient to restrict attention to those sentences in $LINSEN(\Sigma)$ with only one atomic formula.

Let $t_1 \equiv t_2$ be an atomic formula. With $t_1(t_2)$, associate a regular set R_1 (resp., R_2) as follows:

(i) if t_1 is a constant term, then $t_1 \in \Sigma^*$ so let $R_1 = \{t_1\}$;

(ii) if t_1 is not a constant term, then t_1 is a concatenation of variable symbols and constants, that is, $t_1 \in (V_E \cup V_U \cup \Sigma)^*$; let R_1 be the regular set obtained from t_1 by substituting for each variable symbol v_j in t_1 the regular set S_j that is the domain of v_j, so that R_1 is the concatenation of regular sets (domains) and sets containing only a single string (constants) in the order specified by t_1.

In order to determine whether the sentence containing $t_1 \equiv t_2$ is true for the congruence generated by T, it is necessary to obtain information about the sets $[R_1] = \{y \mid$ for some $x \in R_1,\ x \xleftrightarrow{*}_T y\}$ and $[R_2] = \{y \mid$ for some $x \in R_2,\ x \xleftrightarrow{*}_T y\}$. Since T is confluent, it is sufficient to consider the sets of irreducible representatives of R_1 and R_2, that is, the set of irreducible descendants of R_1 and R_2.

Let $IR_1 = \Delta^*(R_1) \cap IRR(T)$ and let $IR_2 = \Delta^*(R_2) \cap IRR(T)$. Since T is finite, $IRR(T)$ is a regular set. Since T is finite and monadic, R_1 and R_2 regular implies $\Delta^*(R_1)$ and $\Delta^*(R_2)$ are regular. Thus, IR_1 and IR_2 are regular sets of irreducible strings and

$$[IR_1] = \nabla^*(IR_1) = [R_1] \text{ and } [IR_2] = \nabla^*(IR_2) = [R_2].$$

Further, from T and regular expressions for R_1 and R_2, one can construct regular expressions for IR_1 and IR_2.

Consider the atomic formula $t_1 \equiv t_2$. There are four cases.

Case 1. If this formula is universal, then one can ignore existential quantifiers, so the sentence is $\forall u_1 \ldots \forall u_q (t_1 \equiv t_2)$. This sentence is true under the interpretation for $\equiv$ if and only if every string in $[R_1]$ is congruent to every string in $[R_2]$. Since T is confluent, every string is congruent to exactly one irreducible string. Thus, every string in $[R_1]$ is congruent to every string in $[R_2]$ if and only if both IR_1 and IR_2 are singleton sets and also $IR_1 = IR_2$.

Case 2. If this formula is existential, then one can ignore universal quantifiers, so the sentence is $\exists v_1 \ldots \exists v_p (t_1 \equiv t_2)$. This sentence is true under the interpretation for $\equiv$ if and only if there exists a string in $[R_1]$ that is congruent to some string in $[R_2]$. Since T is confluent, every string is congruent to exactly one irreducible string. Thus, there exists a string in $[R_1]$ that is congruent to some string in $[R_2]$ if and only if $IR_1 \cap IR_2 \neq \emptyset$.

Case 3. If this formula is constant, then it follows from Cases 1 and 2 that the sentence is true if and only if $IR_1 = IR_2$.

Case 4. If this formula is mixed, then one of t_1, t_2 is universal and the other is existential, say t_1 is universal. There are two subcases depending on whether the quantifiers are in the order $\forall^q \exists^p$ or the order $\exists^p \forall^q$.

Subcase 4.1. If the sentence is

$$\forall u_1 \ldots \forall u_q \exists v_1 \ldots \exists v_p (t_1 \equiv t_2),$$

then the sentence is true under the interpretation for $\equiv$ if and only if every string in $[R_1]$ is congruent to some string in $[R_2]$ if and only if $IR_1 \subseteq IR_2$.

Subcase 4.2. If the sentence is

$$\exists v_1 \ldots \exists v_q \forall u_1 \ldots \forall u_p (t_1 \equiv t_2),$$

then the sentence is true under the interpretation for $\equiv$ if and only if there is some string in $[R_2]$ that is congruent to every string in $[R_1]$.

Since T is confluent, every string is congruent to exactly one irreducible string. Thus, there is some string in $[R_2]$ that is congruent to every string in $[R_1]$ if and only if IR_1 is a singleton set and also $IR_1 \subseteq IR_2$.

Since one can construct regular expressions for IR_1 and IR_2, one can effectively decide whether $IR_1 = IR_2$, whether $IR_1 \cap IR_2 \neq \emptyset$ or whether $IR_1 \subseteq IR_2$, and one can effectively decide whether IR_1 is a singleton set and whether IR_2 is a singleton set. Thus, the procedure correctly determines whether the sentence is true for $\overset{*}{\longleftrightarrow}_T$ and $S_1, \ldots, S_m$.

Consider the complexity of this decision procedure.

Specifications for the sets IR_1 and IR_2 can be constructed in time that is polynomial in the size of the specifications of R_1 and R_2 and the size of T. Consider each of the four possibilities for the atomic formula $t_1 \equiv t_2$.

Case 1. The specifications for IR_1 and IR_2 need not use any symbols for the empty set. Thus one can use breadth-first search to determine whether IR_1 and IR_2 are singletons. If so, they can be compared for equality. This is a polynomial time-bounded procedure.

Case 2. It is sufficient to determine whether $IR_1 \cap IR_2$ is empty. A nondeterministic finite state acceptor specifying $IR_1 \cap IR_2$ can be constructed in time $0(n^2)$, and then emptiness can be tested in time $0(n^2)$, where n is the maximum of the size of the specifications of IR_1 and IR_2.

Case 3. In this case there are no variables, and both IR_1 and IR_2 contain a single string only. Thus, testing for the equality of IR_1 and IR_2 can be done in polynomial time.

Case 4.

Subcase 4.1. Testing whether $IR_1 \subseteq IR_2$ when IR_2 is infinite is a **PSPACE**-complete problem. Thus, in this case the decision procedure is very complex.

Subcase 4.2. As above, determining whether IR_1 is a singleton can be done in polynomial time. If so, testing whether $IR_1 \subseteq IR_2$ is simply testing for membership in IR_2.

Thus, this decision procedure can be carried out in polynomial time in all cases except the $\forall\exists$ case. Now consider the situation where the string-rewriting system T has no rules. Then $[R_1] = IR_1 = R_1$ and $[R_2] = IR_2 = R_2$. Thus, the problem is reduced to determining whether R_1 is included in R_2. Since the inclusion problem for regular sets is **PSPACE**-complete, this problem is inherently difficult, that is, it is not just that this problem cannot be solved easily by the decision procedure but rather the problem itself is inherently difficult. $\square$ 4.3.1

Corollary 4.3.2 *Let T be a string-rewriting system on the alphabet Σ. Suppose that T is finite, monadic and confluent. Then the following problem is decidable in polynomial time:*

Instance: *A sentence φ in $LINSEN(\Sigma)$ containing variables $v_1, v_2, \ldots,$ v_m and regular sets $S_1, \ldots, S_m \subseteq \Sigma^*$ that are specified by regular ex-*

pressions, and such that either φ contains no mixed atomic formulas or the quantifiers are of the form $\exists \ldots \exists \forall \ldots \forall$.

Question: *Is φ true under the interpretation induced by T and $S_1, \ldots, S_m$?*

Observe that the above decision procedure is uniform in T, that is, Theorem 4.3.1 and Corollary 4.3.2 remain true if the finite, monadic and confluent string-rewriting system T is part of the problem instance.

4.4 Applications of the Decision Procedure

Assume a fixed finite alphabet Σ and a fixed finite monadic string-rewriting system T on Σ that is confluent. In the following we give some examples of decision problems for T that can be solved by expressing them through linear sentences.

A. The Extended Word Problem (polynomial time)

Instance: *Two regular sets R_1, $R_2 \subseteq \Sigma^*$.*

Question: *Do there exist $w_1 \in R_1$ and $w_2 \in R_2$ such that w_1 is congruent to w_2?*

Solution: For $i = 1, 2$, let v_i be an existential variable with domain R_i; the desired sentence is $\exists v_1 \exists v_2 (v_1 \equiv v_2)$; the answer is "yes" if and only if this sentence is true for T and R_1, R_2.

B. The Power Problem (polynomial time)

Instance: *Two strings w and z.*

Question: *Does there exist an integer p such that w is congruent to z^p?*

Solution: Let $R_1 = \{w\}$ and $R_2 = \{z\}^*$; the problem reduces to the generalized word problem for R_1 and R_2.

C. Left (right) Divisibility Problem (polynomial time)

Instance: *Two strings w and z.*

Question: *Does there exist a string y such that wy (yw) is congruent to z?*

Solution: Let $R_1 = \{w\}$, $R_2 = \{z\}$, and $R_3 = \Sigma^*$; the problem reduces to the generalized word problem for $R_1 R_3$ and R_2.

D. The Submonoid Problem (polynomial space)

Instance: *Regular sets R_1 and R_2.*

Question: *Is the submonoid generated by R_1 included in the submonoid generated by R_2?*

Solution: Let v_1 be a universal variable with domain R_1 and let v_2 be an existential variable with domain R_2^*; the desired sentence is

$$\forall v_1 \exists v_2 (v_1 \equiv v_2).$$

The answer is "yes" if and only if this sentence is true for T and R_1, R_2^*.

E. The Independent Set Problem (polynomial time)

Instance: *A finite set $A = \{w_1, \ldots, w_n\}$ with each $w_i \neq e$.*

Question: *Is it the case that for each i, $1 \leq i \leq n$, w_i is not congruent to any string in $(A - \{w_i\})^*$? (that is, for each i, $1 \leq i \leq n$, $[w_i]$ is not in the submonoid generated by $(A - \{w_i\})$).*

Solution: For each i, $1 \leq i \leq n$, let v_i be an existential variable with domain $R_i = (A - \{w_i\})^*$; the desired sentence is

$$\exists v_1 \ldots \exists v_n ((w_1 \equiv v_1) \vee \ldots \vee (w_n \equiv v_n)).$$

The answer is "no" if and only if this sentence is true for T and $R_1, \ldots, R_n$.

F. The Subgroup Problem (polynomial time)

Instance: *A finite set $A = \{w_1, \ldots, w_n\}$ with $w_i \neq e$, $i \leq i \leq n$.*

Question: *Is the submonoid generated by A a subgroup?*

Solution: For each i, $1 \leq i \leq n$, let $v_{i,1}$ and $v_{i,2}$ be existential variables with domain A^*; the desired sentence is

$$\exists v_{1,1} \exists v_{1,2} \ldots \exists v_{n,1} \exists v_{n,2} ((v_{1,1} w_1 \equiv e) \wedge$$

$$(w_1 v_{1,2} \equiv e) \wedge \ldots \wedge (v_{n,1} w_n \equiv e) \wedge (w_n v_{n,2} \equiv e).$$

The answer is "yes" if and only if this sentence is true for T.

G. The Right Ideal Problem (polynomial space)

Instance: *A regular set R.*

Question: *Is the submonoid generated by R a right ideal?*

Solution: let v_1 be a universal variable with domain R, let v_2 be a universal variable with domain Σ^*, and let v_3 be an existential variable with domain R^*; the desired sentence is

$$\forall v_1 \forall v_2 \exists v_3 (v_1 v_2 \equiv v_3).$$

The answer is "yes" if and only if this sentence is true for T and R, Σ^*, R^*.

Clearly, the Left Ideal Problem and the Two-Sided Ideal Problem can be solved in a similar manner. Now consider Green's relations.

In a monoid $\mathcal{M}$, Green's relations are defined as follows:

(a) $x\mathbf{R}y$ if and only if $\{xz \mid z \in \mathcal{M}\} = \{yz \mid z \in \mathcal{M}\}$;

(b) $x\mathbf{L}y$ if and only if $\{zx \mid z \in \mathcal{M}\} = \{zy \mid z \in \mathcal{M}\}$;

(c) $x\mathbf{I}y$ if and only if $\{z_1xz_2 \mid z_1, z_2 \in \mathcal{M}\} = \{z_1yz_2 \mid z_1, z_2 \in \mathcal{M}\}$;

(d) $x\mathbf{D}y$ if and only if $x\mathbf{R}y$ or $x\mathbf{L}y$;

(e) $x\mathbf{H}y$ if and only if $x\mathbf{R}y$ and $x\mathbf{L}y$.

Consider the monoid $\mathcal{M}_T$. Green's relations are decidable in polynomial space for $\mathcal{M}_T$, as shown by the following remarks. Let v_1 and v_2 be universal variables and let v_3 and v_4 be existential variables; all variables have domain Σ^*. Consider any x, y in Σ^*.

(a) $x\mathbf{R}y$ holds in $\mathcal{M}_T$ if and only if both the sentence $\forall v_1 \exists v_3 (xv_1 \equiv yv_3)$ and the sentence $\forall v_2 \exists v_4 (yv_2 \equiv xv_4)$ are true for T;

(b) $x\mathbf{L}y$ holds in $\mathcal{M}_T$ if and only if both the sentence $\forall v_1 \exists v_3 (v_1x \equiv v_3y)$ and the sentence $\forall v_2 \exists v_4 (v_2y \equiv v_4x)$ are true for T;

(c) that $x\mathbf{D}y$ and $x\mathbf{H}y$ are decidable follows from (a) and (b);

(d) $x\mathbf{I}y$ holds in $\mathcal{M}_T$ if and only if both the sentence

$$\forall v_1 \forall v_2 \exists v_3 \exists v_4 (v_1xv_2 \equiv v_3yv_4)$$

and the sentence

$$\forall v_1 \forall v_2 \exists v_3 \exists v_4 (v_1yv_2 \equiv v_3xv_4)$$

are true for T.

4.5   Limitations of the Decision Procedure

Let Σ be an alphabet, and let T be a finite monadic string-rewriting system on Σ that is confluent. If φ is a sentence over Σ containing the variables $v_1, \ldots, v_p$, then by providing subsets $S_1, \ldots, S_p \subseteq \Sigma^*$ as domains for these variables, we obtain an interpretation for this sentence, that is, φ is either true or false as a statement on the Thue congruence $\longleftrightarrow^*_T$ and the sets $S_1, \ldots, S_p$. The decision procedure presented in Theorem 4.3.1 determines this value in case the sentence φ is linear and the subsets $S_1, \ldots, S_p$ are regular. In the following we discuss the importance of these two restrictions.

Let us first consider the question of which subsets of Σ^* should be taken to serve as domains for the variables occuring in a linear sentence. Let T

be empty, and so $x \longleftrightarrow^*_T y$ if and only if $x = y$. For $w \in \Sigma^*$, consider the linear sentence $\varphi_w := \exists v (v \equiv w)$. Then this sentence is true under the interpretation induced by T and a subset $S \subseteq \Sigma^*$ if and only if w is in S. Thus, in order to decide whether a linear sentence is satisfied by an interpretation as described in Section 4.3, the sets serving as domains for the variables must be recursive, that is, membership in these sets must be decidable.

Next, consider the linear sentence $\forall v_1 \exists v_2 (v_1 \equiv v_2)$. This sentence is true under the interpretation induced by T and subsets $S_1, S_2 \subseteq \Sigma^*$ if and only if $S_1 \subseteq S_2$. Thus, the inclusion problem (and, thus the equivalence problem) must be decidable for the class of languages admitted as domains for the variables. Hence, we cannot admit arbitrary deterministic context-free languages for this task, since it is well-known that the inclusion problem for such languages is undecidable.

Let us examine non-linear sentences. First consider the sentence $\exists v_1 \exists v_2 \exists v_3 (v_1 \$ v_1 \equiv v_2 \$ v_3)$, where $\$$ is an additional symbol not in Σ, and let $R_1, R_2, R_3 \subseteq \Sigma^*$ be regular sets. Then this sentence is satisfied under the interpretation induced by T and R_1, R_2, R_3 if and only if there are strings $w_i \in R_i$, $i = 1, 2, 3$, such that $w_1 \longleftrightarrow^*_T w_2$ and $w_1 \longleftrightarrow^*_T w_3$, since the rules of T do not contain any occurrence of the symbol $\$$. Since T is confluent, this holds if and only if $(\Delta^*_T(R_1) \cap IRR(T)) \cap (\Delta^*_T(R_2) \cap IRR(T)) \cap (\Delta^*_T(R_3) \cap IRR(T)) \neq \emptyset$, which is decidable, since T is finite and monadic. Thus, for some non-linear sentences this problem is also decidable in this setting. However, we will see that this is not true in general for non-linear sentences.

It is well-known that the undecidability of the Post Correspondence Problem (PCP) can be proved by a reduction from the halting problem for Turing machines. (At this point the reader may wish to review Section 2.1). In fact, if $\mathcal{M} = (Q, \Sigma, \delta, q_0, q_a)$ is a single-tape Turing machine, then from $\mathcal{M}$ one can effectively construct a set of pairs of non-empty words $S_M = \{(x_i, y_i) \mid i = 2, \ldots, k\} \subseteq \Gamma^* \times \Gamma^*$, where $\Gamma = Q \cup \Sigma_b \cup \{\#\}$, such that the following two statements are equivalent for each string $w \in \Sigma^*$:

(1) $\mathcal{M}$ accepts on input w, that is, $w \in L(\mathcal{M})$, and

(2) the instance $S_{M,w} = \{(\#, \#q_0 w\#)\} \cup S_M$ of the Modified Post Correspondence Problem has a solution, that is, there exists a sequence of integers $i_1, i_2, \ldots, i_n \in \{2, \ldots, k\}$ such that $\#x_{i_1} x_{i_2} \ldots x_{i_n} = \#q_0 w \# y_{i_1} \ldots y_{i_n}$.

In the following "$S_{M,w}$ has a solution" will be expressed as "$MPCP(S_{M,w})$ holds".

Let $\alpha : \Gamma^* \to \{a, b\}^*$ be an encoding such that $\alpha(\Gamma) \subseteq \{a, b\}^r$ for some integer $r \geq 1$, and let $S^\alpha_M = \{(\alpha(x_i), \alpha(y_i)) \mid i = 2, \ldots, k\} \subseteq \{a, b\}^* \times \{a, b\}^*$. Then the following two statements are equivalent for each string $w \in \Sigma^*$:

(1) $w \in L(\mathcal{M})$, and

(2) $MPCP(S^\alpha_{M,w})$ holds, where $S^\alpha_{M,w} = \{(\alpha(\#), \alpha(\#q_0w\#))\} \cup S^\alpha_M$.

If $\mathcal{M}$ is a Turing machine such that the language $L(\mathcal{M})$ is non-recursive, we see the following.

Lemma 4.5.1 *There exists a set of pairs* $S = \{(x_i, y_i) \mid i = 2, \ldots, k\} \subseteq \{a, b\}^* \times \{a, b\}^*$ *such that the following problem is undecidable:*

Instance: *Two non-empty strings* $x_1, y_1 \in \{a, b\}^*$.

Question: *Does* $MPCP(\{(x_1, y_1)\} \cup S)$ *hold, that is, does there exist a sequence of integers*

$$i_1, i_2, \ldots, i_n \in \{2, \ldots, k\} \text{ such that } x_1 x_{i_1} x_{i_2} \ldots x_{i_n} = y_1 y_{i_1} y_{i_2} \ldots y_{i_n}?$$

From S, define a finite monadic string-rewriting system $T(S)$ on $\Sigma = \{a, b, \$, \&, \#, 0, 1\}$:

(1) Rules to simulate the x-part of a solution:

$$\begin{aligned}
x_2\$\text{bin}(2)\# &\rightarrow \$ \\
x_3\$\text{bin}(3)\# &\rightarrow \$ \\
&\vdots \\
x_k\$\text{bin}(k)\# &\rightarrow \$
\end{aligned}$$

(2) Rules to simulate the y-part of a solution:

$$\begin{aligned}
y_2\&\text{bin}(2)\# &\rightarrow \& \\
y_3\&\text{bin}(3)\# &\rightarrow \& \\
&\vdots \\
y_k\&\text{bin}(k)\# &\rightarrow \&
\end{aligned}$$

Here, for $i = 1, \ldots, k$, $\text{bin}(i)$ stands for the binary representation of the integer i. It is easily seen that $T(S)$ is finite, monadic, and confluent, since there are no non-trivial critical pairs at all for $T(S)$.

Consider the following decision problem for $T(S)$:

Instance: *Two strings* $x_1, y_1 \in \{a, b\}^*$.

Question: $\exists u, v \in \Sigma^* (u\$v \xleftrightarrow{\;*\;}_{T(S)} x_1\$ \text{ and } u\&v \xleftrightarrow{\;*\;}_{T(S)} y_1\&)$?

We claim that this problem is undecidable.

Lemma 4.5.2 *Let* $x_1, y_1 \in \{a, b\}^*$. *If* $MPCP(\{(x_1, y_1)\} \cup S)$ *holds, then there are strings* $u, v \in \Sigma^*$ *such that* $u\$v \longleftrightarrow_{T(S)}^* x_1\$$ *and* $u\&v \longleftrightarrow_{T(S)}^* y_1\&$.

Proof. Let $i_1, i_2, \ldots, i_n \in \{2, \ldots, k\}$ such that $x_1 x_{i_1} \ldots x_{i_n} = y_1 y_{i_1} \ldots y_{i_n}$. We choose $u = x_1 x_{i_1} \ldots x_{i_n}$ and $v = \mathrm{bin}(i_n)\# \ldots \mathrm{bin}(i_1)\#$. Then we obtain the following reductions:

$$u\$v = x_1 x_{i_1} \ldots x_{i_n} \$ \mathrm{bin}(i_n)\# \ldots \mathrm{bin}(i_1)\# \xrightarrow{*}_{T(S)} x_1\$ \quad \text{and}$$

$$u\&v = y_1 y_{i_1} \ldots y_{i_n} \& \mathrm{bin}(i_n)\# \ldots \mathrm{bin}(i_1)\# \xrightarrow{*}_{T(S)} y_1\&.$$

$\square$ 4.5.2

Lemma 4.5.3 *Let* $u, v \in \Sigma^*$ *such that* $u\$v \longleftrightarrow_{T(S)}^* x_1\$$ *and* $u\&v \longleftrightarrow_{T(S)}^* y_1\&$ *for some strings* $x_1, y_1 \in \{a, b\}^*$. *Then* $MPCP(\{(x_1, y_1)\} \cup S)$ *holds.*

Proof. If $x_1, y_1 \in \{a, b\}^*$, then $x_1\$$ and $y_1\&$ are irreducible, that is, we can choose $u, v \in IRR(T(S))$ such that $u\$v \xrightarrow{*}_{T(S)} x_1\$$ and $u\&v \xrightarrow{*}_{T(S)} y_1\&$. If $x_1 = y_1$, then obviously $MPCP(\{(x_1, y_1)\} \cup S)$ holds. So let us assume that $x_1 \neq y_1$. Then at least one of the above sequences of reductions is non-empty, and therefore they both are non-empty. Hence, $v = \mathrm{bin}(i_n)\# \ldots \mathrm{bin}(i_1)\#v_1$ for some $i_1, \ldots, i_n \in \{2, \ldots, k\}$ and $v_1 \notin \{\mathrm{bin}(2), \ldots, \mathrm{bin}(k)\} \cdot \{\#\} \cdot \Sigma^*$, and $u = u_1 x_{i_1} \ldots x_{i_n} = u_2 y_{i_1} \ldots y_{i_n}$:

$$u\$v = u_1 x_{i_1} \ldots x_{i_n} \$ \mathrm{bin}(i_n)\# \ldots \mathrm{bin}(i_1)\#v_1 \xrightarrow{*}_{T(S)} u_1\$v_1 \xrightarrow{*}_{T(S)} x_1\$ \quad \text{and}$$

$$u\&v = u_2 y_{i_1} \ldots y_{i_n} \& \mathrm{bin}(i_n)\# \ldots \mathrm{bin}(i_1)\#v_1 \xrightarrow{*}_{T(S)} u_2\&v_1 \xrightarrow{*}_{T(S)} y_1\&.$$

Since v is irreducible, and since occurrences of the symbols $\$$ and $\&$ are neither generated nor deleted, we can conclude that $v_1 = e$, that is, $u_1\$v_1 = u_1\$ = x_1\$$, while $u_2\&v_1 = u_2\& = y_1\&$. Hence, $x_1 x_{i_1} \ldots x_{i_n} = u = y_1 y_{i_1} \ldots y_{i_n}$, and thus $MPCP(\{(x_1, y_1)\} \cup S)$ holds. $\square$ 4.5.3

The choice of S together with Lemmas 4.5.2 and 4.5.3 give the result.

Theorem 4.5.4 *The following problem is undecidable for the finite monadic and confluent string-rewriting system* $T(S)$:

Instance: *Two strings* $x_1, y_1 \in \{a, b\}^*$.

Question: $\exists u, v \in \Sigma^* (u\$v \longleftrightarrow_{T(S)}^* x_1\$$ *and* $u\&v \longleftrightarrow_{T(S)}^* y_1\&)$?

Observe that the formula above is not an interpretation of a syntactically correct sentence from $SEN(\Sigma)$, since the expression "$\exists v_1 \exists v_2 (v_1\$v_2 \equiv x_1\$ \wedge v_1\&v_2 = y_1\&)$" contains the conjunction of two atomic formulas that have existential variables in common.

Finally take the alphabet $\Delta := \Sigma \cup \{\S\}$, where $\S$ is a new symbol. For $x_1, y_1 \in \{a, b\}^*$, consider the non-linear sentence $\varphi(x_1, y_1) := \exists v_1 \exists v_2$ $(v_1 \$ v_2 \S v_1 \& v_2 \equiv x_1 \$ \S y_1 \&)$. We claim that this sentence is true under the interpretation induced by $T(S)$ and $S_1 = S_2 = \Delta^*$ if and only if $MPCP$ $(\{(x_1, y_1)\} \cup S)$ holds. Clearly, if $MPCP(\{(x_1, y_1)\} \cup S)$ holds, then $u \$ v \overset{*}{\longleftrightarrow}_{T(S)} x_1 \$$ and $u \& v \overset{*}{\longleftrightarrow}_{T(S)} y_1 \&$ for some $u, v \in \Sigma^*$, and hence, $u \$ v \S u \& v \overset{*}{\longleftrightarrow}_{T(S)} x_1 \$ \S y_1 \&$. Conversely, assume that $u \$ v \S u \& v \overset{*}{\longleftrightarrow}_{T(S)}$ $x_1 \$ \S y_1 \&$ for some $u, v \in \Delta^*$. Since $x_1, y_1 \in \{a, b\}^*$, and since the symbol $\S$ does not occur in the rules of $T(S)$, we have $u, v \in \Sigma^*$, and $u \$ v \overset{*}{\longleftrightarrow}_{T(S)} x_1 \$$ and $u \& v \overset{*}{\longleftrightarrow}_{T(S)} y_1 \&$. Thus, $MPCP(\{(x_1, y_1)\} \cup S)$ holds. Hence, there is no decision procedure that applies to such nonlinear sentences.

Thus, we have shown that the result of Theorem 4.3.1 cannot be extended to the class of sentences $SEN(\Delta)$ and therefore the restriction to linear sentences is necessary. In addition, in Chapter 5 we will show that even for linear sentences, the hypotheses of the string-rewriting system being both monadic and confluent are necessary for the result of Theorem 4.3.1 to hold. The reader should note that we are not just claiming that these hypotheses are necessary for the *method* presented in the proof of Theorem 4.3.1 to work but rather that these hypotheses are necessary for the theorem itself to hold.

4.6   Bibliographic Remarks

Monadic string-rewriting systems have arisen in numerous places. It appears that the first systematic studies of their properties were carried out by Book, Jantzen, and Wrathall [BJW82], Ó'Dúnlaing [Ó'Dú81, Ó'Dú83b], Jantzen [Jan88], and Book et al [BJMO'DW81]. Theorem 4.1.2 is from [BoOt85a] and is related to a result of Berstel [Ber79]. Other results in Section 4.1 are from [BJW82]. Theorem 4.2.2 is due to Berstel [Ber77]. Theorem 4.2.7 and Corollary 4.2.8 are due to Book [Boo82a]. A very different approach to the specification of formal languages by string-rewriting systems (that are not monadic) was developed by McNaughton, Narendran, and Otto [MNO88].

The decision procedure presented in Sections 4.3 and the discussion and applications in Section 4.4 are based on [Boo83]. Otto [Ott84a] studied the limitations of the decision procedure and Section 4.5 is based on his work.

It should be noted that the decision procedure of Section 4.4 has been referred to as the "method of linear sentences." No claims are made that it is of interest to logicians, but the applications presented in Section 4.5 suggest that it should be considered by those who are interested in algorithms for deciding questions about finitely-presented monoids (or groups). The fact that the general method has applicability in settings that are less restrictive than that of Theorem 4.3.1 is attested to by results of Madlener, Narendran, Otto, and Zhang [MNOZ93] and of Gilleron [Gil91].

It is likely that the reader has noticed that context-free grammars are special cases of monadic string-rewriting systems. One might think that results about string-rewriting systems and techniques developed for studying string-rewriting systems could be of use in studying context-free grammars and languages. However, there are few examples of this. Indeed, it would be of interest to determine precisely how the string-rewriting theory can be applied to formal language theory in general (including L-systems).

5

Length-Reducing Non-Monadic String-Rewriting Systems

In the previous chapter we saw that there is a decision procedure to determine if a linear sentence is true for a monoid presented by a finite, monadic and confluent string-rewriting system. By using linear sentences many decision problems can be solved for these systems (see Section 4.4). Here we will show that in general for finite, length-reducing and confluent string-rewriting systems the truth of linear sentences in the monoids so prescribed is undecidable; in fact, many decision problems like the extended word problem, that can be expressed through linear sentences, are undecidable in this setting. All these undecidability results will be derived from a presentation of recursively enumerable languages through finite, length-reducing, and confluent string-rewriting systems.

5.1 Presenting Recursively Enumerable Languages

The goal of this section is to establish the following technical result.

Theorem 5.1.1 *Let $L \subseteq \Sigma^*$ be recursively enumerable, and let $\$, s_0$ and $\pounds$ be three additional symbols. Then there exist a finite alphabet Γ containing $\Sigma \cup \{\$, s_0, \pounds\}$, a finite, length-reducing and confluent string-rewriting system T on Γ with $\mathrm{range}(T) \subseteq \Gamma \cup \Gamma^2$, and a regular set $R \subseteq \Gamma^*$ such that $\Delta_T^*(R) \cap \{\$s_0\} \cdot \Sigma^* \cdot \{\pounds\} = [R]_T \cap (\{\$s_0\} \cdot \Sigma^* \cdot \{\pounds\}) = \{\$s_0\} \cdot L \cdot \{\pounds\}.$*

Let $L \subseteq \Sigma^*$ be a recursively enumerable language. Then there exists a single-tape Turing machine $\mathcal{M} = (Q, \Sigma, \delta, q_0, q_a)$ that accepts this language. From this Turing machine we construct an alphabet Γ, a string-rewriting system $T = T(\mathcal{M})$ and a regular set R satisfying the properties stated in the theorem. Although the system T could be constructed directly from the transition function δ of $\mathcal{M}$, it would be technically involved to prove that T has the desired properties. Therefore we construct T in several steps.

First, we assume without loss of generality that $\mathcal{M}$ is a "five-tuple" Turing machine, which means that in each step $\mathcal{M}$ performs a print operation as well as a move of its head, so the transition function δ has the form

$$\delta : (Q - \{q_a\}) \times \Sigma_b \to Q \times \Sigma_b \times \{L, R\}.$$

In addition, we assume that $q_0 \neq q_a$, which implies that no initial configuration of $\mathcal{M}$ is halting, and in order to simplify the discussion, we assume that the states of $\mathcal{M}$ are numbered: $Q = \{q_0, q_1, q_2, \ldots, q_n\}$ for some $n \geq 1$, and q_n is the accepting state.

The construction will now proceed as follows. First the Turing machine $\mathcal{M}$ is simulated by a **two-stack machine** $\mathcal{M}_1$. Essentially, a two-stack machine is a two-tape Turing machine that uses its tapes only as stacks. Then a string-rewriting system S_1 is presented that simulates the stepwise behavior of the machine $\mathcal{M}_1$. However, most of the rules of S_1 are length-preserving. So in the next step additional symbols called **dummy symbols** are introduced, and a string-rewriting system S_2 is constructed from S_1 by adding an occurrence of one of these dummy symbols to the right-hand side of each rule of S_1. In fact, the dummy symbols will be used in such a way that the right-hand side of each rule of S_2 uniquely determines the corresponding left-hand side. Obviously, S_2 will contain length-increasing rules only. Finally, the desired system $T := T(\mathcal{M})$ is obtained from S_2 by turning each rule of S_2 around and by adding some extra length-reducing rules to resolve all critical pairs.

Now we describe this construction in detail. Let $\mathcal{M} = (Q, \Sigma, \delta, q_0, q_n)$ be the Turing machine accepting the language L, where $Q = \{q_0, q_1, \ldots, q_n\}$ and let $\Sigma_b = \Sigma \cup \{b\}$ be its tape alphabet. From $\mathcal{M}$ we obtain a two-stack machine $\mathcal{M}_1$ as follows. The two pushdown stacks will be called **prefix** and **suffix**, respectively. It is convenient to think of **prefix** as a "push-left" stack and of **suffix** as a "push-right" stack, so we can picture $\mathcal{M}_1$ as follows:

The two-stack Machine $\mathcal{M}_1$

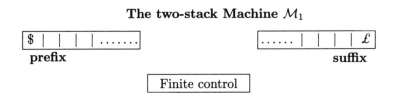

We introduce two new symbols \$ and $\pounds$, and take $\Pi := \Sigma_b \cup \{\$, \pounds\}$. The symbol \$ will serve as the bottom marker of the stack **prefix**, while $\pounds$ will serve as the bottom marker of **suffix**. The set of states of $\mathcal{M}_1$ is $Q_1 := Q_P \cup Q_S$, where $Q_P = \{p_0, \ldots, p_n\}$ and $Q_S = \{s_0, \ldots, s_n\}$ are disjoint copies of Q. Thus, to each state q_i of $\mathcal{M}$ there correspond two states p_i and s_i of $\mathcal{M}_1$. As initial state of $\mathcal{M}_1$ we choose the state s_0. Thus, it remains to define the transition function δ_1 of $\mathcal{M}_1$. Before doing so let us describe the correspondence between the configurations of $\mathcal{M}$ and $\mathcal{M}_1$.

The general configuration of $\mathcal{M}_1$ is as follows:

(a) $\$u$ on the stack **prefix** with $\$$ on bottom and $u \in \Sigma_b^*$,

(b) $v\mathcal{L}$ on the stack **suffix** with $\mathcal{L}$ on bottom and $v \in \Sigma_b^*$, and

(c) state p_i or s_i for some i, $0 \leq i \leq n$.

For simplicity this configuration will be written as $\$up_iv\mathcal{L}$ or $\$us_iv\mathcal{L}$, respectively. It corresponds to the following configuration of $\mathcal{M}$:

(a) tape contents uv,

(b) state q_i,

(c) tape head scanning the rightmost symbol of bu (which is b if $u = e$), if the state of $\mathcal{M}_1$ is p_i, or the leftmost symbol of vb (which is b if $v = e$), if the state of $\mathcal{M}_1$ is s_i.

The initial configuration of the Turing machine $\mathcal{M}$ on input $x \in \Sigma^*$ is q_0x. Accordingly, as initial configuration of the two-stack machine $\mathcal{M}_1$ on input x we choose the configuration $\$s_0x\mathcal{L}$.

Now we define the transition function of $\mathcal{M}_1$. This will be done in such a way as to ensure that at any step the transition of $\mathcal{M}_1$ is determined by the actual state and by the symbol on top of one of the two stacks, not both stacks. In fact, if $\mathcal{M}_1$ is in state p_i for some i, $0 \leq i \leq n - 1$, then its transition depends on the symbol on top of **prefix**; if $\mathcal{M}_1$ is in state s_i for some i, $0 \leq i \leq n - 1$, then it depends on the symbol on the top of **suffix**. For each transition $\delta(q_i, a) = (q_j, c, \varepsilon)$ $(q_i, q_j \in Q, a, c \in \Sigma_b, \varepsilon \in \{L, R\})$ we need a transition with state p_i as well as one with state s_i for $\mathcal{M}_1$. The following table describes the transition function μ of $\mathcal{M}_1$;

1. $\mu(p_i, a)$: replace a by c on **prefix**;
    next state : s_j,

    $\mu(s_i, a)$: pop a from **suffix**;
    push c on **prefix**;
    next state : s_j,

    $\Big\}$ if $\delta(q_i, a) = (q_j, c, R)$;

2. $\mu(p_i, a)$: pop a from **prefix**;
    push c on **suffix**;
    next state : p_j,

    $\mu(s_i, a)$: replace a by c on **suffix**;
    next state : p_j,

    $\Big\}$ if $\delta(q_i, a) = (q_j, c, L)$;

3. $\mu(p_i, \$)$: push c on **prefix**;
    next state : s_j,

    $\mu(s_i, \mathcal{L})$: push c on **prefix**;
    next state : s_j,

    $\Big\}$ if $\delta(q_i, b) = (q_j, c, R)$;

4. $\mu(p_i, \$)$:   push c on **suffix**;
             next state : p_j,

   $\mu(s_i, \pounds)$:   push c on **suffix**;
             next state : p_j,
$$\left.\begin{array}{l}\\\\\\\\\end{array}\right\} \text{if } \delta(q_i, b) = (q_j, c, L).$$

Here $a, c \in \Sigma_b$, and $i \in \{0, 1, \ldots, n-1\}$.

Note that the correspondence between the configurations of $\mathcal{M}$ and $\mathcal{M}_1$ is not one-to-one; for example, the configurations $\$p_0\pounds$, $\$s_0\pounds$, $\$bp_0bb\pounds$, and so forth, all correspond to the same configuration of $\mathcal{M}$. However, the correspondence is sufficiently close to verify easily that $\mathcal{M}_1$ simulates $\mathcal{M}$ step by step. In particular, $\mathcal{M}_1$ halts if and only if it enters state p_n or s_n.

Thus, we have the following consequence of the above construction.

Lemma 5.1.2 *For all $x \in \Sigma^*$, $\mathcal{M}_1$ halts on input x if and only if $\mathcal{M}$ halts on input x.*

In fact, if $\mathcal{M}$ makes exactly m steps on input x, then so does $\mathcal{M}_1$. Observe that the set of descriptions of all possible configurations of $\mathcal{M}_1$ is the set

$$\text{CONFIG}_1 := \{\$\} \cdot \Sigma_b^* \cdot Q_1 \cdot \Sigma_b^* \cdot \{\pounds\},$$

which is a regular subset of $(Q_1 \cup \Pi)^*$, and the set of descriptions of halting configurations of $\mathcal{M}_1$ is

$$\text{HALTING}_1 := \{\$\} \cdot \Sigma_b^* \cdot \{p_n, s_n\} \cdot \Sigma_b^* \cdot \{\pounds\},$$

which is a regular set as well.

The two-stack machine $\mathcal{M}_1$ is simulated by a string-rewriting system S_1 on the alphabet $Q_1 \cup \Pi$. The system S_1 consists of the following rules:

1. $ap_i \rightarrow cs_j$
    $s_i a \rightarrow cs_j$ $\quad\left.\right\}$ if $\delta(q_i, a) = (q_j, c, R)$;

2. $ap_i \rightarrow p_j c$
    $s_i a \rightarrow p_j c$ $\quad\left.\right\}$ if $\delta(q_i, a) = (q_j, c, L)$;

3. $\$p_i \rightarrow \$cs_j$
    $s_i \pounds \rightarrow cs_j \pounds$ $\quad\left.\right\}$ if $\delta(q_i, b) = (q_j, c, R)$;

4. $\$p_i \rightarrow \$p_j c$
    $s_i \pounds \rightarrow p_j c \pounds$ $\quad\left.\right\}$ if $\delta(q_i, b) = (q_j, c, L)$.

Here $a, c \in \Sigma_b$ and $i \in \{0, 1, \ldots, n-1\}$.

It is easily verified that, when restricted to the set CONFIG_1 of descriptions of configurations of $\mathcal{M}_1$, the single-step reduction relation $\rightarrow_{S_1}$ induced by S_1 simulates the stepwise behavior of $\mathcal{M}_1$. Hence, we conclude the following.

Lemma 5.1.3 *For all $x \in \Sigma^*$, the following two statements are equivalent:*

(1) $\mathcal{M}$ *halts on input* x;

(2) $\$s_0 x \pounds \xrightarrow{*}_{S_1} w$ *for some* $w \in \mathrm{HALTING}_1$.

Most of the rules of S_1 are length-preserving. Now S_1 will be simulated by a string-rewriting system S_2 that contains length-increasing rules only. To this end we introduce some additional symbols called **dummy symbols**: $D := \{\langle ap_i \rangle, \langle s_i a \rangle \mid a \in \Pi, \ 0 \le i \le n-1\} \cup \{\langle A \rangle, \langle B \rangle\}$. The system S_2 is obtained from S_1 by adding an occurrence of a dummy symbol to each right-hand side. In addition, S_2 contains some rules to handle the situation that a dummy symbol is immediately to the left of a state symbol from Q_p or immediately to the right of a state symbol from Q_S. Here is a listing of S_2:

1.
$$\left.\begin{array}{rcl} ap_i & \to & \langle ap_i \rangle cs_j \\ s_i a & \to & \langle s_i a \rangle cs_j \end{array}\right\} \text{ if } \delta(q_i, a) = (q_j, c, R);$$

2.
$$\left.\begin{array}{rcl} ap_i & \to & p_j c \langle ap_i \rangle \\ s_i a & \to & p_j c \langle s_i a \rangle \end{array}\right\} \text{ if } \delta(q_i, a) = (q_j, c, L);$$

3.
$$\left.\begin{array}{rcl} \$p_i & \to & \$\langle \$p_i \rangle cs_j \\ s_i \pounds & \to & \langle s_i \pounds \rangle cs_j \pounds \end{array}\right\} \text{ if } \delta(q_i, b) = (q_j, c, R);$$

4.
$$\left.\begin{array}{rcl} \$p_i & \to & \$p_j c \langle \$p_i \rangle \\ s_i \pounds & \to & p_j c \langle s_i \pounds \rangle \pounds \end{array}\right\} \text{ if } \delta(q_i, b) = (q_j, c, L);$$

5.
$$\begin{array}{rcl} \langle d \rangle p_i & \to & p_i \langle d \rangle \langle A \rangle, \\ s_i \langle d \rangle & \to & \langle B \rangle \langle d \rangle s_i. \end{array}$$

Here $a, c \in \Sigma_b$, $\langle d \rangle \in D$ and $i \in \{0, 1, \ldots, n-1\}$.

Consider the sets

$$\mathrm{CONFIG}_2 := \{\$\} \cdot (\Sigma_b \cup D)^* \cdot Q_1 \cdot (\Sigma_b \cup D)^* \cdot \{\pounds\}$$

and

$$\mathrm{HALTING}_2 := \{\$\} \cdot (\Sigma_b \cup D)^* \cdot \{p_n, s_n\} \cdot (\Sigma_b \cup D)^* \cdot \{\pounds\},$$

and the homomorphism $\alpha : (Q_1 \cup \Pi \cup D)^* \to (Q_1 \cup \Pi)^*$ induced by the mapping $f \mapsto f$ (for $f \in Q_1 \cup \Pi$) and $\langle d \rangle \mapsto e$ (for $\langle d \rangle \in D$). Then $\alpha(\mathrm{CONFIG}_2) = \mathrm{CONFIG}_1$ and $\alpha(\mathrm{HALTING}_2) = \mathrm{HALTING}_1$. Further, if $w \in \mathrm{CONFIG}_2$ such that $w = w_0 \to_{S_2} w_1 \to_{S_2} \cdots \to_{S_2} w_m$, then $w_1, \ldots, w_m$

are from CONFIG$_2$, too, and $\alpha(w) = \alpha(w_0) \xrightarrow{\varepsilon}_{S_1} \alpha(w_1) \xrightarrow{\varepsilon}_{S_1} \cdots \xrightarrow{\varepsilon}_{S_1}$ $\alpha(w_m)$. Here $u \xrightarrow{\varepsilon}_{S_1} v$ stands for $u \rightarrow_{S_1} v$ or $u = v$, that is, zero or one step is performed. Conversely, if $u \in$ CONFIG$_1$ such that $u = u_0 \rightarrow_{S_1}$ $u_1 \rightarrow_{S_1} \cdots \rightarrow_{S_1} u_m$, then there are $w_0, \ldots, w_m \in$ CONFIG$_2$ such that $\alpha(w_i) = u_i (0 \le i \le m)$, and $w_0 \xrightarrow{+}_{S_2} w_1 \xrightarrow{+}_{S_2} \cdots \xrightarrow{+}_{S_2} w_m$. Hence, there is a correspondence between the reduction sequences of S_1 and those of S_2. This yields the following.

Lemma 5.1.4 *For all $x \in \Sigma^*$, the following two statements are equivalent:*

(1) $\mathcal{M}$ *halts on input x.*

(2) $\$s_0 x \pounds \xrightarrow{*}_{S_2} w$ *for some $w \in$ HALTING$_2$.*

Notice that the dummy symbols are used in such a way as to ensure that the right-hand side of each rule of S_2 uniquely determines the corresponding left-hand side.

Now we are ready to define the desired string-rewriting system $T :=$ $T(\mathcal{M})$. Let Γ be the following alphabet $\Gamma := Q_1 \cup \Pi \cup D \cup \{\langle C \rangle\}$, and let S_2^{-1} denote the string-rewriting systems $S_2^{-1} := \{u \rightarrow v \mid (v \rightarrow u) \in S_2\}$. Then T is the following system:

$$T := S_2^{-1} \cup \{\langle B \rangle p_i s_j \rightarrow \langle C \rangle, \ p_i s_j \langle A \rangle \rightarrow \langle C \rangle \mid 0 \le i, j \le n\}$$

$$\cup \{\langle C \rangle \langle A \rangle \rightarrow \langle C \rangle, \ \langle B \rangle \langle C \rangle \rightarrow \langle C \rangle\}.$$

Obviously, T is a finite string-rewriting system satisfying the following conditions:

(a) T is length-reducing,

(b) range$(T) \subseteq \Gamma \cup \Gamma^2$,

(c) if $w \in$ CONFIG$_2$ and if $w \xrightarrow{*}_T z$, then $z \in$ CONFIG$_2$, and

(d) $\{\$s_0\} \cdot \Sigma^* \cdot \{\pounds\} \subseteq IRR(T)$.

Furthermore, it is easily checked that

(e) T is confluent.

Finally, since the rules in $T - S_2^{-1}$ do not apply to strings from the set CONFIG$_2$, Lemma 5.1.4 yields the following.

Corollary 5.1.5 *For all $x \in \Sigma^*$, the following two statements are equivalent:*

(1) $\mathcal{M}$ *halts on input x.*

(2) *There exists some $w \in$ HALTING$_2$ such that $w \xrightarrow{*}_{T(\mathcal{M})} \$s_0 x \pounds$.*

Let R denote the set HALTING$_2$. Then R is a regular subset of Γ^*, and by Corollary 5.1.5 and (d) we see that, for $x \in \Sigma^*$, $\mathcal{M}$ halts on input x if and only if $\$s_0x\pounds \in \Delta^*_{T(M)}(R)$ if and only if $\$s_0x\pounds \in [R]_{T(M)}$. Since L is the language accepted by the Turing machine $\mathcal{M}$, this shows that $\Delta^*_{T(M)}(R) \cap \{\$s_0\} \cdot \Sigma^* \cdot \{\pounds\} = \{\$s_0\} \cdot L \cdot \{\pounds\} = [R]_{T(M)} \cap \{\$s_0\} \cdot \Sigma^* \cdot \{\pounds\}$ holds. This completes the proof of Theorem 5.1.1.

From Theorem 5.1.1 we immediately obtain the following representation theorem for recursively enumerable languages.

Corollary 5.1.6 *Let $L \subseteq \Sigma^*$ be recursively enumerable. Then there exist a finite, length-reducing and confluent string-rewriting system T on some alphabet Γ properly containing Σ and two regular sets $R_1, R_2 \subseteq \Gamma^*$ such that $\Pi_\Sigma(\Delta^*_T(R_1) \cap R_2) = \Pi_\Sigma([R_1]_T \cap R_2) = L$, where Π_Σ denotes the projection from Γ^* onto Σ^*.*

As an application of Theorem 5.1.1 we will prove in the next section that, for finite, length-reducing and confluent string-rewriting systems that are non-monadic, the decision problem for linear sentences (see Section 4.3) is undecidable in general.

5.2   Some Undecidability Results

For a finite monadic string-rewriting system T the set $\Delta^*_T(R)$ of descendants of a regular set R is itself regular (Corollary 4.1.3). But it is possible that the set $\Delta^*_T(R)$ of descendants of a regular set R is non-recursive if T is a finite, length-reducing and confluent string-rewriting system that is not monadic (Theorem 5.1.1). Since sets of the form $\Delta^*_T(R)$ played a fundamental role in the proof of Theorem 4.3.1 the following result is not surprising.

Theorem 5.2.1 *There exists a finite, length-reducing and confluent string-rewriting system T on some alphabet Γ such that the following problem is undecidable:*

>**Instance:** *A sentence $\varphi \in$ LINSEN(Γ) containing the variables v_1, $\ldots, v_p \in V_E \cup V_U$, and regular sets $R_1, \ldots, R_p \subseteq \Gamma^*$.*

>**Question:** *Is φ true under the interpretation induced by T and $R_1, \ldots, R_p$?*

Proof. Let $L \subseteq \Sigma^*$ be recursively enumerable but non-recursive. Then by Theorem 5.1.1 there exist a finite alphabet Γ containing $\Sigma \cup \{\$, s_0, \pounds\}$, where $\$$, s_0 and $\pounds$ are additional symbols, a finite length-reducing and confluent string-rewriting system T on Γ, and a regular subset $R \subseteq \Gamma^*$ such that $\Delta^*_T(R) \cap (\{\$s_0\} \cdot \Sigma^* \cdot \{\pounds\}) = [R]_T \cap (\{\$s_0\} \cdot \Sigma^* \cdot \{\pounds\}) = \{\$s_0\} \cdot L \cdot \{\pounds\}$. Thus, for $x \in \Sigma^*$, $\$s_0x\pounds \in [R]_T$ if and only if $x \in L$.

For $x \in \Sigma^*$ we define the linear sentence $\theta(x) := \exists v \, (\$s_0 x \pounds \equiv v)$. Then this sentence $\theta(x)$ is true under the interpretation induced by T and the regular set R if and only if $\$s_0 x \pounds \in [R]_T$, which according to the choices of T and R holds if and only if $x \in L$. Hence, L not recursive implies that the decision problem for linear sentences is undecidable for T.   □5.2.1

Hence, the method of linear sentences (Theorem 4.3.1) cannot be used to prove that certain problems are decidable in the setting of finite, length-reducing and confluent string-rewriting systems that are non-monadic. Of course, this does not imply that all the problems that can be expressed by linear sentences (see Section 4.4) are undecidable in this setting, since there could be other ways to obtain algorithms for solving these problems. However, we will see that in general many of these problems are in fact undecidable for finite, length-reducing and confluent string-rewriting systems.

First, we consider the **generalized word problem**, which is the following variant of the extended word problem for a string-rewriting system T on Σ:

Instance: *A finite subset $U \subseteq \Sigma^*$, and a string $w \in \Sigma^*$.*

Question: *Does $w \in \langle U \rangle_T$ hold?*

Here $\langle U \rangle_T$ denotes the submonoid generated by U, that is, $\langle U \rangle_T = \{u \in \Sigma^* \mid \exists n \geq 0 \, \exists u_1, \ldots, u_n \in U \text{ such that } u \xleftrightarrow{*}_T u_1 \ldots u_n\}$. In addition, since they are closely related, we consider the extended word problem, the submonoid problem, and the independent set problem (see Section 4.4).

Corollary 5.2.2 *There is a finite, length-reducing and confluent string-rewriting system T such that*

(a) *the generalized word problem,*

(b) *the extended word problem,*

(c) *the submonoid problem, and*

(d) *the independent set problem*

are undecidable for T.

Proof. Let $L \subseteq \Sigma^*$ be recursively enumerable but not recursive. By Theorem 5.1.1 there exist an alphabet $\Gamma = \Sigma \cup \{b, \$, \pounds\} \cup \{p_0, p_1, \ldots, p_n, s_0, s_1, \ldots, s_n\} \cup D \cup \{\langle C \rangle\}$, a regular set $R = \{\$\} \cdot (\Sigma \cup \{b\} \cup D)^* \cdot \{p_n, s_n\} \cdot (\Sigma \cup \{b\} \cup D)^* \cdot \{\pounds\}$ and a finite, length-reducing and confluent string-rewriting system T on Γ such that $\Delta_T^*(R) \cap (\{\$s_0\} \cdot \Sigma^* \cdot \{\pounds\}) = \{\$s_0\} \cdot L \cdot \{\pounds\}$, and $\{\$s_0\} \cdot \Sigma^* \cdot \{\pounds\} \subseteq IRR(T)$.

Part (a): Take $U := \Sigma \cup D \cup \{b, \$, p_n, s_n, \pounds\}$, so $R \subseteq U^*$. For $w \in \Sigma^*$ we can conclude the following: $\$s_0 w \pounds \in \langle U \rangle_T$ if and only if $\exists u \in U^* \, (u \xleftrightarrow{*}_T$

$\$s_0w\pounds$), which in turn holds if and only if $\exists u \in U^*(u \xrightarrow{*}_T \$s_0w\pounds)$, since T is confluent and $\{\$s_0\} \cdot \Sigma^* \cdot \{\pounds\} \subseteq IRR(T)$.

The definition of the system T in the proof of Theorem 5.1.1 shows that if $u \xrightarrow{*}_T \$s_0w\pounds$ for some $u \in U^*$, then u already belongs to the regular set R. Thus, $\$s_0w\pounds \in \langle U \rangle_T$ if and only if $\exists u \in R : u \xrightarrow{*}_T \$s_0w\pounds$ if and only if $\$s_0w\pounds \in \Delta_T^*(R) \cap (\{\$s_0\} \cdot \Sigma^* \cdot \{\pounds\}) = \{\$s_0\} \cdot L \cdot \{\pounds\}$ if and only if $w \in L$. Since L is not recursive, we see that the generalized word problem for T is undecidable.

Part (b): Take $R_1 := \{\$s_0w\pounds\}$ and $R_2 := U^*$. Then there exist $w_1 \in R_1$ and $w_2 \in R_2$ such that $w_1 \xleftrightarrow{*}_T w_2$ if and only if $\$s_0w\pounds \in \langle U \rangle_T$. Thus, the generalized word problem reduces to the extended word problem, and hence the latter is undecidable.

Part (c): Take $R_1 := \{\$s_0w\pounds\}$ and $R_2 := U$. Then $\langle R_1 \rangle_T \subseteq \langle R_2 \rangle_T$ if and only if $\$s_0w\pounds \in \langle R_2 \rangle_T$, that is, if and only if $\$s_0w\pounds \in \langle U \rangle_T$.

Part (d): For $w \in \Sigma^*$ let $A(w)$ denote the set $A(w) := U \cup \{\$s_0w\pounds\}$. Since $\text{range}(T) \subseteq \Gamma \cup \Gamma^2$, $[e]_T = \{e\}$, and hence, for all $a \in \Gamma$, $[a]_T \neq \{a\}$ if and only if $a \in \text{range}(T)$. Since $U \subseteq \Gamma$, and since $U \cap \text{range}(T) = \emptyset$, we can conclude that $[a]_T = \{a\}$ for all $a \in U$. Thus, for all $a \in U$, $a \notin \langle A(w) \backslash \{a\} \rangle_T$. Hence, the set $A(w)$ is independent mod T if and only if $\$s_0w\pounds \notin \langle U \rangle_T$, which in turn holds if and only if $w \notin L$. Since L is not recursive, this implies that the independent set problem is undecidable for T.   □5.2.2

For the next undecidability result we must modify the construction given in the proof of Theorem 5.1.1.

Let Σ be an alphabet, let $L \subseteq \Sigma^*$ be recursively enumerable, and let $\mathcal{M} = (Q, \Sigma, \delta, q_0, q_a)$ be a single-tape Turing machine accepting L. As above, we assume that $\mathcal{M}$ moves its head in every step, and that $q_0 \neq q_a$, so that no initial configuration is halting. In addition, we now assume that $\mathcal{M}$ cannot print the blank symbol b. Thus, whenever the head of $\mathcal{M}$ leaves a tape square, then this square contains some letter $a \in \Sigma$. Finally, we assume that when $\mathcal{M}$ is about to halt, then it moves its head to the left until it finds the first occurrence of the blank symbol b, it prints a special symbol c, and then moves its head again one step to the left while it enters the final state $q_n = q_a$. Thus, for each $w \in \Sigma^*$, we obtain that $q_0w \vdash^* q_nbcw_1$ for some $w_1 \in \Sigma^*$, $|w_1| \geq |w|$, if and only if $w \in L$.

To this Turing machine we apply the construction described in detail in the proof of Theorem 5.1.1. Thus, we have a finite alphabet $\Gamma = \Sigma \cup Q_1 \cup \{\pounds, \$\} \cup D \cup \{\langle C \rangle\}$, a regular set R describing the halting configurations of some two-stack machine simulating $\mathcal{M}$, where occurrences of the dummy symbols from D are interspersed with the stacks' contents, and a finite, length-reducing and confluent string-rewriting system T on Γ such that $\Delta_T^*(R) \cap (\{\$s_0\} \cdot \Sigma^* \cdot \{\pounds\}) = \{\$s_0\} \cdot L \cdot \{\pounds\}$. Since $\mathcal{M}$ cannot print the blank symbol b, no configuration of the two-stack machine can contain an occurrence of b. Therefore, Γ need not contain the symbol b. Furthermore, since $\mathcal{M}$ moves its head to the left end of its tape inscription before it halts, we see that $R = \{\$p_n\} \cdot \{\Sigma \cup D\}^* \cdot \{\mathcal{L}\}$ can be taken.

Finally, let $\Delta := \Gamma \cup \{\#\}$, where $\#$ is a new symbol, and let S denote the string-rewriting system.

$$S := T \cup \{a\mathcal{L}\# \to \mathcal{L}\# \mid a \in \Sigma\} \cup \{\$s_0\mathcal{L}\# \to \$p_n\}.$$

It is easy to check that there are no overlaps between the rules of T and the additional rules in S. Thus, S is a finite, length-reducing and confluent system. This system has the following properties.

Lemma 5.2.3 *Let $w \in \Sigma^*$.*

(a) $\$s_0 w \mathcal{L}\# \xrightarrow{*}_S \$p_n$.

(b) *There exists a string $z \in \Delta^*$ such that $\$p_n z \xrightarrow{*}_S \$s_0 w \mathcal{L}$ if and only if $w \in L$.*

Proof.

(a) This is immediate from the rules in $S - T$.

(b) Assume that z is a string from Δ^* such that $\$p_n z \xrightarrow{*}_S \$s_0 w \mathcal{L}$.

Checking all the rules of S we see that a $\$$-symbol cannot be deleted. Thus, $|z|_\$ = 0$. The number of occurrences of symbols from Q_1 can only be reduced by applying a rule from the subset $\{\langle B\rangle p_i s_j \to \langle C\rangle,\ p_i s_j \langle A\rangle \to \langle C\rangle \mid 0 \le i,\ j \le n\}$ of T. However, an application of one of these rules introduces an occurrence of the dummy symbol $\langle C\rangle$ which cannot be deleted again. Hence, $|z|_{Q_1} = 0$, that is, z contains no state symbol. Thus, $z \in (\Sigma \cup D \cup \{\mathcal{L}, \#\})^*$.

The number of occurrences of the symbol $\#$ can be reduced only by applying the rule $\$s_0 \mathcal{L}\# \to \$p_n$. Let $\$p_n z = v_0 \to_S v_1 \to_S \cdots \to_S v_m = \$s_0 w \mathcal{L}$, and let $i = \min\{j \mid |v_j|_\# = 0\}$, that is, v_i is the first string in this reduction that does not contain any occurrences of the symbol $\#$. Then either $0 < i \le m$ and $v_{i-1} = \$s_0 \mathcal{L}\# z_i \to_S \$p_n z_i = v_i$, where $|z_i|_\# = 0$, or $|z|_\# = 0$ implying that $z_i = z$. In either case $z_i \in (\Sigma \cup D)^* \cdot \{\mathcal{L}\}$, and $\$p_n z_i \xrightarrow{*}_T \$s_0 w \mathcal{L}$. Hence, $\$p_n z_i \in R$, and therefore $\$s_0 w \mathcal{L} \in \Delta^*_T(R)$. This yields $w \in L$.

Conversely, let $w \in L$. Then $\$s_0 w \mathcal{L} \in \Delta^*_T(R)$, that is, there exists some $u \in R$ such that $u \xrightarrow{*}_T \$s_0 w \mathcal{L}$. From the form of R we conclude that $u = \$p_n z$ for some $z \in (\Sigma \cup D)^* \cdot \{\mathcal{L}\}$. Since $T \subseteq S$, this completes the proof of Lemma 5.2.3.   □5.2.3

From the above construction we will now deduce the following undecidability results.

Theorem 5.2.4 *There is a finite, length-reducing and confluent string-rewriting system S such that*

(a) *the left-divisibility problem,*

(b) *Green's relation* **R**,

(c) *Green's relation* **I**, *and*

(d) *Green's relation* **D**

are undecidable for S.

Proof. Let $L \subseteq \Sigma^*$ be recursively enumerable but non-recursive, and let S be the finite, length-reducing and confluent string-rewriting system on Δ constructed above.

Part (a): Let $w \in \Sigma^*$. Then the string $\$s_0 w \pounds$ is left-divisible by $\$p_n$ mod S if and only if $\$s_0 w \pounds \xrightarrow{*}_S \$p_n z$ for some $z \in \Gamma^*$. Since S is confluent, and since $\$s_0 w \pounds$ is irreducible, this holds if and only if $\$p_n z \xrightarrow{*}_S \$s_0 w \pounds$. By Lemma 5.2.3(b), this is equivalent to $w \in L$. Thus, the left-divisibility problem is undecidable for S.

Part (b): For $x, y \in \Delta^*$, $[x]_S \mathbf{R} [y]_S$ if and only if $[x]_S \cdot \mathcal{M}_S = [y]_S \cdot \mathcal{M}_S$. We can present this relation through the following relation R_Δ on $\Delta^* \times \Delta^*$: $x R_\Delta y$ if and only if $[x]_S \mathbf{R} [y]_S$. It can be verified easily that $x R_\Delta y$ holds if and only if x is left-divisible by y, and y is left-divisible by x mod S.

Let $w \in \Sigma^*$. Then $\$s_0 w \pounds \# \xrightarrow{*}_S \$p_n$ by Lemma 5.2.3 (a), and hence, $\$p_n$ is left-divisible by $\$s_0 w \pounds$ mod S. On the other hand, the proof of part (a) shows that $\$s_0 w \pounds$ is left-divisible by $\$p_n$ mod S if and only if $w \in L$. Thus, $\$s_0 w \pounds R_\Delta \$p_n$ if and only if $w \in L$, and hence, Green's relation **R** is undecidable for S.

Part (c): We first establish the following claim:

Claim. For $w \in \Sigma^*$, there exist strings $z_1, z_2 \in \Delta^*$ such that $z_1 \$p_n z_2 \xrightarrow{*}_S$ $\$s_0 w \pounds$ if and only if $w \in L$.

Proof. If $w \in L$, then $\$p_n z \xrightarrow{*}_S \$s_0 w \pounds$ for some $z \in \Delta^*$ by Lemma 5.2.3 (b). Conversely, if $z_1 \$p_n z_2 \xrightarrow{*}_S \$s_0 w \pounds$, then z_1 must be the empty string e, since $[e]_S = \{e\}$, and since no rule of S moves any symbol across an occurrence of the symbol $\$$. Thus $\$p_n z_2 \xrightarrow{*}_S \$s_0 w \pounds$, and hence, $w \in L$ by Lemma 5.2.3 (b). □ Claim

For $x, y \in \Delta^*$, $[x]_S \mathbf{I} [y]_S$ if and only if $\mathcal{M}_S \cdot [x]_S \cdot \mathcal{M}_S = \mathcal{M}_S \cdot [y]_S \cdot \mathcal{M}_S$. Hence, Green's relation **I** corresponds to the following binary relation I_Δ on $\Delta^* \times \Delta^*$: $x I_\Delta y$ if and only if $[x]_S \mathbf{I} [y]_S$. It is easily seen that $x I_\Delta y$ holds if and only if there exist $z_1, z_2, z_3, z_4 \in \Delta^*$ such that $x \xleftrightarrow{*}_S z_1 y z_2$ and $y \xleftrightarrow{*}_S z_3 x z_4$.

For $w \in \Sigma^*$, $\$s_0 w \pounds \# \xleftrightarrow{*}_S \$p_n$, and there are $z_1, z_2 \in \Delta^*$ such that $z_1 \$p_n z_2 \xleftrightarrow{*}_S \$s_0 w \pounds$ if and only if $w \in L$. Hence, Green's relation **I** is undecidable for S.

Part (d): For $x, y \in \Delta^*$, $[x]_S \mathbf{D} [y]_S$ if and only if $[x]_S \mathbf{R} [y]_S$ or $[x]_S \mathbf{L} [y]_S$, that is, if and only if $[x]_S \cdot \mathcal{M}_S = [y]_S \cdot \mathcal{M}_S$ or $\mathcal{M}_S \cdot [x]_S = \mathcal{M}_S \cdot [y]_S$ holds.

Let $w \in \Sigma^*$. If $[\$p_n]_S L[\$s_0 w \mathcal{L}]_S$ holds, then $\$p_n$ is right-divisible by $\$s_0 w \mathcal{L}$ and vice versa, $\$s_0 w \mathcal{L}$ is right-divisible by $\$p_n$ mod S. However, $\$s_0 w \mathcal{L}$ is irreducible, and $z\$p_n$ cannot reduce to $\$s_0 w \mathcal{L}$ mod S. Hence, $[\$p_n]_S L[\$s_0 w \mathcal{L}]_S$ does not hold for any $w \in \Sigma^*$. Thus, $[\$p_n]_S D[\$s_0 w \mathcal{L}]_S$ holds if and only if $[\$p_n]_S R[\$s_0 w \mathcal{L}]_S$ holds. By part (b) this is undecidable, and therefore Green's relation D is undecidable for S.   □5.2.4

By considering the string-rewriting system $S^R := \{u^R \rightarrow v^R \mid (u \rightarrow v) \in S\}$, where w^R denotes the reversal of the string w, we immediately obtain the following.

Corollary 5.2.5 *There is a finite, length-reducing and confluent string-rewriting system S^R such that*

(a) *the right-divisibility problem,*

(b) *Green's relation L,*

(c) *Green's relation I, and*

(d) *Green's relation D*

are undecidable for S^R.

By using variants and extensions of the construction presented in the proof of Theorem 5.1.1 various other problems have been shown to be undecidable for finite, length-reducing and confluent string-rewriting systems. In the following we present some of these results without proofs; instead we give detailed references to the original papers. First, let us define the decision problems of interest.

Definition 5.2.6

(a) *Let T be a string-rewriting system on Σ. Two strings $u, v \in \Sigma^*$ are called* **cyclically equal** *mod $T (u \approx_T v)$ if there exist $x, y \in \Sigma^*$ such that $u \xleftrightarrow{*}_T xy$ and $v \xleftrightarrow{*}_T yx$.*
The **problem of cyclic equality** *for T is the following:*

   Instance: *Two strings $u, v \in \Sigma^*$.*

   Question: *Are u and v cyclically equal mod T?*

(b) *A string-rewriting system T on Σ is called* **left-cancellative** *if, for all $u, v, w \in \Sigma^*$, $uv \xleftrightarrow{*}_T uw$ implies that $v \xleftrightarrow{*}_T w$. It is* **right-cancellative** *if, for all $u, v, w \in \Sigma^*$, $uv \xleftrightarrow{*}_T wv$ implies that $u \xleftrightarrow{*}_T w$. Finally, it is* **cancellative** *if it is both left- and right-cancellative.*

The following undecidability results concerning these notions have been obtained by using the technique presented in Section 5.1.

Theorem 5.2.7 *There exists a finite, length-reducing and confluent string-rewriting system T such that the problem of cyclic equality is undecidable for T.*

The system T constructed in the proof of this undecidability result is non-monadic. In fact, it is an open question whether the problem of cyclic equality is decidable for finite, monadic and confluent string-rewriting systems.

Theorem 5.2.8 *It is undecidable in general whether a finite, length-reducing and confluent string-rewriting system is (left-,right-) cancellative.*

We close this section with two more undecidability results for finite, length-reducing and confluent string-rewriting systems. These undecidability results are proved in a way different to the technique used above, and therefore we present them in some detail.

Definition 5.2.9

(a) *Let T be a string-rewriting system, and let $u, v \in \Sigma^*$. We say that u and v have a **common right-multiplier** mod T if there exists a string $x \in \Sigma^*$ such that $ux \overset{*}{\longleftrightarrow}_T vx$. They have a **common left-multiplier** mod T if there exists a string $x \in \Sigma^*$ such that $xu \overset{*}{\longleftrightarrow}_T xv$.*

(b) *The **uniform common right-multiplier (left-multiplier) problem** for finite, length-reducing and confluent string-rewriting systems is the following decision problem:*

> **Instance:** *A finite, length-reducing and confluent string-rewriting system T on Σ, and two strings $u, v \in \Sigma^*$.*
>
> **Question:** *Do u and v have a common right-multiplier (left-multiplier) mod T?*

Theorem 5.2.10 *The uniform common right-multiplier problem and the uniform common-left-multiplier problem are undecidable for finite, length-reducing and confluent string-rewriting systems.*

Now we prove the undecidability of the common right-multiplier problem by a reduction from the Correspondence Problem (see Section 2.1).

Lemma 5.2.11 *The Correspondence Problem is reducible to the common right-multiplier problem for finite, length-reducing and confluent string-rewriting systems.*

Proof. Let Σ be a finite alphabet, and let $S = (x_1, y_1), (x_2, y_2), \dots, (x_n, y_n)$ be a nonempty finite sequence of ordered pairs of nonempty strings over Σ. We construct a finite length-reducing string-rewriting system $T(S)$ on the alphabet $\Gamma := \Sigma \cup \{\$, \$_0, \pounds, \pounds_0, \#, \S, L, R, M, \ell, r, 0, 1\}$, where $\$, \$_0, \pounds, \pounds_0,$ $\#, \S, L, R, M, \ell, r, 0, 1$ are 13 new symbols not contained in Σ.

The system $T(S)$ consists of the following two groups of rules:

1.
$$
\begin{aligned}
\$ \, \text{bin}(i) \, MMM &\to L \, \text{bin}(i) \, R\$ \\
\$ \, \text{bin}(i) \, \#\#\# &\to L \, \text{bin}(i) \, R\$_0 \\
L \, \text{bin}(i) \, R\$_0 x_i &\to \$_0 \\
\$_0\# &\to \S
\end{aligned}
\quad\Bigg\}\quad \text{for } i = 1, 2, \ldots, n
$$

2.
$$
\begin{aligned}
\pounds \, \text{bin}(i) \, MMM &\to \ell \, \text{bin}(i) \, r\pounds \\
\pounds \, \text{bin}(i) \, \#\#\# &\to \ell \, \text{bin}(i) \, r\pounds_0 \\
\ell \, \text{bin}(i) \, r\pounds_0 y_i &\to \pounds_0 \\
\pounds_0\# &\to \S
\end{aligned}
\quad\Bigg\}\quad \text{for } i = 1, 2, \ldots, n.
$$

Here $\text{bin}(i)$ denotes the binary representation of the integer i without leading zeros. Obviously, $T(S)$ is a finite length-reducing string-rewriting system on Γ that can be constructed effectively from S. Further, since $|x_i|, |y_i| \geq 1$ for all $i = 1, 2, \ldots, n$, the left-hand side of no rule of $T(S)$ overlaps with the left-hand side of any rule of $T(S)$ implying that there are no critical pairs for $T(S)$. Hence, the system $T(S)$ is confluent.

For integers $i_1, i_2, \ldots, i_m \in \{1, 2, \ldots, n\}$, let $x(i_1, i_2, \ldots, i_m)$ denote the string

$$
\begin{aligned}
x(i_1, i_2, \ldots, i_m) = {}&\text{bin}(i_m)MMM\ldots \\
&\text{bin}(i_2)MMM\text{bin}(i_1)\#\#\# x_{i_1} x_{i_2} \ldots x_{i_m}\#,
\end{aligned}
$$

and let $y(i_1, i_2, \ldots, i_m)$ denote the string

$$
\begin{aligned}
y(i_1, i_2, \ldots, i_m) = {}&\text{bin}(i_m)MMM\ldots \\
&\text{bin}(i_2)MMM\text{bin}(i_1)\#\#\# y_{i_1} y_{i_2} \ldots y_{i_m}\#.
\end{aligned}
$$

Using the rules of group (1) we can establish the following.

Claim 1. For all $i_1, i_2, \ldots, i_m \in \{1, 2, \ldots, n\}$, $\$x(i_1, i_2, \ldots, i_m) \xrightarrow{*}_{T(S)} \S$.

Proof. $\$x(i_1, i_2, \ldots, i_m) =$

$\underbrace{\$\text{bin}(i_m)MMM}\,\text{bin}(i_{m-1})MMM\ldots\text{bin}(i_1)\#\#\# x_{i_1} x_{i_2} \ldots x_{i_m}\# \to_{T(S)}$

$L\text{bin}(i_m)R\$\text{bin}(i_{m-1})MMM\ldots\text{bin}(i_1)\#\#\# x_{i_1} x_{i_2} \ldots x_{i_m}\# \xrightarrow{m-2}_{T(S)}$

$L\text{bin}(i_m)RL\text{bin}(i_{m-1})R\ldots L\text{bin}(i_2)R\,\underbrace{\$\text{bin}(i_1)\#\#\#}\, x_{i_1} x_{i_2} \ldots x_{i_m}\# \to_{T(S)}$

$L\text{bin}(i_m)RL\text{bin}(i_{m-1})R\ldots L\text{bin}(i_2)R\,\underbrace{L\text{bin}(i_1)R\$_0 x_{i_1}}\, x_{i_2} \ldots x_{i_m}\# \to_{T(S)}$

$L\text{bin}(i_m)RL\text{bin}(i_{m-1})R\ldots L\text{bin}(i_2)R\$_0 x_{i_2} \ldots x_{i_m}\# \xrightarrow{m-2}_{T(S)}$

$\underbrace{L\text{bin}(i_m)R\$_0 x_{i_m}}\# \to_{T(S)} \$_0\# \to_{T(S)} \S$ $\square$Claim 1

Using the rules of group (2) we obtain accordingly the following.

Claim 2. For all $i_1, i_2, \ldots, i_m \in \{1, 2, \ldots, n\}$, $\pounds y(i_1, i_2, \ldots, i_m) \xrightarrow{*}_{T(S)} \S$.

Assume that S has a solution, that is, there exists a nonempty sequence $i_1, i_2, \ldots, i_m \in \{1, 2, \ldots, n\}$ such that $x_{i_1} x_{i_2} \ldots x_{i_m} = y_{i_1} y_{i_2} \ldots y_{i_m}$. Then $x(i_1, i_2, \ldots, i_m) = y(i_1, i_2, \ldots, i_m)$, and hence, $\$x(i_1, i_2, \ldots, i_m) \xleftrightarrow{*}_{T(S)} \S \xleftrightarrow{*}_{T(S)} \pounds y(i_1, i_2, \ldots, i_m)$, that is, \$ and $\pounds$ have a common right-multiplier mod $T(S)$.

Conversely, assume that \$ and $\pounds$ have a common right-multiplier, say $z \in \Gamma^*$, mod $T(S)$, that is, $\$z \xleftrightarrow{*}_{T(S)} \pounds z$. We shall prove that from this assumption we can conclude that the instance S of the Correspondence Problem has a solution. To prove this we need the following two claims.

Claim 3. Let $u, v \in \Gamma^*$ be irreducible with $|u|_a \geq |v|_a$ for all $a \in \{\$, \$_0, L, R\}$. If $\$u \xrightarrow{*}_{T(S)} v$, then there exists a nonempty sequence $i_1, i_2, \ldots, i_k \in \{1, 2, \ldots, n\}$ such that $u = x(i_1, i_2, \ldots, i_k)u_2$ for some $u_2 \in \Gamma^*$.

Proof. Since $|v|_\$ \leq |u|_\$ < |\$u|_\$$, we see that the number of occurrences of the symbol \$ is reduced in the reduction $\$u \xrightarrow{*}_{T(S)} v$. Hence, we can conclude from the form of the rules of $T(S)$ that u can be factored as $u = \mathrm{bin}(i_k)MMM \ldots \mathrm{bin}(i_2)MMM\, \mathrm{bin}(i_1)\#\#\#u_1$ for a nonempty sequence $i_1, i_2, \ldots, i_k \in \{1, 2, \ldots, n\}$ and some string $u_1 \in \Gamma^*$. Thus, $\$u \xrightarrow{k}_{T(S)} L\,\mathrm{bin}(i_k)R \ldots L\,\mathrm{bin}(i_2)R\, L\,\mathrm{bin}(i_1)R\$_0 u_1 =: w$. Now, $|w|_{\$_0} = |u|_{\$_0} + 1 > |v|_{\$_0}, |w|_L > |u|_L \geq |v|_L$, and $|w|_R > |u|_R \geq |v|_R$, and $w \xrightarrow{*}_{T(S)} v$, since $T(S)$ is confluent, and v is irreducible. Since u_1 is also irreducible as a suffix of u, we see from the form of the rules of $T(S)$ that $u_1 = x_{i_1} x_{i_2} \ldots x_{i_k}\#u_2$ for some $u_2 \in \Gamma^*$, that is, $u = x(i_1, i_2, \ldots, i_k)u_2$. □ Claim 3.

Analogously, the following symmetric result is obtainable.

Claim 4. Let $u, v \in \Gamma^*$ be irreducible with $|u|_a \geq |v|_a$ for all $a \in \{\pounds, \pounds_0, \ell, r\}$. If $\pounds u \xrightarrow{*}_{T(S)} v$, then there exists a non-empty sequence $i_1, i_2, \ldots, i_k \in \{1, 2, \ldots, n\}$ such that $u = y(i_1, i_2, \ldots, i_k)u_2$ for some $u_2 \in \Gamma^*$.

Based on these observations we can now complete the proof of Lemma 5.2.11. Assume that $\$z \xleftrightarrow{*}_{T(S)} \pounds z$ for some $z \in \Gamma^*$. Without loss of generality we may assume that z is irreducible. Since $T(S)$ is confluent, there exists an irreducible string $v \in \Gamma^*$ such that $\$z \xrightarrow{*}_{T(S)} v$ and $\pounds z \xrightarrow{*}_{T(S)} v$. Since in the reduction $\pounds z \xrightarrow{*}_{T(S)} v$ only rules from group (2) are applicable, and since the symbols $a \in \{\$, \$_0, L, R\}$ do not occur in these rules, we can conclude that $|v|_a \leq |\pounds z|_a = |z|_a$ for all $a \in \{\$, \$_0, L, R\}$. Hence, by Claim 3 there exist a non-empty sequence $i_1, i_2, \ldots, i_k \in \{1, 2, \ldots, n\}$ and a string $u_2 \in \Gamma^*$ such that $z = x(i_1, i_2, \ldots, i_k)u_2$. Analogously, $|v|_a \leq |z|_a$ for all $a \in \{\pounds, \pounds_0, \ell, r\}$, and so by Claim 4 there exist a non-empty sequence $j_1, j_2, \ldots, j_p \in \{1, 2, \ldots, n\}$ and a string $u_3 \in \Gamma^*$ such that $z = y(j_1, j_2, \ldots, j_p)u_3$. Hence, $x(i_1, i_2, \ldots, i_k)u_2 = z = y(j_1, j_2, \ldots, j_p)u_3$, which implies that $k = p, i_1 = j_1, \ldots, i_k = j_k$, and $x_{i_1} x_{i_2} \ldots x_{i_k} = y_{i_1} y_{i_2} \ldots y_{i_k}$. Thus, the instance S of the Correspondence Problem has a solution.

We have thus shown that S has a solution if and only if there exists a string $z \in \Gamma^*$ satisfying $\$z \xleftrightarrow{*}_{T(S)} \pounds z$. Hence, the given construction is an effective reduction of the Correspondence Problem to the uniform common right-multiplier problem for finite, length-reducing and confluent string-rewriting systems.   □5.2.11

Since the Correspondence Problem is undecidable in general, Lemma 5.2.11 yields the undecidability of the uniform common right-multiplier problem for finite, length-reducing and confluent string-rewriting systems. The undecidability of the corresponding left-multiplier problem follows by a symmetric argument.

5.3   Some Questions on Congruential Languages

Recall from Section 4.2 that a language $L \subseteq \Sigma^*$ is congruential if there is a finite string-rewriting system T on Σ such that L is the union of finitely many of T's congruence classes. Thus, the string-rewriting system T together with finitely many strings $x_1, \ldots, x_m \in \Sigma^*$ gives a specification for the congruential language $L = \bigcup_{i=1,\ldots,m} [x_i]_T$. Here we are interested in the problem of deciding certain properties of congruential languages that are specified through finite, length-reducing and confluent string-rewriting systems.

In Section 4.2 we saw that a congruential language that is specified through a finite, monadic and confluent string-rewriting system is necessarily deterministic context-free (Corollary 4.2.6). In addition, if T is finite and monadic, then, given a string x, it is decidable whether x has infinitely many ancestors mod T (Corollary 4.2.5). Thus, if T is also confluent, then it is decidable whether $[x]_T$ is finite. For finite, length-reducing and confluent string-rewriting systems that are not monadic, the situation is different. The congruential languages specified through a system of this form are decidable in linear time (Theorem 3.1.4) and so they are context-sensitive, but they are in general not context-free as shown by the example given at the end of Section 4.2. In fact, by using still another variant of the construction presented in the proof of Theorem 5.1.1, the following undecidability result can be established.

Theorem 5.3.1 *There exists a finite, length-reducing and confluent string-rewriting system T on alphabet Σ such that the following problem is undecidable:*

Instance: *A string $x \in \Sigma^*$.*

Question: *Is the congruence class $[x]_T$ finite?*

Thus, for those congruential languages that are specified through finite, length-reducing and confluent string-rewriting systems the finiteness problem is undecidable.

For a finite, monadic and confluent string-rewriting system T there exists a string x such that the congruence class $[x]_T$ is infinite if and only if $[e]_T$ is infinite, or if there exists a symbol $a \in \Sigma$ such that $[a]_T$ is infinite (see Lemma 4.2.3). Hence, by the above mentioned result it is decidable whether or not T admits an infinite congruence class. In contrast the following is in general true for non-monadic systems.

Theorem 5.3.2 *The following problem is undecidable:*

Instance: *A finite, length-reducing and confluent string-rewriting system T on alphabet Σ.*

Question: *Does T admit any infinite congruence class, that is, is there some string $x \in \Sigma^*$ such that the congruence class $[x]_T$ is infinite?*

Since the congruential languages that are specified through finite, length-reducing and confluent string-rewriting systems are in general not context-free, this raises the question of whether there is a way to recognize those congruential languages of this form that are context-free. Unfortunately, even this is not possible as we shall see in the following. To this end let Ω be any family of context-free languages that includes all the finite sets.

Theorem 5.3.3

(a) *There exists a finite, length-reducing and confluent string-rewriting system T on alphabet Σ such that the following problem is undecidable:*

    Instance: *A string $x \in \Sigma^*$.*

    Question: *Does the congruence class $[x]_T$ belong to the family Ω?*

(b) *The following problem is undecidable:*

    Instance: *A finite, length-reducing, and confluent string-rewriting system T on alphabet Σ.*

    Question: *Does every congruence class $[x]_T$ belong to the family Ω?*

The families of context-free languages that can be considered here include the family of all context-free languages and the family of all deterministic context-free languages, but also the family of all regular languages. Thus, it is in particular undecidable in general whether a congruence class $[x]_T$ is a regular set, if T is a finite, length-reducing and confluent string-rewriting system.

5.4   Bibliographic Remarks

Theorem 5.1.1 was first described by Jantzen and Monien in [BJMO'DW81]. Later Ó'Dúnlaing [Ó'Dú81] gave a detailed presentation and it is his presentation that is given here.

Theorem 5.2.1 and its corollaries are due to Otto [Ott84a]. Theorem 5.2.7 is from Narendran and Otto [NaOt86]. Theorem 5.2.8 is due to Narendran and Ó'Dúnlaing [NaÓ'Dú89]. Contrasting the undecidability result given by Theorem 5.2.8, Narendran and Ó'Dúnlaing (in the same paper) showed that if the system is finite, confluent, and monadic, then the question of being left-cancellative (right-cancellative) is not just decidable but is tractable. Theorem 5.2.10 is due to Otto [Ott86c], where it is also shown that the common right-multiplier (left-multiplier) problem is decidable for finite, monadic and confluent systems. In fact, in this setting these problems are tractable [NaOt89].

Theorems 5.3.1 and 5.3.2 are due to Narendran, Ó'Dúnlaing, and Rolletschek [NOR85].

6

Algebraic Protocols

The topic of public key cryptosystems is important in the study of security of data in networks as well as cryptography. In this section we consider protocols for such systems, in particular we consider "algebraic" protocols whose syntax and semantics are given by finite string-rewriting systems that are monadic and confluent.

Public key encryption systems are effective against eavesdroppers who merely tap communication lines and try to decipher the intercepted message. However, an improperly designed protocol may be compromised in a complex way and sometimes informal arguments asserting the security for a protocol are in error. Thus, one would like to have a formal model in which security (and other) issues can be discussed precisely.

The material in this chapter is not part of the study of string-rewriting systems. This material is presented as just one example of how one can use string-rewriting systems.

6.1 Basic Properties

In a public key system there is a finite set of "users." Each user X has an encryption function E_X and a decryption function D_X. Both are functions from Δ^* to Δ^* for some fixed finite alphabet Δ, usually $\{0, 1\}$. A secure public directory (that is, a directory that is known to all users and that cannot be altered) contains all pairs $\langle X, E_X \rangle$ while the decryption function D_X is known only to X. By definition, $D_X E_X = 1$ (where 1 is the identity function) and it is often assumed that $E_X D_X = 1$, especially when these are functions on the natural numbers. An important requirement is that knowing $E_X(M)$ and the public directory does not reveal anything about the value of the plaintext message $M \in \Delta^*$. There is a public channel so that all users can read $E_X(M)$ as a string in Δ^* and X can decode the message by applying D_X, that is, $D_X(E_X(M)) = 1(M) = M$. But, in general, no user other than X can determine M from $E_X(M)$.

Formal models of protocols will be defined along with a formal definition of "security." An algorithm for testing whether a protocol is secure will be described as well as characterizations of the syntax of secure protocols of a certain type. Attention will be restricted to two-person protocols.

There are certain basic assumptions that we wish to make clear.

(1) In a public key system the one-way functions are unbreakable, the public directory is secure, and each user has access to every encryption function but only his own decryption function.

(2) In a two-party protocol, only the two users who wish to communicate are involved in the transmission process.

(3) The protocol is uniform in the sense that the same format is used for every pair of users.

(4) An eavesdropper who wishes to discover the plaintext message — called a "saboteur" — is a legitimate user who can initiate an exchange with any other user and can be a receiver for any other user.

What is emphasized here are the definitions of the model and the results that can be obtained by understanding the previous material in this book. We begin with formal definitions of protocols.

Consider a finite set Δ of symbols. We assume a finite set of users. Thus, we can assume that for some integer $m > 0$, every user has a name that is a string of length m in Δ^*. For any $w \in \Delta^*$, if $|w| > m$, then write $w = \text{head}(w)\text{tail}(w)$ where $|\text{tail}(w)| = m$. Consider the following functions, each of which has Δ^* as its domain and its co-domain:

(a) for each user X, the encryption function E_X and the decryption function D_X;

(b) for each user X, the name-appending function i_X, where for every $w \in \Delta^*$, $i_X(w) = wX$ (we use X for the name of X), and the name-matching function d_X, where for every $w \in \Delta^*$,

$$d_X(w) = \begin{cases} \text{head}(w) & \text{if tail}(w) = X \\ \text{undefined} & \text{otherwise;} \end{cases}$$

(c) the deletion function d where for every $w \in \Delta^*$,

$$d(w) = \begin{cases} \text{head}(w) & \text{if } |w| > m \\ \text{undefined} & \text{otherwise.} \end{cases}$$

Let $D = \{D_X \mid X \text{ is a user}\}$, $E = \{E_X \mid X \text{ is a user}\}$, $I = \{i_X \mid X \text{ is a user}\}$, and $J = \{d_X \mid X \text{ is a user}\}$, and let $\Gamma = D \cup E \cup I \cup J \cup \{d\}$.

Since Δ^* is the domain and co-domain of every function in Γ, arbitrary compositions of functions in Γ are well-defined. We assume that for every choice of two users X and Y, the set $\{D_X, E_X, i_X, d_X, D_Y, E_Y, i_Y, d_Y, d\}$ contains nine different functions. Thus, we lose no generality by writing Γ^* for the set of all compositions of functions in Γ, assuming the property of associativity of composition and the properties of the identity function on Γ^* (written here as 1), and, hence, treating Γ^* as the free monoid generated by Γ.

What relations exist between the functions in Γ^*? These are given by sets of rewriting rules that specify the semantics to be applied to Γ^*. The following is a list of potential cancellation rules:

(a) for every user X, D_X composed with E_X is 1;

(b) for every user X, E_X composed with D_X is 1;

(c) for every user X, d_X composed with i_X is 1;

(d) for every user X, d composed with i_X is 1.

Since we are viewing Γ^* as the free monoid generated by Γ, we can take any subset of the set of cancellation rules and view this as a string-rewriting system T on Γ. This method of attack will be used throughout this section, and the following theorem (whose proof follows immediately from the technique used to prove Theorem 2.3.1) provides the fundamental tool.

Theorem 6.1.1 *Every subset of the set of cancellation rules forms a string-rewriting system that is confluent.*

To define protocols, we consider two syntactic types, "name-stamp" and "cascade".

Definition 6.1.2 *A* **two-party cascade protocol** P *is specified by a finite sequence of strings over the alphabet* $\{z_1, z_2, z_3, z_4\}$:

$$\tilde{\alpha}_i \in \{z_1, z_2, z_3\}, \quad 1 \le i \le t,$$
$$\tilde{\beta}_j \in \{z_1, z_2, z_4\}, \quad 1 \le j \le t',$$

where $t' = t$ *or* $t' = t - 1$. *For each pair* X, Y *of distinct users, let* $\alpha_i(X, Y)$, $\beta_j(X, Y)$ *denote the strings* $\tilde{\alpha}_i$, $\tilde{\beta}_j$ *under the substitution*

$$
\begin{aligned}
z_1 &:= E_X \\
z_2 &:= E_Y \\
z_3 &:= D_X \\
z_4 &:= D_Y
\end{aligned}
$$

Definition 6.1.3 *A* **two-party name-stamp protocol** P *is specified by a finite sequence of strings over the alphabet* $\{z_1, z_2, z_3, z_4, z_5, z_6, z_7, z_8, z_9\}$:

$$\tilde{\alpha}_i \in \{z_1, z_2, z_3, z_5, z_6, z_7, z_8, z_9\}^*, \quad 1 \le i \le t,$$
$$\tilde{\beta}_j \in \{z_1, z_2, z_4, z_5, z_6, z_7, z_8, z_9\}^*, \quad 1 \le j \le t',$$

where $t' = t$ or $t' = t - 1$. For each pair X, Y of distinct users, let $\alpha_i(X, Y)$ and $\beta_j(X, Y)$ denote the strings $\tilde{\alpha}_i$, $\tilde{\beta}_j$ under the substitution

$$
\begin{aligned}
z_1 &:= E_X \\
z_2 &:= E_Y \\
z_3 &:= D_X \\
z_4 &:= D_Y \\
z_5 &:= i_X \\
z_6 &:= i_Y \\
z_7 &:= d_X \\
z_8 &:= d_Y \\
z_9 &:= d
\end{aligned}
$$

There is another aspect of the definition of protocols. The underlying semantics determine additional relations on the functions in Γ^*. Besides the associativity of composition and properties of the identity function, the only other relations on the functions in Γ^* are those that follow from the string-rewriting systems that describe certain cancellation rules.

Definition 6.1.4 *Consider the following string-rewriting systems on Γ:*

$$
\begin{aligned}
T_1 &= \{(E_X D_X, 1),\ (D_X E_X, 1) \mid X \text{ is a user}\}, \\
T_2 &= \{(D_X E_X, 1) \mid X \text{ is a user}\}, \\
T_3 &= \{(E_X D_X, 1),\ (D_X E_X, 1),\ (d_X i_X, 1),\ (d i_X, 1) \mid X \text{ is a user}\}, \\
T_4 &= \{(D_X E_X, 1),\ (d_X i_X, 1),\ (d i_X, 1),\mid X \text{ is a user}\}.
\end{aligned}
$$

Define the following protocols:

(a) *A cascade protocol is* **symmetric** *if the semantics are given by T_1 and is* **nonsymmetric** *if the semantics are given by T_2.*

(b) *A name-stamp protocol is* **symmetric** *if the semantics are given by T_3 and is* **nonsymmetric** *if the semantics are given by T_4.*

Thus there are four distinct types of two-party algebraic protocols: symmetric cascade, nonsymmetric cascade, symmetric name-stamp, and nonsymmetric name-stamp. In each case we assume that the $\tilde{\alpha}_i$, $\tilde{\beta}_j$ are such that for every pair X, Y of distinct users, $\alpha_i(X, Y)$ and $\beta_j(X, Y)$ are irreducible with respect to the string-rewriting system that specifies the semantics of that type of protocol.

Recall that if two functions are in Γ, then they are indeed two different functions on Δ^*, that is, Γ is a set of functions, not a set of names of functions. Thus, if γ and δ are in Γ and $\gamma \neq \delta$, then γ and δ are not congruent with respect to any set of cancellation rules. Also, any element of Γ is irreducible with respect to every set of cancellation rules. On the other hand, if γ and δ are different elements of Γ^*, then they may be different names for the same function or they may represent different functions; the given semantics determines this. For any string-rewriting system T that represents a set of cancellation rules on Γ (such as T_1, T_2, T_3, or T_4), $\gamma \xleftrightarrow{*} \delta$ (mod T) if and only if for every $M \in \Delta^*$, $\gamma(M) = \delta(M)$; thus, γ and δ are congruent (mod T) if and only if they represent the same function on Δ^*. The systems are confluent (Theorem 6.1.1) so that for every $\gamma \in \Gamma^*$ there is a unique irreducible element in $[\gamma]$: we denote this irreducible element by $\overline{\gamma}$ and recall that it is the unique irreducible (leftmost) descendant of γ.

Consider a (symmetric or nonsymmetric, cascade or name-stamp) two-party protocol P with semantics given by string-rewriting system T. When user X wants to initiate an exchange to transmit a secret plaintext message M to user Y, they exchange messages according to P in the following way:

X sends to Y the message $\alpha_1(X,Y)(M)$;
Y sends to X the message $\beta_1(X,Y)(\alpha_1(X,Y)(M))$;
X sends to Y the message $\alpha_2(X,Y)(\beta_1(X,Y)(\alpha_1(X,Y)(M)))$;

.

.   .

.

This process is uniform in the sense that $\alpha_i(A,B)$ and $\beta_j(A,B)$ for any users A, B can be obtained from $\widetilde{\alpha}_i$ and $\widetilde{\beta}_j$ as described in Definitions 6.1.2 and 6.1.3 above.

Definition 6.1.5 *Let P be a two-party (symmetric or nonsymmetric, cascade or name-stamp) protocol specified by $\{\widetilde{\alpha}_i, \widetilde{\beta}_j \mid 1 \le i \le t,\ 1 \le j \le t'\}$ and some choice of string-rewriting system T taken from $\{T_1, T_2, T_3, T_4\}$. Let X, Y be a pair of distinct users. Define*

$$
\begin{aligned}
N_1(X,Y) \quad &:= \alpha_1(X,Y), \\
N_{2j}(X,Y) \quad &:= \beta_j(X,Y)N_{2j-1}(X,Y), \quad 1 \le j \le t', \\
N_{2i+1}(X,Y) \quad &:= \alpha_{i+1}(X,Y)N_{2i}(X,Y), \quad 1 \le i \le t-1.
\end{aligned}
$$

We assume that when P is name-stamp, for each k, $\overline{N}_k(X,Y)$ contains no occurrence of a symbol in $J \cup \{d\}$. (Recall that for any γ, $\overline{\gamma}$ denotes the unique irreducible descendant of γ.)

We will be interested in the situation where $\gamma, \delta \in \Gamma^*$ and according to $T(= T_i$ for some $i \in \{1, \ldots, 4\})$, $\gamma\delta \xleftrightarrow{*} 1$. In this situation γ is a left-inverse of δ and δ is a right-inverse of γ. If $\gamma\delta \xleftrightarrow{*} \delta\gamma \xleftrightarrow{*} 1$, then $\gamma(\delta)$ is a two-sided inverse of $\delta(\gamma)$. Notice that if γ has a two-sided inverse, then $\overline{\gamma}$ has a unique irreducible two-sided inverse which is denoted γ^{-1}. In certain contexts we will also use γ^{-1} to denote any irreducible right (left) inverse of γ if γ has a right (left) inverse but not a left (right) inverse; the context will guarantee that no ambiguity is introduced.

Consider each of the four string-rewriting systems $T_1 - T_4$:

(a) For symmetric cascade protocols, only the subset $\Gamma_0 = \{D_X, E_X \mid X \text{ is a user}\}$ of Γ is relevant. Consider strings in Γ_0^* under T_1. Then every $\gamma \in \Gamma_0^*$ has a two-sided inverse.

(b) For nonsymmetric cascade protocols, only Γ_0 is relevant. Consider strings in Γ_0^* under T_2. Then every $\overline{\gamma} \in D^*$ has a unique irreducible right-inverse and every $\overline{\gamma} \in E^*$ has a unique irreducible left-inverse.

(c) For symmetric name-stamp protocols, every string in Γ^* is relevant. Under T_3, every $\gamma \in (E \cup D)^*$ has a two-sided inverse. Every $\overline{\gamma} \in (E \cup D \cup I)^*$ has a left-inverse which is not unique if there is an occurrence of a function in I in $\overline{\gamma}$. Every $\overline{\gamma} \in (E \cup D \cup J)^*$ has a unique right-inverse. Every $\overline{\gamma} \in ((E \cup D \cup J \cup \{d\})^* - (E \cup D \cup J)^*)$ has a right-inverse which is not necessarily unique.

(d) For nonsymmetric name-stamp protocols, every string in Γ^* is relevant. Under T_4 only the identity function 1 has a two-sided inverse. Every $\overline{\gamma} \in (E \cup I)^*$ has a left-inverse which is not unique if there is an occurrence of a function in I in $\overline{\gamma}$. Every $\overline{\gamma} \in (D \cup J)^*$ has a unique right-inverse. Every $\overline{\gamma} \in (D \cup J \cup \{d\})^*$ has a right-inverse which is not unique if there is an occurrence of the function d in $\overline{\gamma}$.

The role of inverses becomes clear when the notion of security is described.

Consider some examples.

(a) Let P be the two-party symmetric cascade protocol specified by $\{\widetilde{\alpha}_1, \widetilde{\beta}_1\}$ where $\widetilde{\alpha}_1 = z_2 z_3$ and $\widetilde{\beta}_1 = z_1 z_4 z_1 z_1 z_4$. Then for any two users X, Y, $\alpha_1(X, Y) = E_Y D_X$ and $\beta_1(X, Y) = E_X D_Y E_X E_X D_Y$. For any plaintext message M,

$$\begin{aligned} N_1(X, Y)(M) &= E_Y D_X(M) \text{ and} \\ N_2(X, Y)(M) &= E_X D_Y E_X E_X D_Y E_Y D_X(M). \end{aligned}$$

Since $E_X D_Y E_X E_X D_Y E_Y D_X$ reduces to $E_X D_Y E_X$ (and the latter is irreducible), we see that $N_2(X, Y)(M) = E_X D_Y E_X(M)$. We will see that this protocol is secure.

(b) Let P be the two-party name-stamp protocol specified by $\{\widetilde{\alpha}_i, \widetilde{\beta}_j \mid 1 \le i \le t, \quad 1 \le j \le t'\}$ where for any two users X, Y,

$$\begin{aligned} \alpha_1(X, Y) &= E_X i_X i_Y, \\ \beta_1(X, Y) &= E_X i_X i_Y, \\ \alpha_2(X, Y) &= E_Y i_Y i_X d_Y d_X D_X d_Y d_X D_X, \\ \beta_j(X, Y) &= E_X i_X i_Y d_X d_Y D_Y, \ j \ge 2, \\ \alpha_i(X, Y) &= E_Y i_Y i_X d_Y d_X D_X, \ i \ge 3. \end{aligned}$$

Then $\overline{N}_1(X, Y) = \overline{N}_{2i}(X, Y) = E_X i_X i_Y$ for $i \ge 2$, $\overline{N}_2(X, Y) = E_X i_X i_Y E_X i_X i_Y$, and $\overline{N}_3(X, Y) = \overline{N}_{2i-1}(X, Y) = E_Y i_Y i_X$ for $i \ge 3$.

Thus, for every k, $\overline{N}_k(X,Y) \in (E \cup I)^*$ and so P is a valid two-party name-stamp protocol. One can check that for all $j \geq 1$, X can decrypt $N_{2j}(X,Y)(M)$ for any $M \in \Delta^*$, receiver Y cannot decrypt $N_1(X,Y)(M)$ for any $M \in \Delta^*$, and for all $i \geq 2$, receiver Y can decrypt $N_{2i-1}(X,Y)(M)$ for any $M \in \Delta^*$. We will see that that this protocol is secure.

6.2   Security and Cascade Protocols

In this section we will develop an algorithm for determining whether a two-party protocol is secure.

Recall that any user X has access to every function in $\{D_X\} \cup E \cup I \cup J \cup \{d\}$ and, hence, to arbitrary compositions of functions taken from this set. However, functions in $I \cup J \cup \{d\}$ are not used in cascade protocols. Hence, for cascade protocols let $\Gamma_X = \{D_X\} \cup E$ for every user X, and for name-stamp protocols let $\Gamma_X = \{D_X\} \cup E \cup I \cup J \cup \{d\}$ for every user X.

We must describe the role of a potential saboteur in order to define the notion of security.

A saboteur Z is a legitimate user of the system and hence has access to all the functions in Γ_Z and all compositions of functions in Γ_Z. The saboteur Z knows the rules of the given protocol $P = \{\widetilde{\alpha}_i, \widetilde{\beta}_j \mid 1 \leq i \leq t,\ 1 \leq j \leq t'\}$. The saboteur can read the encrypted text as it is communicated in the public channel, that is, if user X initiates an exchange with user Y to transmit plaintext message M, then Z is able to obtain $N_i(X,Y)(M)$ (which is a string in Δ^*) for every i. The definition of security is based on other functions in Γ^* that Z may be able to obtain by using some ingenuity.

Suppose that user X is trying to send plaintext message M to user Y using protocol P with semantics given by T. For any i, Z has a chance to transform $N_i(X,Y)(M)$ in three possible ways:

(a) apply any function σ in Γ_Z;

(b) apply any function σ in $\{\beta_j(A,B) \mid A,B \in \{X,Y,Z\},\ A \neq B,$ and $j \geq 1\}$;

(c) apply any function σ in $\{\alpha_i(A,B) \mid A,B \in \{X,Y,Z\},\ A \neq B,$ and $i \geq 2\}$.

While it follows immediately from the definitions that Z has the ability to apply the functions in case (a), the other two cases need explanation.

Case (b). Since Z is a user, he can initiate an exchange with a user B claiming himself to be A. If Z wishes to apply $\beta_j(A,B)$ to the string Π, then at the appropriate time during the exchange Z simply sends Π to B as the (2j-1)st message. User B sees this message as a string in Δ^*, and if B follows the protocol, then B replies by sending $\beta_j(A,B)(\Pi)$. Thus, Z obtains the string in Δ^* that is the result of applying $\beta_j(A,B)$ to Π.

Case (c). If Z wishes to apply $\alpha_i(A, B)$ to the string Π, then Z observes all exchanges to determine whether A ever initiates an exchange with B. If so, Z obtains the (i-1)st reply from B to A and sends Π to A while claiming to be B; if Z does this quickly, then A has no reason not to believe that Π is the reply message from B that complies with the protocol, and so A replies. Now A's reply message is $\alpha_i(A, B)(\Pi)$ so that Z obtains the string in Δ^* that is the result of applying $\alpha_i(A, B)$ to Π.

Thus, Z has the opportunity to transform $N_i(X, Y)(M)$ by applying any of the functions in $\Gamma_Z \cup \{\beta j(A, B) \mid A, B \in \{X, Y, Z\}, \ A \neq B, \text{ and } j \geq 1\} \cup \{\alpha_i(A, B) \mid A, B \in \{X, Y, Z\}, \ A \neq B, \text{ and } i \geq 2\}$.

The definition of security should not depend on the choice of users or on the plaintext message. This factor plays a role in our choice of definition which applies to both cascade and name-stamp protocols and to both symmetric and nonsymmetric protocols.

Definition 6.2.1 *Let* $P = \{\widetilde{\alpha}_i, \widetilde{\beta}_j\}$ *be a protocol with semantics specified by* T. *The protocol* P *is* **secure** *if for every choice of three distinct users* X, Y, Z, *there exists no* k *such that* $N_k(X, Y)$ *has a left-inverse in* $(\Gamma_Z \cup \{\alpha_i(A, B), \beta_j(A, B) \mid A, B \in \{X, Y, Z\}, \ A \neq B, \ i \geq 2, \ j \geq 1\})^*$; *otherwise,* P *is* **insecure**.

If P is an insecure protocol, then for some choice of three distinct users X, Y, Z there exists k such that Z can compute some α with the property that $\alpha \overline{N_k(X, Y)} \overset{*}{\longleftrightarrow} 1$. Hence, for every message M, if X initiates an exchange with Y in order to transmit M, then Z can learn M since $\alpha N_k(X, Y)(M) = 1(M) = M$, where α and k depend only on P and not on M. Further, if we consider the definitions of potential protocols (as in Definitions 6.1.2–6.1.4), then we see that in terms of the variables z_1-z_4 or z_1-z_g, the form of α does not depend on the choice of X, Y, Z.

At first glance it appears that functions in Γ involving users other than X, Y, Z play a role. But in fact the form of the cancellation rules making up T (Definition 6.1.4) is such that it is sufficient to restrict attention to $\{E_A, D_A, i_A, d_A \mid A \in \{X, Y, Z\}\} \cup \{d\}$. This helps in the following result.

Theorem 6.2.2 *Consider the following problem:*

Instance: *A two-party protocol* $P = \{\widetilde{\alpha}_i, \widetilde{\beta}_j\}$ *with semantics specified by* T.

Question: *Is* P *secure?*

There is an $0(((t + t') \parallel P \parallel)^3)$ *algorithm to solve this problem, where*

$$\parallel P \parallel = \left\{ \sum_{i=1}^{t} \mid \widetilde{\alpha}_i \mid + \sum_{j=1}^{t'} \mid \widetilde{\beta}_j \mid \right\}.$$

It is worth observing that Theorem 6.2.2 applies to protocols that are cascade or name-stamp and that are symmetric or nonsymmetric.

Proof of Theorem 6.2.2. Notice that if $P = \{\tilde{\alpha}_i, \tilde{\beta}_j\}$, then for every pair X, Y of users, $|N_1(X, Y)| \leq |\alpha_1(X, Y)|$, $|N_2(X, Y)| = |\beta_1(X, Y)\alpha_1(X, Y)| \leq |\beta_1(X, Y)| + |\alpha_1(X, Y)|$, ... so that for every k, $1 \leq k \leq t + t'$,

$$|N_k(X, Y)| \leq \left\{ \sum_{i=1}^{t} |\tilde{\alpha}_i| + \sum_{j=1}^{t'} |\tilde{\beta}_j| \right\}.$$

User Z can compute any function in $\Pi_Z = \{E_A, i_A, d_A \mid A \in \{X, Y, Z\}\} \cup \{D_Z, d\} \cup \{\alpha_i(A, B) \mid A, B \in \{X, Y, Z\}, A \neq B, i \geq 2\} \cup \{\beta_j(A, B) \mid A, B \in \{X, Y, Z\}, A \neq B, i \geq 1\}$. Notice that

$$|\Pi_Z| = O\left\{ \sum_{i=1}^{t} |\tilde{\alpha}_i| + \sum_{j=1}^{t'} |\tilde{\beta}_j| \right\}.$$

By the above discussion, P is insecure if and only if there exist $k > 0$ and $\gamma \in \Pi_Z^*$ such that $\gamma N_k(X, Y) \overset{*}{\longleftrightarrow} 1$. Thus, P is insecure if and only if there exists $w \in \Pi_Z^*\{N_1(X, Y), \ldots, N_{t+t'}(X, Y)\}$ such that $w \overset{*}{\longleftrightarrow} 1$, and this happens if and only if $\Pi_Z^*\{N_1(X, Y), \ldots, N_{t+t'}(X, Y)\}$ and $\{1\}$ have a common descendant. There is a nondeterministic finite-state acceptor specifying $\Pi_Z^*\{N_1(X, Y), \ldots, N_{t+t'}(X, Y)\}$ that has

$$O\left\{ \sum_{i=1}^{t} |\tilde{\alpha}_i| + \sum_{j=1}^{t'} |\tilde{\beta}_j| + (t + t') \left\{ \sum_{i=1}^{t} |\tilde{\alpha}_i| + \sum_{j=1}^{t'} |\tilde{\beta}| \right\} \right\}$$

$$= O\left\{ (t + t') \left\{ \sum_{i=1}^{t} |\tilde{\alpha}_i| + \sum_{j=1}^{t'} |\tilde{\beta}_j| \right\} \right\}$$

states. There is a nondeterministic finite state acceptor specifying $\{1\}$ that has one state. By Theorem 4.1.2, there is an $0(((t + t') \|P\|)^3)$ algorithm to determine whether $\Pi_Z^*\{N_1(X, Y), \ldots, N_{t+t'}(X, Y)\}$ and $\{1\}$ have a common descendant.   □6.2.2

There is a small improvement to this result which can be obtained easily. First, as in the proof of Theorem 6.2.2, let $\Pi_Z = \{E_A, i_A, d_A \mid A \in \{X, Y, Z\}\} \cup \{D_Z, d\} \cup \{\alpha_i(A, B), \beta_j(A, B) \mid A, B \in \{X, Y, Z\}, A \neq B, i \geq 2, j \geq 1\}$. Second, recall that if $k > 1$, then $N_k(X, Y) = \delta N_1(X, Y) = \delta \alpha_1(X, Y)$ where $\delta \in \{\alpha_i(X, Y), \beta_j(X, Y) \mid 2 \leq i \leq k, 1 \leq j \leq k\}^* \subset \Pi_Z^*$. Thus, if $N_k(X, Y)$ has a left-inverse $\gamma \in \Pi_Z^*$, then $\gamma\delta$ is a left-inverse of $\alpha_1(X, Y)$ and $\gamma\delta \in \Pi_Z^*$.

Lemma 6.2.3 *Let* $P = \{\widetilde{\alpha}_i, \widetilde{\beta}_j\}$ *be a protocol with semantics specified by* T. *Let* X, Y, Z *be three distinct users. Then* P *is insecure if and only if* $\alpha_1(X, Y)$ *has a left-inverse in* Π_Z^*.

Corollary 6.2.4 *Consider the following problem:*

> **Instance:** *A two-party protocol* $P = \{\widetilde{\alpha}_i, \widetilde{\beta}_j\}$ *with semantics specified by* T.

> **Question:** *Is* P *secure?*

There is an algorithm to solve this problem with running time

$$O(\|P\|^3).$$

Proof.   By Lemma 6.2.3 it is sufficient to determine whether Π_Z^* $\{\alpha_1(X, Y)\}$ and $\{1\}$ have a common descendant. There is a nondeterministic finite-state acceptor to specify $\Pi_Z^*\{\alpha_1(X, Y)\}$ that has $0(\| P \|)$ states. The result now follows, as in the proof of Theorem 6.2.2, by Theorem 4.1.2.   □6.2.4

In the case of the cascade protocols, a much more efficient algorithm is known. This method is based on an intrinsic characterization of secure cascade protocols, that is, a characterization that involves concepts that are not part of the definition of security itself. The characterization has conditions that can be checked by inspection. Thus, the existence of a linear-time algorithm is trivial once the characterization theorem is developed.

Definition 6.2.5

(a) *For each* $\gamma \in \Gamma^*$, *let* $lt(\gamma)$ *be the set of elements in* Γ *that occur in* γ.

(b) *For* $\gamma \in (E \cup D)^*$ *and user name* A, γ *has the* **balancing property** *with respect to* A *if* $D_A \in lt(\gamma)$ *implies* $E_A \in lt(\gamma)$.

(c) *A two-party cascade protocol* $P = \{\widetilde{\alpha}_i, \widetilde{\beta}_j\}$ *is* **balanced** *if for any choice of two user names* X, Y, *the following hold:*

> (i) *for every* $i \geq 2$, $\alpha_i(X, Y)$ *has the balancing property with respect to* X, *and*

> (ii) *for every* $j \geq 1$, $\beta_j(X, Y)$ *has the balancing property with respect to* Y.

Now we have the first characterization theorem.

Theorem 6.2.6 *A two party symmetric cascade protocol* $P = \{\widetilde{\alpha}_i, \widetilde{\beta}_j\}$ *is secure if and only if for any choice of two user names* X, Y, $lt(\alpha_1(X, Y)) \cap \{E_X, E_Y\} \neq \emptyset$ *and* P *is balanced.*

Notice that checking the two conditions in Theorem 6.2.6 is quite simple. Thus, we have the following result.

Corollary 6.2.7 *There is a linear-time algorithm to solve the following problem:*

Instance: *A two party symmetric cascade protocol* $P = \{\tilde{\alpha}_i, \tilde{\beta}_j\}$.

Question: *Is P secure?*

Proof of Theorem 6.2.6. The definition of two-party cascade protocols and the notion of security are such that one only needs to verify the conditions in Theorem 6.2.6 for some choice $X, Y, X \neq Y$, and one need consider only a single saboteur Z. Thus, we assume three user names, X, Y, Z.

Let $F = \{\Pi \in (\Gamma_X \cup \Gamma_Y \cup \Gamma_Z)^* \mid \Pi$ is irreducible; $lt(\Pi) \cap \{D_X, D_Y, D_Z\}$ has at most one element; if $A = X$ or $A = Y$ and $D_Z \notin lt(\Pi)$, then Π has the balancing property with respect to $A\}$.

Claim 1. For every $\gamma_1, \gamma_2, \in F$, either $\overline{\gamma_1\gamma_2} \in F$ or there exist $\delta_1, \delta_2 \in F$ such that $\delta_1 \neq 1$, δ_1 is a prefix of γ_1, and $\overline{\gamma_1\gamma_2} = \overline{\delta_1\delta_2} = \delta_1\delta_2$.

Proof. If $\gamma_1\gamma_2$ is irreducible, then let $\delta_1 = \gamma_1$ and $\delta_2 = \gamma_2$. Assume $\gamma_1\gamma_2$ is reducible so that $\gamma_1 \neq 1$ and $\gamma_2 \neq 1$.

If $lt(\gamma_1) \cap D = \emptyset$ or $lt(\gamma_2) \cap D = \emptyset$, then $\overline{\gamma_1\gamma_2} \in F$. Otherwise, there exist $A, B \in \{X, Y, Z\}$ such that $D_A \in lt(\gamma_1)$ and $D_B \in lt(\gamma_2)$. Consider cases.

Case 1. $A = B = Z$. Then, $\overline{\gamma_1\gamma_2} \in F$.

Case 2. $A = B \neq Z$. Then either γ_1 has a suffix $(D_A)^r$ and γ_2 has a prefix $(E_A)^s$, or γ_1 has a suffix $(E_A)^s$ and γ_2 has a prefix $(D_A)^r$; in either case, $r, s > 0$. We lose no generality by assuming the former. Let $\gamma_1 = \mu_1(D_A)^r$ and $\gamma_2 = (E_A)^s\mu_2$. Since $\gamma_1, \gamma_2 \in F$, μ_1 does not end in an element of D and μ_2 does not begin with an element of $\{E_A, D_A\}$. Since γ_1 has the balancing property with respect to A, $E_A \in lt(\mu_1)$. Thus, $\overline{\gamma_1\gamma_2} = \mu_1\mu_2$ if $s = r$, $\overline{\gamma_1\gamma_2} = \mu_1(D_A)^{r-s}\mu_2$ if $r > s$, and $\overline{\gamma_1\gamma_2} = \mu_1(E_A)^{s-r}\mu_2$ if $r < s$. Since $E_A \in lt(\mu_1)$, E_A is in $lt(\overline{\gamma_1\gamma_2})$. Thus, $\overline{\gamma_1\gamma_2} \in F$.

Case 3. $A \neq Z$. Then there exist a prefix δ_1 of γ_1 and a suffix δ_2 of γ_2 such that $\overline{\gamma_1\gamma_2} = \delta_1\delta_2$.

If $A \neq B$, then $B \neq A$ and $D_B \in lt(\gamma_2)$ imply that no occurrence of E_A in γ_1 can be cancelled by any symbol in γ_2. Thus, E_A occurs in δ_1, $\delta_1 \neq 1$, and $\delta_1 \in F$. If $B = Z$, then $\delta_2 \in F$. If $B \neq Z$, a similar argument yields E_B in $lt(\delta_2)$ so that $\delta_2 \in F$.

If $A = Z$, then $\delta_1 \in F$ and $B \neq Z$. Thus, just as in the last paragraph, $\delta_2 \in F$.   □ Claim 1.

Claim 2. If $\gamma \in F^*$, then $\overline{\gamma} \in F^*$.

Proof. Let $\gamma = \gamma_1 \ldots \gamma_n$ where $\gamma_i \in F$ for each i, $1 \leq i \leq n$. We will prove that there exist $\delta_1, \ldots, \delta_k \in F$ with $k \leq n$ such that $\overline{\gamma} = \delta_1 \ldots \delta_k$. Clearly this is true for $n = 1$. Suppose that this is true for $n < m$ where m is a positive integer.

Consider $\gamma_1, \ldots, \gamma_{m+1} \in F$. By the induction hypothesis, there exist $k \leq m$ and $\delta_1, \ldots, \delta_k \in F$ such that $\overline{\gamma_1 \ldots \gamma_m} = \delta_1 \ldots \delta_k$. Let $\gamma = \overline{\gamma_1 \ldots \gamma_{m+1}}$ so that $\gamma = \overline{\delta_1 \ldots \delta_k \gamma_{m+1}} = \delta_1 \ldots \delta_{k-1} \overline{\delta_k \gamma_{m+1}}$. Now $\delta_k, \gamma_{m+1} \in F$ so by Claim 1 there are two cases.

Case 1. If $\overline{\delta_k \gamma_{m+1}} \in F$, then the induction hypothesis applies to $\delta_1, \ldots, \delta_{k-1}, \overline{\delta_k \gamma_{m+1}}$ to yield the result.

Case 2. If $\overline{\delta_k \gamma_{m+1}} = \mu_1 \mu_2$ where $\mu_1, \mu_2 \in F$, $\mu_1 \neq 1$, μ_1 is a prefix of δ_k, and $\mu_1 \mu_2 = \overline{\mu_1 \mu_2}$, then $\gamma = \delta_1 \ldots \delta_{k-1} \overline{\delta_k \gamma_{m+1}} = \delta_1 \ldots \delta_{k-1} \mu_1 \mu_2 = \delta_1 \ldots \delta_{k-1} \mu_1 \mu_2$ since $\overline{\gamma_1 \ldots \gamma_m} = \delta_1 \ldots \delta_k$, μ_1 is a prefix of δ_k, and $\overline{\mu_1 \mu_2} = \mu_1 \mu_2$. $\square$ Claim 2.

Let us return to the statement of Theorem 6.2.6. Suppose that $lt(\alpha_1(X, Y)) \cap \{E_X, E_Y\} \neq \emptyset$, P is balanced, and P is insecure. Then there exists $\gamma \in \Pi_Z{}^*$ such that $\overline{\gamma}$ is a left-inverse of $\alpha_1(X, Y)$ (see the proof of Lemma 6.2.3). Now $\Gamma_Z \subseteq F$ so $\Pi_Z \subseteq F$ since P is balanced. Thus, $\overline{\gamma} = \alpha_1(X, Y)^{-1}$ is in F^* by Claim 2. This means that $\alpha_1(X, Y)^{-1}$ must have the balancing property with respect to X and with respect to Y.

Since $D_Y \notin \Gamma_X$, $D_Y \notin lt(\alpha_1(X, Y))$ so that $E_Y \notin lt(\alpha_1(X, Y)^{-1})$. Since $\alpha_1(X, Y)^{-1}$ has the balancing property with respect to Y, this means $D_Y \notin lt(\alpha_1(X, Y)^{-1})$. Hence, $E_Y \notin lt(\alpha_1(X, Y))$. Thus, $E_X \in lt(\alpha_1(X, Y))$ since $lt(\alpha_1(X, Y)) \cap \{E_X, E_Y\} \neq \emptyset$, so that $lt(\alpha_1(X, Y)) = \{E_X\}$ since $\alpha_1(X, Y)$ is irreducible. Thus, $lt(\alpha_1(X, Y)^{-1}) = \{D_X\}$ and $\alpha_1(X, Y)^{-1}$ does not have the balancing property with respect to X, a contradiction.

For the converse, suppose P is secure. If $lt(\alpha_1(X, Y)) \cap \{E_X, E_Y\} = \emptyset$, then $\alpha_1(X, Y) = (D_X)^r$ for some $r > 0$ so that $\alpha_1(X, Y)^{-1} = (E_X)^r$ and P is insecure. Hence, $lt(\alpha_1(X, Y)) \cap \{E_X, E_Y\} \neq \emptyset$. If P is not balanced, then either for some $i \geq 2$, $\alpha_i(X, Y)$ does not have the balancing property with respect to X, or for some $j \geq 1$, $\beta_j(X, Y)$ does not have the balancing property with respect to Y; the arguments are similar so we assume the former. Thus, there exists $i \geq 2$ such that $D_X \in lt(\alpha_i(X, Y))$ but $E_X \notin lt(\alpha_i(X, Y))$, so $lt(\alpha_i(X, Y)) \subseteq \{D_X, E_Y\}$. This implies that $lt(\alpha_i(X, Z)) \subseteq \{D_X, E_Z\}$ and $lt(\alpha_i(Y, Z)) \subseteq \{D_Y, E_Z\}$. It follows from the discussion above describing the power of a saboteur that in this case Z has the power to compute the effect of applying the D_X or D_Y to any message. (Caution: This does not say that Z has D_X or D_Y, only that by performing a sequence of interchanges, Z can compute the result of applying these functions to any message.) Since Z can already compute E_X (and E_Y), this means that Z has the power of applying any function in $\Gamma_X{}^*$ to any message, so that for any plaintext message M, Z can compute $\alpha_1(X, Y)^{-1}(\alpha_1(X, Y)(M)) = M$ since $lt(\alpha_1(X, Y)^{-1}) \subseteq \{D_X, E_Y, E_X\}$. Hence, P is insecure, a contradiction. $\square$ 6.2.6

For nonsymmetric protocols we have a similar result.

Theorem 6.2.8 *A two-party nonsymmetric cascade protocol* $P = \{\widetilde{\alpha}_i, \widetilde{\beta}_j\}$ *is secure if and only if for every choice of two user names* X, Y, *either*

(a) $\ell t(\alpha_1(X,Y)) \cap D \neq \emptyset$, or

(b) $\ell t(\alpha_1(X,Y)) \cap D = \emptyset$, $\ell t(\alpha_1(X,Y) \cap E) \neq \emptyset$, and (i) and (ii) hold, where

    (i) for every i, $2 \leq i \leq t$, $\alpha_i(X,Y)$ is balanced with respect to X or $\alpha_i(X,Y)$ contains a factor $D_X E_Y$,

    (ii) for every j, $1 \leq j \leq t'$, $\beta_j(X,Y)$ is balanced with respect to Y or $\beta_j(X,Y)$ contains a factor $D_Y E_X$.

The proof of Theorem 6.2.8 is left as an exercise for the reader. Checking the conditions in Theorem 6.2.8 is quite simple.

Corollary 6.2.9 *There is a linear-time algorithm to solve the following problem:*

Instance: *Two-party nonsymmetric cascade protocol $P = \{\widetilde{\alpha_i}\,\widetilde{\beta_j}\}$.*

Question: *Is P secure?*

6.3 Security and Name-Stamp Protocols

Now we turn to name-stamp protocols. We show that there is no characterization of secure name-stamp protocols that has a form similar to the characterizations of secure cascade protocols given in Theorems 6.2.6 and 6.2.8 above. This implies that name-stamp protocols are essentially more complicated than cascade protocols since there is no "simple" characterization of security. Of course, Theorem 6.2.2 still applies, that is, there is an algorithm that allows one to determine if a name-stamp protocol is secure.

We will develop a sequence of facts about a family of protocols whose definition depends on the parameter n. To begin we choose $n \geq 2$ and let $P_0 = \{\widetilde{\alpha_i}, \widetilde{\beta_j} \mid 1 \leq i,\ j \leq n+1\}$ be the two-party name-stamp protocol specified as follows:

$$
\begin{aligned}
\alpha_1(X,Y) &= (E_Y)^{n+1} i_Y i_X, \\
\beta_1(X,Y) &= (E_Y)^n i_Y i_X d_Y (D_Y)^{n+1}, \\
\alpha_i(X,Y) &= 1,\ i = 2,\ldots,n+1 \\
\beta_j(X,Y) &= (E_Y)^{n+1-j} i_Y i_X d_X d_Y (D_Y)^{n+2-j},\ j = 2,\ldots,n, \\
\beta_{n+1}(X,Y) &= E_X i_Y i_X d_X d_Y D_Y.
\end{aligned}
$$

It is easy to see that P_0 is a valid two-party name-stamp protocol, that is, X can compute each of the $\alpha_i(X,Y)$, Y can compute each of the $\beta_j(X,Y)$, and for every i, $\overline{N_i(X,Y)} \in (E \cup D \cup I)^*$. Further, it is easy to see that P_0 is insecure:

If $\alpha = d_X d_Z d_Y D_Z \beta_{n+1}(Z,Y) \beta_n(Z,Y)\ldots\beta_2(Z,Y)\beta_1(Z,Y)$, then $\gamma\alpha_1(X,Y) \xrightarrow{*} 1$.

Now we consider $n+1$ different protocols that are defined from the protocol P_0.

(i) Let $(\widetilde{\beta}_1)'$ be such that for every two user names $A, B, (\widetilde{\beta}_1)'(A, B) = (E_B)^n i_B i_A d_A d_B (D_B)^{n+1}$. Let $P_1 = \{\widetilde{\alpha}_i, \widetilde{\beta}_j \mid 1 \leq i \leq n+1, \ 2 \leq j \leq n+1\} \cup \{(\widetilde{\beta}_1)'\}$.

(ii) For each $k \in \{2, \ldots, n\}$, let $(\widetilde{\beta}_k)'$ be such that for every two user names A, B, $(\beta_k)'(A, B) = (E_B)^{n+1-k} i_B i_A (E_B)^{n+2-k} i_B i_A d_A d_B (D_B)^{n+2-k}$. Let $P_k = \{\widetilde{\alpha}_i, \widetilde{\beta}_j \mid 1 \leq i \leq n+1, \ 1 \leq j \leq n+1$ with $j \neq k\} \cup \{(\widetilde{\beta}_k)'\}$.

(iii) Let $(\widetilde{\beta}_{n+1})'$ be such that for every two user names A, B, $(\beta_{n+1})'(A,B) = E_B i_B i_A d_A d_B D_B$. Let $P_{n+1} = \{\widetilde{\alpha}_i, \widetilde{\beta}_j \mid 1 \leq i \leq n+1, 1 \leq j \leq n\} \cup \{(\widetilde{\beta}_{n+1})'\}$.

Consider P_1. It is straightforward to show that P_1 is a valid name-stamp protocol, either as a symmetric or a nonsymmetric name-stamp protocol. Further, we claim that P_1 is secure. To prove this, let $H_1 = \Gamma_Z \cup \{\beta_j(A, B) \mid j = 2, \ldots, n+1, \ A \neq B, \ A \in \{X, Y, Z\}, \ B \in \{X, Y\}\} \cup \{\beta'_1(A, B) \mid A \neq B, \ A \in \{X, Y, Z\}, \ B \in \{X, Y\}\}$. Then it suffices to show (by induction on $|\gamma|$) that for all $\gamma \in (H_1)^*$, $\ell t(\overline{\gamma \alpha_1(X, Y)}) \cap J \neq \emptyset$ or there exists $w \in \Gamma^*$, $k \geq 1$, $C \in \{X, Y\}$ such that $\gamma \alpha_1(X, Y) = w(E_C)^k i_Y i_X$.

Similarly, for each k, $2 \leq k \leq n$, P_k is a valid two-party name-stamp protocol and P_k is secure. The security of P_k is shown by letting $H_k = \Gamma_Z \cup \{\beta_j(A, B) \mid j \neq k, \ j \in \{1, \ldots, n+1\}, \ A \neq B, \ A \in \{X, Y, Z\}, \ B \in \{X, Y\}\} \cup \{(\beta_k)'(A, B) \mid A \neq B, \ A \in \{X, Y, Z\}, \ B \in \{X, Y\}\}$ and showing that for all $\gamma \in H_k^*$, $\ell t(\overline{\gamma \alpha_1(X, Y)}) \cap J \neq \emptyset$ or there exist $w \in \Gamma^*$ and $u \in \{i_X, i_Z\}^*$, with $\overline{\gamma \alpha_1(X, Y)}) = w(E_Y)^{n+2-k} i_Y u$.

Finally, it is clear that P_{n+1} is a valid two-party name-stamp protocol, either as a symmetric or a nonsymmetric name-stamp protocol. Furthermore, P_{n+1} is secure. To show that P_{n+1} is secure, it suffices to prove that for all $\gamma \in H_{n+1}$, $E_Y \in \ell t(\overline{\gamma \alpha_1(X, Y)})$ where $H_{n+1} = \Gamma_Z \cup \{\beta_j(A, B) \mid j = 1, \ldots, n, \ A \neq B, \ A \in \{X, Y, Z\}, \ B \in \{X, Y\}\} \cup \{(\beta_{n+1})'(A, B) \mid A \neq B, \ A \in \{X, Y, Z\}, \ B \in \{X, Y\}\}$.

We will use the protocols $P_0, P_1, \ldots, P_{n+1}$ to show that there is no "simple" characterization of name-stamp protocols that are secure.

Definition 6.3.1 (a) *Let $P = \{\widetilde{\alpha}_i, \widetilde{\beta}_j \mid 1 \leq i \leq t, 1 \leq j \leq t'\}$ be a two-party protocol. For any choice of two user names X and Y, the words $\alpha_i(X, Y)$, and $\beta_j(X, Y)$, $2 \leq i \leq t$, $1 \leq j \leq t'$, are **primitive (X, Y)-operators** of the protocol P. For each $\alpha_i(X, Y), 1 \leq$*

$i \leq t$, let $\rho(\alpha_i(X,Y)) = X$, and for each $\beta_j(X,Y)$, $1 \leq j \leq t'$, let $\rho(\beta_j(X,Y)) = Y$.

(b) Let $k \geq 1$. A k-**characterization of security** is a predicate C_k of $2k+1$ arguments $(x_0, x_1, x_2, \ldots, x_k, y_1, \ldots, y_k)$ satisfying the following: for every two-party protocol $P = \{\widetilde{\alpha}_i, \widetilde{\beta}_j \mid 1 \leq i \leq t, 1 \leq j \leq t'\}$, P is secure if and only if for every sequence $(\gamma_1, \ldots, \gamma_k)$ of k primitive (X,Y)-operators from $\{\alpha_i(X,Y), \beta_j(X,Y) \mid 2 \leq i \leq t, 1 \leq j \leq t'\}$, $C_k(\alpha_1(X,Y), \gamma_1, \ldots, \gamma_k, \rho(\gamma_1), \ldots, \rho(\gamma_k))$ is true.

Consider the characterization of two-party symmetric cascade protocols that are secure as given in Theorem 6.2.6: P is secure if and only if $\ell t(\alpha_1(X,Y) \cap E) \neq \emptyset$ and for all $i = 2, \ldots, t$, $\alpha_i(X,Y)$ has the balancing property with respect to X, and for every $j = 1, \ldots, t'$, $\beta_j(X,Y)$ has the balancing property with respect to Y. This is a 1-characterization of security as witnessed by the predicate $C_1(x_0, x_1, y_1)$ which is defined to be true if $\ell t(x_0 \cap E) \neq \emptyset$ and both [if $y_1 = X$, then x_1 has the balancing property with repect to X] and [if $y_1 = Y$, then x_1 has the balancing property with respect to Y]. Thus, we have a 1-characterization of security for such protocols. Similarly, there is a 1-characterization of security for two-party non-symmetric cascade protocols; this follows from the characterization of secure protocols of this type given by Theorem 6.2.8

The reader will note that there is a certain ambiguity in Definition 6.3.1. It is possible that for some protocol P, there exist i and j such that $\alpha_i(X,Y) = \beta_j(X,Y)$. Then ρ is multi-valued since it is intended that $\rho(\alpha_i(X,Y)) = X$ and $\rho(\beta_j(X,Y)) = Y$. This portion of the definition can be rewritten to avoid this ambiguity but since we will use these notions only in the proof of the next theorem we will not do so here.

Theorem 6.3.2 There is no $k \geq 1$ such that there exists a k-characterization of security for two-party name-stamp protocols, either symmetric or non-symmetric.

Proof. Assume to the contrary that for some $k \geq 1$, such a k-characterization of security for two-party name-stamp protocols exists. Let C_k be a predicate of $2k + 1$ arguments that witnesses that characterization. Let $n = k+1$ and consider for this value of $n \geq 2$ the protocols $P_0, P_1, \ldots, P_{n+1}$ defined above.

As noted above, P_0 is insecure. Thus, there exists a k-tuple $\gamma_1, \ldots, \gamma_k$ of primitive (X,Y)-operators of P_0 such that $C_k(\alpha_1(X,Y), \gamma_1, \ldots, \gamma_k, \rho(\gamma_1) \ldots, \rho(\gamma_k))$ is false. Since $n > k$, there exists a j such that $\beta_j(X,Y)$ is not one of the primitive (X,Y)-operators $\gamma_1, \ldots, \gamma_k$ in this k-tuple.

Now consider the protocol P_j. This protocol differs from P_0 only by containing $(\beta_j)'(X,Y)$ instead of $\beta_j(X,Y)$. Since $\beta_j(X,Y)$ does not occur in the k-tuple $\gamma_1, \ldots, \gamma_k$, this k-tuple is a legitimate choice when evaluating the predicate C_k for protocol P_j. But $C_k(\alpha_1(X,Y), \gamma_1, \ldots, \gamma_k, \rho(\gamma_1), \ldots$

$\rho(\gamma_k))$ is false so that P_j must be insecure by the assumption that C_k witnesses a k-characterization of security for two-party name-stamp protocols. However, we have seen that for each $j \geq 1$, P_j is secure, a contradiction.   □6.3.2

Note that we are making no claims about other methods of characterizing security for name-stamp protocols. Our attention has been restricted to characterizations involving a uniformly bounded number of primitive (X, Y)-operators, and our result (Theorem 6.3.2) asserts that no such characterization exists.

6.4 Bibliographic Remarks

The model for public key encryption systems studied here is due to Dolev and Yao [DoYa83]. Nonsymmetric protocols were introduced by Book and Otto [BoOt85c]. The formal definition of security and the characterization of secure two party symmetric cascade protocols given in Theorem 6.2.6 is due to Dolev and Yao, but the proof of Theorem 6.2.6 given here is due to Pan [Pan86, Pan88]. The material in Section 6.3 is from [BoOt85b].

7

Algebraic Properties

In this chapter we first review the notion in detail that string-rewriting systems can be seen as presentations of monoids. In particular, we will learn about the so-called Tietze transformations which are a means to change presentations without changing the monoid presented. Then we will address the following question: Given a finite string-rewriting system R on Σ, how much information on the algebraic structure of the monoid presented by $(\Sigma; R)$ can be obtained from R? We will establish a general undecidability result due to Markov and give some applications of it, before we finally derive some decidability results for presentations $(\Sigma; R)$, for which R satisfies certain additional restrictions, like being noetherian and confluent.

7.1   Finite Monoid-Presentations

Let R be a string-rewriting system on Σ. Then the Thue congruence $\xleftrightarrow{*}_R$ generated by R is in fact a **congruence relation** on Σ^*, that is, it is reflexive, symmetric, and transitive (an **equivalence relation**), and it satisfies the following implication:

$$\forall x, y, u, v \in \Sigma^* : u \xleftrightarrow{*}_R v \text{ implies } xuy \xleftrightarrow{*}_R xvy.$$

Definition 7.1.1 *Let R be a string-rewriting system on Σ. The set $\{[w]_R \mid w \in \Sigma^*\}$ of congruence classes mod R is denoted by $\mathcal{M}_R$.*

Lemma 7.1.2 *The set $\mathcal{M}_R$ is a monoid under the operation $[u]_R \circ [v]_R := [uv]_R$ with identity $[e]_R$.*

Proof. The operation $\circ$ is well-defined, because: if $u, v, x, y \in \Sigma^*$ are such that $u \xleftrightarrow{*}_R x$ and $v \xleftrightarrow{*}_R y$, then $uv \xleftrightarrow{*}_R uy \xleftrightarrow{*}_R xy$ by the congruence property of $\xleftrightarrow{*}_R$. Since the operation of concatenation is associative with identity e, the operation $\circ$ is associative with identity $[e]_R$. Thus, $\mathcal{M}_R$ is a monoid under $\circ$ with identity $[e]_R$. $\square$ 7.1.2

In fact, $\mathcal{M}_R$ is the **factor monoid** of the free monoid Σ^* modulo the congruence $\xleftrightarrow{*}_R$, that is, $\mathcal{M}_R = \Sigma^* / \xleftrightarrow{*}_R$.

Definition 7.1.3 *Let $\mathcal{M}$ be a monoid.*

(a) *Let R be a string-rewriting system on alphabet Σ. If $\mathcal{M}$ is isomorphic to the factor monoid $\mathcal{M}_R$ ($\mathcal{M} \cong \mathcal{M}_R$), then the ordered pair $(\Sigma; R)$ is called a **monoid-presentation** of the monoid $\mathcal{M}$.*

(b) *The monoid $\mathcal{M}$ is* **finitely generated** *if there exist a finite alphabet Σ and a string-rewriting system R on Σ such that $(\Sigma; R)$ is a monoid-presentation of $\mathcal{M}$.*

(c) *The monoid $\mathcal{M}$ is* **finitely presented** *if there exist a finite alphabet Σ and a finite string-rewriting system R on Σ such that $(\Sigma; R)$ is a monoid-presentation of $\mathcal{M}$.*

If $(\Sigma; R)$ is a monoid-presentation, then Σ is the **set of generators**, and R is the set of **defining relations** of this presentation.

Examples 7.1.4

(a) *Let Σ be an alphabet, and let $R := \emptyset$. Then $(\Sigma; R)$ is a monoid-presentation of the free monoid Σ^*, since for all $u, v \in \Sigma^*$, $u \overset{*}{\longleftrightarrow}_R v$ if and only if $u = v$, that is, $[u]_R = \{u\}$ for each $u \in \Sigma^*$, and the mapping $u \mapsto [u]_R$ induces an isomorphism from Σ^* onto $\Sigma^*/\overset{*}{\longleftrightarrow}_R$.*

(b) *The* **bicyclic monoid** *$C(a,b)$ is given through the presentation $(\{a,b\}; \{(ab, e)\})$, which is usually written as $(a, b; ab = e)$ or as $(a, b; ab)$ for short. Each congruence class contains exactly one string of the form $b^i a^j (i, j \geq O)$. Hence, $\{b^i a^j \mid i, j \geq O\}$ is a* **set of representatives** *for the monoid $C(a, b)$.*

(c) *Let Σ be an alphabet, and let $\overline{\Sigma} = \{\overline{a} \mid a \in \Sigma\}$ be another alphabet in one-to-one correspondence with Σ and such that $\Sigma \cap \overline{\Sigma} = \emptyset$. Let $R := \{(a\overline{a}, e), (\overline{a}a, e) \mid a \in \Sigma\}$ be a string-rewriting system on Σ. Then the monoid $F_{|\Sigma|}$ given through the presentation $(\Sigma \cup \overline{\Sigma}; R)$ is the* **free group of rank** *$|\Sigma|$. Define a mapping $^{-1} : (\Sigma \cup \overline{\Sigma})^* \to (\Sigma \cup \overline{\Sigma})^*$ through $e^{-1} := e$, $(wa)^{-1} := \overline{a}w^{-1}$, and $(w\overline{a})^{-1} := aw^{-1}$ for $a \in \Sigma$, $w \in (\Sigma \cup \overline{\Sigma})^*$. Then for $w \in (\Sigma \cup \overline{\Sigma})^*$, $ww^{-1} \overset{*}{\longleftrightarrow}_R e \overset{*}{\longleftrightarrow}_R w^{-1}w$, and therefore w^{-1} is called the* **formal inverse** *of w. A string $w \in (\Sigma \cup \overline{\Sigma})^*$ is called* **freely reduced** *if it does not contain a factor of the form $a\overline{a}$ or $\overline{a}a (a \in \Sigma)$. Each congruence class contains exactly one freely reduced string, and so $\{w \in (\Sigma \cup \overline{\Sigma})^* \mid w \text{ is freely reduced}\}$ is a set of representatives for the group $F_{|\Sigma|}$.*

Lemma 7.1.5 *Let $(\Sigma; R)$ be a monoid-presentation, and let $\varphi : \Sigma^* \to \mathcal{M}_R$ be defined by $\varphi(w) := [w]_R$ for all $w \in \Sigma^*$. Then φ is a monoid-homomorphism from the free monoid Σ^* onto the monoid $\mathcal{M}_R$, and for all $x, y \in \Sigma^*$, $\varphi(x) = \varphi(y)$ if and only if $x \overset{*}{\longleftrightarrow}_R y$.*

Proof. Let $u, v \in \Sigma^*$. Then $\varphi(u) \circ \varphi(v) = [u]_R \circ [v]_R = [uv]_R = \varphi(uv)$, and $\varphi(e) = [e]_R$, that is, φ is a monoid-homomorphism from Σ^* onto $\mathcal{M}_R$.

Further, for $x, y \in \Sigma^*$, $\varphi(x) = \varphi(y)$ if and only if $[x]_R = [y]_R$ if and only if $x \xleftrightarrow{*}_R y$. $\qquad\qquad$ □7.1.5

The following lemma characterizes the situation that a monoid-presentation $(\Sigma; R)$ presents a given monoid $\mathcal{M}$.

Lemma 7.1.6 *Let $(\Sigma; R)$ be a monoid-presentation, and let $\mathcal{M}$ be a monoid. If there exists a homomorphism Ψ from the free monoid Σ^* onto $\mathcal{M}$ satisfying $\Psi(u) = \Psi(v)$ if and only if $u \xleftrightarrow{*}_R v$, then $(\Sigma; R)$ is a presentation of $\mathcal{M}$, that is, $\mathcal{M} \cong \mathcal{M}_R$.*

Proof. Assume that $\Psi : \Sigma^* \to \mathcal{M}$ is a homomorphism that is onto and with the property that for all $u, v \in \Sigma^*$, $\Psi(u) = \Psi(v)$ if and only if $u \xleftrightarrow{*}_R v$. Define a mapping $\chi : \mathcal{M}_R \to \mathcal{M}$ through $\chi([w]_R) := \Psi(w)$, and let $\varphi : \Sigma^* \to \mathcal{M}_R$ be the homomorphism given through $\varphi(w) := [w]_R$, that is, we have the following situation:

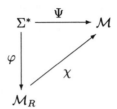

Claim. χ is an isomorphism.

Proof. $\chi([u]_R) \circ \chi([v]_R) = \Psi(u) \circ \Psi(v) = \Psi(uv) = \chi([uv]_R) = \chi([u]_R \circ [v]_R)$, and $\chi([e]_R) = \Psi(e) = 1_{\mathcal{M}}$, where $1_{\mathcal{M}}$ denotes the identity of $\mathcal{M}$. Hence, χ is a monoid-homomorphism from $\mathcal{M}_R$ into $\mathcal{M}$. Since $\chi([w]_R) = \Psi(w)$, and since Ψ is onto, χ is an onto-mapping. Finally assume that $\chi([u]_R) = \chi([v]_R)$. Then $\Psi(u) = \chi([u]_R) = \chi([v]_R) = \Psi(v)$ implying $u \xleftrightarrow{*}_R v$ by hypothesis. Thus, $[u]_R = [v]_R$, that is, χ is also one-to-one. Hence, χ is an isomorphism from $\mathcal{M}_R$ onto $\mathcal{M}$, that is, $\mathcal{M}_R \cong \mathcal{M}$. $\qquad$ □7.1.6

Using Lemma 7.1.6 we can prove the following result which establishes the fact that monoid-presentations of the form $(\Sigma; R)$ are powerful enough to present each and every monoid.

Theorem 7.1.7 *Each monoid $\mathcal{M}$ has a presentation of the form $(\Sigma; R)$.*

Proof. Let $\mathcal{M} = (M, \circ, 1_{\mathcal{M}})$ be a monoid with operation $\circ$ and identity $1_{\mathcal{M}}$, and let $M_0 := M - \{1_{\mathcal{M}}\} = \{m_i \mid i \in I\}$ be the set of elements of $\mathcal{M}$ other than the identity. For each pair $m_i, m_j \in M_0$ there exists a unique element $m_{k(i,j)} \in M$ such that $m_i \circ m_j = m_{k(i,j)}$. The system $\{m_i \circ m_j = m_{k(i,j)} \mid i, j \in I\}$ is the **multiplication table** of $\mathcal{M}$. Let $\Sigma = \{a_i \mid i \in I\}$ be an alphabet in one-to-one correspondence with M_0,

and let $R := \{(a_i a_j, a_{k(i,j)}) \mid i, j \in I\}$, where e is chosen for $a_{k(i,j)}$ in case $m_{k(i,j)} = 1_{\mathcal{M}}$. Then R is an encoding of the multiplication table of $\mathcal{M}$.
Claim. $(\Sigma; R)$ is a monoid-presentation of $\mathcal{M}$.

Proof. We must verify that $\mathcal{M}_R \cong \mathcal{M}$. In order to do so we define a homomorphism $\Psi : \Sigma^* \to \mathcal{M}$ as follows: $\Psi(e) := 1_{\mathcal{M}}, \Psi(a_i) := m_i$ ($i \in I$), $\Psi(wa_i) := \Psi(w) \circ m_i$ ($w \in \Sigma^*$, $i \in I$). Since $\mathcal{M} = \{m_i \mid i \in I\} \cup \{1_{\mathcal{M}}\}$, Ψ is onto. By Lemma 7.1.6 it remains to show that, for all $u, v \in \Sigma^*$, $\Psi(u) = \Psi(v)$ if and only if $u \overset{*}{\longleftrightarrow}_R v$. Let $i, j \in I$. Then $\Psi(a_i a_j) = m_i \circ m_j = m_{k(i,j)} = \Psi(a_{k(i,j)})$, and so $\Psi(\ell) = \Psi(r)$ for all $(\ell, r) \in R$. Thus, for all $u, v \in \Sigma^*$, if $u \overset{*}{\longleftrightarrow}_R v$, then $\Psi(u) = \Psi(v)$.

For all $i, j \in I$ there is an element $a_{k(i,j)} \in \Sigma \cup \{e\}$ such that $a_i a_j \overset{*}{\longleftrightarrow}_R a_{k(i,j)}$. Hence, each congruence class $[w]_R$ contains at least one element from $\Sigma \cup \{e\}$. Let $u, v \in \Sigma^*$ such that $\Psi(u) = \Psi(v)$. Then there are elements $a, b \in \Sigma \cup \{e\}$ satisfying $a \overset{*}{\longleftrightarrow}_R u$ and $b \overset{*}{\longleftrightarrow}_R v$. Hence, $\Psi(a) = \Psi(u) = \Psi(v) = \Psi(b)$. Since Ψ is one-to-one on $\Sigma \cup \{e\}$, this yields $a = b$, that is, $u \overset{*}{\longleftrightarrow}_R v$. Thus, $(\Sigma; R)$ is a presentation of $\mathcal{M}$. □7.1.7

A monoid $\mathcal{M}$ has many different presentations. The following lemma is useful to compare presentations to each other.

Lemma 7.1.8 Let $(\Sigma_1; R_1)$ and $(\Sigma_2; R_2)$ be two monoid-presentations, and let $\varphi : \Sigma_1 \to \Sigma_2^*$ be a mapping. Then φ induces a monoid-homomorphism $\hat{\varphi} : \Sigma_1^* \to \mathcal{M}_{R_2}$, which is defined by $\hat{\varphi}(w) := [\varphi(w)]_{R_2}$. The induced mapping $\tilde{\varphi} : [w]_{R_1} \mapsto \hat{\varphi}(w)$ ($w \in \Sigma_1^*$) is a monoid-homomorphism from $\mathcal{M}_{R_1}$ into $\mathcal{M}_{R_2}$ if and only if $\varphi(\ell) \overset{*}{\longleftrightarrow}_{R_2} \varphi(r)$ holds for all rules $(\ell, r) \in R_1$.

Proof. Let $(\Sigma_1; R_1)$, $(\Sigma_2; R_2)$, and $\varphi : \Sigma_1 \to \Sigma_2^*$ be as above. The mapping φ can be extended to Σ_1^* as follows: $\varphi(e) := e$, $\varphi(wa) := \varphi(w)\varphi(a)$ for all $w \in \Sigma_1^*, a \in \Sigma_1$. Let $\varphi_2 : \Sigma_2^* \to \mathcal{M}_{R_2}$ be the canonical projection defined by $\varphi_2(x) := [x]_{R_2}$. Then $\hat{\varphi} := \varphi_2 \circ \varphi : \Sigma_1^* \to \mathcal{M}_{R_2}$ is a monoid-homomorphism satisfying $\hat{\varphi}(w) = \varphi_2(\varphi(w)) = [\varphi(w)]_{R_2}$ for all $w \in \Sigma_1^*$.

Define $\tilde{\varphi}([w]_{R_1}) := \hat{\varphi}(w)$ for each $w \in \Sigma_1^*$. If $\varphi(\ell) \overset{*}{\longleftrightarrow}_{R_2} \varphi(r)$ holds for each rule $(\ell, r) \in R_1$, then $u \overset{*}{\longleftrightarrow}_{R_1} v$ implies $\varphi(u) \overset{*}{\longleftrightarrow}_{R_2} \varphi(v)$ for all $u, v \in \Sigma_1^*$. Thus, $\tilde{\varphi}$ is a well-defined mapping from $\mathcal{M}_{R_1}$ into $\mathcal{M}_{R_2}$. Further, $\tilde{\varphi}([e]_{R_1}) = \hat{\varphi}(e) = [\varphi(e)]_{R_2} = [e]_{R_2}$, and $\tilde{\varphi}([u]_{R_1}) \circ \tilde{\varphi}([v]_{R_1}) = \hat{\varphi}(u) \circ \hat{\varphi}(v) = [\varphi(u)]_{R_2} \circ [\varphi(v)]_{R_2} = [\varphi(u)\varphi(v)]_{R_2} = [\varphi(uv)]_{R_2} = \hat{\varphi}(uv) = \tilde{\varphi}([uv]_{R_1}) = \tilde{\varphi}([u]_{R_1} \circ [v]_{R_1})$, and hence, $\tilde{\varphi}$ is a monoid-homomorphism from $\mathcal{M}_{R_1}$ into $\mathcal{M}_{R_2}$. Conversely, if $\tilde{\varphi}$ is a monoid-homomorphism from $\mathcal{M}_{R_1}$ into $\mathcal{M}_{R_2}$, then $u \overset{*}{\longleftrightarrow}_{R_1} v$ implies $\varphi(u) \overset{*}{\longleftrightarrow}_{R_2} \varphi(v)$. In particular, for $(\ell, r) \in R_1$, this yields $\varphi(\ell) \overset{*}{\longleftrightarrow}_{R_2} \varphi(r)$. □7.1.8

Examples 7.1.9

(a) *Let* $(\Sigma_1; R_1) = (a, b; ab)$, *and* $(\Sigma_2; R_2) = (x; x^3)$.

   (i) *Define a mapping* $\varphi_1 : \Sigma_1 \to \Sigma_2^*$ *by taking* $\varphi_1(a) := x$ *and* $\varphi_1(b) := x$. *Then* $\hat{\varphi}_1(ab) = [x^2]_{R_2} \neq [e]_{R_2} = \hat{\varphi}_1(e)$. *Hence,* φ_1 *does not induce a homomorphism from* $\mathcal{M}_{R_1}(= \mathcal{C}(a, b))$ *into* $\mathcal{M}_{R_2}$.

   (ii) *Define a mapping* $\varphi_2 : \Sigma_1 \to \Sigma_2^*$ *by taking* $\varphi_2(a) := x$ *and* $\varphi_2(b) := x^2$. *Then* $\hat{\varphi}_2(ab) = [x^3]_{R_2} = [e]_{R_2} = \hat{\varphi}_2(e)$. *Hence,* φ_2 *induces a monoid-homomorphism* $\tilde{\varphi}_2$ *from* $\mathcal{M}_{R_1}(= \mathcal{C}(a, b))$ *into* $\mathcal{M}_{R_2}$.

(b) *Let* $(\Sigma_1; R_1) = (a, b; a^3, b^2, ab = ba)$, *and* $(\Sigma_2; R_2) = (b, c; (cb)^3, b^2, bcb = c)$. *Define a mapping* $\varphi : \Sigma_1^* \to \Sigma_2^*$ *through* $a \mapsto cb$ *and* $b \mapsto b$. *Then* $\varphi(a^3) = (cb)^3 \longleftrightarrow_{R_2} e = \varphi(e)$, $\varphi(b^2) = b^2 \longleftrightarrow_{R_2} e = \varphi(e)$, *and* $\varphi(ab) = cb^2 \overset{*}{\longleftrightarrow}_{R_2} bcb = \varphi(ba)$. *Hence,* φ *induces a monoid-homomorphism* $\tilde{\varphi} : [w]_{R_1} \to [\varphi(w)]_{R_2}$ *from* $\mathcal{M}_{R_1}$ *into* $\mathcal{M}_{R_2}$.

   Define a mapping $\Psi : \Sigma_2^* \to \Sigma_1^*$ *through* $b \mapsto b$ *and* $c \mapsto ab$. *Then* $\Psi((cb)^3) = ab^2ab^2ab^2 \overset{*}{\longleftrightarrow}_{R_1} e = \Psi(e)$, $\Psi(b^2) = b^2 \longleftrightarrow_{R_1} e = \Psi(e)$, *and* $\Psi(bcb) = bab^2 \overset{*}{\longleftrightarrow}_{R_1} ab = \Psi(c)$. *Hence,* Ψ *induces a monoid-homomorphism* $\tilde{\Psi} : [x]_{R_2} \to [\Psi(x)]_{R_1}$ *from* $\mathcal{M}_{R_2}$ *into* $\mathcal{M}_{R_1}$.

   Since $\Psi \circ \varphi(a) = \Psi(cb) = ab^2 \longleftrightarrow_{R_1} a$ *and* $\Psi \circ \varphi(b) = \Psi(b) = b$, *and since* $\varphi \circ \Psi(b) = \varphi(b) = b$ *and* $\varphi \circ \Psi(c) = \varphi(ab) = cb^2 \longleftrightarrow_{R_2} c$, *we conclude that the homomorphisms* $\tilde{\varphi}$ *and* $\tilde{\Psi}$ *are inverse to each other. Hence,* $\mathcal{M}_{R_1} \cong \mathcal{M}_{R_2}$, *that is,* $(\Sigma_1; R_1)$ *and* $(\Sigma_2; R_2)$ *are two finite presentations of the same monoid.*

If $(\Sigma_1; R_1)$ and $(\Sigma_2; R_2)$ are two presentations of the same monoid, there exists an isomorphism $\tilde{\Psi} : \mathcal{M}_{R_1} \to \mathcal{M}_{R_2}$. If Σ_1 is a finite alphabet, then this isomorphism can be described by a linearly bounded function $f : \Sigma_1^* \to \Sigma_2^*$.

Lemma 7.1.10 *Let* $(\Sigma_1; R_1)$ *and* $(\Sigma_2; R_2)$ *be two presentations such that* $\mathcal{M}_{R_1} \cong \mathcal{M}_{R_2}$. *If* $|\Sigma_1| < \infty$, *then there exist a constant* $c \in \mathcal{N}_+$ *and a mapping* $f : \Sigma_1^* \to \Sigma_2^*$ *satisfying the following two conditions:*

(i) $|f(w)| \leq c \cdot |w|$ *for all* $w \in \Sigma_1^*$, *and*

(ii) f *induces an isomorphism from* $\mathcal{M}_{R_1}$ *onto* $\mathcal{M}_{R_2}$, *that is, the mapping* $[w]_{R_1} \to [f(w)]_{R_2}$ *is an isomorphism from* $\mathcal{M}_{R_1}$ *onto* $\mathcal{M}_{R_2}$.

Proof. We have the following situation:

$$\Sigma_1^* \xrightarrow[\text{onto}]{\Pi_1} \mathcal{M}_{R_1}$$
$$\cong$$
$$\Sigma_2^* \xrightarrow[\text{onto}]{\Pi_2} \mathcal{M}_{R_2}$$

For each $a \in \Sigma_1$ there exists a string $u_a \in \Sigma_2^*$ such that $\Pi_1(a) = \Pi_2(u_a)$. Define $f : \Sigma_1^* \to \Sigma_2^*$ as follows: $f(e) := e$, $f(wa) := f(w)u_a$ for $w \in \Sigma_1^*$, $a \in \Sigma_1$. Then $|f(w)| \le c \cdot |w|$, where $c := \max\{|u_a| \mid a \in \Sigma_1\}$.

Claim. For all $w \in \Sigma_1^*$, $\Pi_1(w) = \Pi_2(f(w))$.

Proof. By induction on $|w|$:

$$\Pi_1(e) = [e]_{R_1} = [e]_{R_2} = \Pi_2(e) = \Pi_2(f(e)), \text{ and } \Pi_1(wa)$$
$$= \Pi_1(w) \circ \Pi_1(a) = \Pi_2(f(w)) \circ \Pi_2(u_a) = \Pi_2(f(w)u_a) = \Pi_2(f(wa)).$$

□

If $(\ell, r) \in R_1$, then $\Pi_2(f(\ell)) = \Pi_1(\ell) = \Pi_1(r) = \Pi_2(f(r))$, and so $f(\ell) \xleftrightarrow{*}_{R_2} f(r)$. Hence, the mapping $\tilde{f} : [w]_{R_1} \mapsto [f(w)]_{R_2}$ is a homomorphism from $\mathcal{M}_{R_1}$ into $\mathcal{M}_{R_2}$. The monoid $\mathcal{M}_{R_1}$ is generated by Σ_1. Further, for $a \in \Sigma_1$, $\Pi_1(a) = \Pi_2(f(a))$. Thus, $\mathcal{M}_{R_2}$ is generated by $f(\Sigma_1)$, and hence, $\tilde{f}$ is onto. Finally, let $u, v \in \Sigma_1^*$ such that $f(u) \xleftrightarrow{*}_{R_2} f(v)$. Then $\Pi_1(u) = \Pi_2(f(u)) = \Pi_2(f(v)) = \Pi_1(v)$, which implies that $u \xleftrightarrow{*}_{R_1} v$. Thus, the homomorphism $\tilde{f}$ induced by f is in fact an isomorphism from $\mathcal{M}_{R_1}$ onto $\mathcal{M}_{R_2}$.   □7.1.10

Using the technique developed in the proof of Lemma 7.1.10 we can easily derive the following interesting observations.

Corollary 7.1.11

(a) Let $\mathcal{M}$ be a finitely generated monoid, and let $(\Sigma; R)$ be a presentation of $\mathcal{M}$ such that $|\Sigma| = \infty$. Then there exists a finite subalphabet $\Sigma_1 \subset \Sigma$ such that Σ_1 generates $\mathcal{M}$, that is, $\langle \Sigma_1 \rangle_{\mathcal{M}} := \{w \in \Sigma^* \mid \exists u \in \Sigma_1^* : u \xleftrightarrow{*}_R w\} = \Sigma^*$.

(b) Let $\mathcal{M}$ be a finitely presented monoid, and let $(\Sigma; R)$ be a finitely generated presentation of $\mathcal{M}$ such that $|R| = \infty$. Then there exists a finite subset $R_1 \subset R$ such that $(\Sigma; R_1)$ is also a presentation of $\mathcal{M}$, and the identity mapping $\text{id}: a \mapsto a(a \in \Sigma)$ induces an isomorphism from $\mathcal{M}_R$ onto $\mathcal{M}_{R_1}$.

Proof.

(a) This is an immediate consequence of the proof of the proceeding lemma.

(b) Let $(\Sigma; R)$ be a finitely generated presentation of a finitely presented monoid $\mathcal{M}$ such that $|R| = \infty$, and let $(\Gamma; S)$ be a finite presentation of $\mathcal{M}$. By Lemma 7.1.10 there exist a constant $c \in \mathcal{N}_+$ and mappings $f : \Sigma^* \to \Gamma^*$ and $g : \Gamma^* \to \Sigma^*$ satisfying the following conditions:

(i) $|f(w)| \le c \cdot |w|$ for all $w \in \Sigma^*$,

(ii) $|g(z)| \le c \cdot |z|$ for all $z \in \Gamma^*$,

(iii) the mapping $[w]_R \mapsto [f(w)]_S$ is an isomorphism from $\mathcal{M}_R$ onto $\mathcal{M}_S$, and

(iv) the mapping $[z]_S \mapsto [g(z)]_R$ is an isomorphism from $\mathcal{M}_S$ onto $\mathcal{M}_R$.

In fact, $\Pi_1(w) = \Pi_2(f(w))$ and $\Pi_2(z) = \Pi_1(g(z))$ for all $w \in \Sigma^*$ and all $z \in \Gamma^*$, where $\Pi_1 : \Sigma^* \to \mathcal{M}_R$ and $\Pi_2 : \Gamma^* \to \mathcal{M}_S$ are the corresponding canonical projections. In particular, this implies that $\Pi_1(a) = \Pi_2(f(a)) = \Pi_1(g(f(a)))$ holds for each $a \in \Sigma$, which yields $a \overset{*}{\longleftrightarrow}_R g(f(a))$.

Let R_2 be the subset of R that is used to prove these congruences. Since Σ is finite, R_2 is a finite subset of R. If $(\ell, r) \in S$, then $g(\ell) \overset{*}{\longleftrightarrow}_R g(r)$. Let R_3 be a subset of R that is sufficient to prove these congruences. Since S is finite, R_3 is a finite subset of R. As seen easily R_3 has the following property: if $u \overset{*}{\longleftrightarrow}_S v$, then $g(u) \overset{*}{\longleftrightarrow}_{R_3} g(v)$. Finally, let $R_1 := R_2 \cup R_3$. Then R_1 is a finite subset of R. We claim that $(\Sigma; R_1)$ is a monoid-presentation of $\mathcal{M}$. In order to verify this claim it suffices to show the following.

Claim. For all $(\ell, r) \in R$, $\ell \overset{*}{\longleftrightarrow}_{R_1} r$.

Proof. If $(\ell, r) \in R_1$, then there is nothing to show. So let $(\ell, r) \in R - R_1$. Then $f(\ell) \overset{*}{\longleftrightarrow}_S f(r)$, and hence, $g(f(\ell)) \overset{*}{\longleftrightarrow}_{R_3} g(f(r))$. Thus, $\ell \overset{*}{\longleftrightarrow}_{R_2} g(f(\ell)) \overset{*}{\longleftrightarrow}_{R_3} g(f(r)) \overset{*}{\longleftrightarrow}_{R_2} r$, that is, $\ell \overset{*}{\longleftrightarrow}_{R_1} r$.   □ 7.1.11

Using the last corollary we can now present examples of monoids that are not finitely generated or that are finitely generated, but not finitely presented.

Examples 7.1.12

(a) *The free monoid Σ^* generated by $\Sigma = \{a_i \mid i \in \mathcal{N}\}$, which is given through the presentation $(\Sigma; \emptyset)$, is not finitely generated.*

(b) *The monoid $\mathcal{M}$ given through the presentation $(\Sigma; R)$, where $\Sigma = \{a, b, c, d, f, g\}$ and $R = \{(ab^n c, df^n g) \mid n \geq 1\}$, is finitely generated, but not finitely presented. Observe that if $R_n := R - \{(ab^n c, df^n g)\}$, then $[ab^n c]_{R_n} = \{ab^n c\} \neq \{ab^n c, df^n g\} = [ab^n c]_R$, that is, R is not equivalent to any proper subsystem of R.*

Thus, finite presentations are not sufficient to present each and every monoid. Nevertheless, we will mainly restrict our attention to finite alphabets and finite string-rewriting systems.

7.2 Tietze Transformations

The Tietze transformations are introduced, and it is shown that two finite presentations of the same abstract monoid can be transformed into each other by applying a sequence of these transformations. In addition, the isomorphism problem is introduced and briefly discussed.

Definition 7.2.1 Let $(\Sigma; R)$ be a monoid-presentation. The following transformations of $(\Sigma; R)$ are called **elementary Tietze transformations**:

(T_1) Let $u, v \in \Sigma^*$ such that $u \overset{*}{\longleftrightarrow}_R v$. Then the presentation $(\Sigma; R \cup \{(u, v)\})$ is obtained from $(\Sigma; R)$ by an elementary Tietze transformation of **type 1**.

(T_2) Let $(\ell, r) \in R$ such that $\ell \overset{*}{\longleftrightarrow}_{R - \{(\ell, r)\}} r$. Then the presentation $(\Sigma; R - \{(\ell, r)\})$ is obtained from $(\Sigma; R)$ by an elementary Tietze transformation of **type 2**.

(T_3) Let $u \in \Sigma^*$, and let a be a new symbol, that is, $a \notin \Sigma$. Then the presentation $(\Sigma \cup \{a\}; R \cup \{(a, u)\})$ is obtained from $(\Sigma; R)$ by an elementary Tietze transformation of **type 3**.

(T_4) Let $a \in \Sigma$, and let $u \in (\Sigma - \{a\})^*$ such that $(a, u) \in R$. Define a homomorphism $\varphi_a : \Sigma^* \to (\Sigma - \{a\})^*$ through

$$\varphi_a(b) = \begin{cases} b & \text{if } b \in \Sigma - \{a\}, \\ u & \text{if } b = a, \end{cases}$$

and let $R_1 := \{(\varphi_a(\ell),\ \varphi_a(r)) \mid (\ell, r) \in R - \{(a, u)\}\}$. Then the presentation $(\Sigma - \{a\}; R_1)$ is obtained from $(\Sigma; R)$ by an elementary Tietze transformation of **type 4**.

That these transformations do not affect the monoid presented is shown by the following lemma.

Lemma 7.2.2 Let $(\Sigma_1; R_1)$ and $(\Sigma_2; R_2)$ be two presentations such that $(\Sigma_2; R_2)$ is obtained from $(\Sigma_1; R_1)$ by an elementary Tietze transformation. Then $\mathcal{M}_{R_1}$ and $\mathcal{M}_{R_2}$ are isomorphic, that is, $\mathcal{M}_{R_1} \cong \mathcal{M}_{R_2}$.

Proof.

(i) $(\Sigma_2; R_2)$ is obtained by an elementary Tietze transformation of type 1, that is, $\Sigma_1 = \Sigma_2$, and $R_2 = R_1 \cup \{(u, v)\}$, where $u \overset{*}{\longleftrightarrow}_{R_1} v$. For all $x, y \in \Sigma_1^*$, $x \overset{*}{\longleftrightarrow}_{R_1} y$ if and only if $x \overset{*}{\longleftrightarrow}_{R_2} y$, and so R_1 and R_2 are equivalent systems. In particular, this implies $\mathcal{M}_{R_1} \cong \mathcal{M}_{R_2}$.

(ii) $(\Sigma_2; R_2)$ is obtained by an elementary Tietze transformation of type 2, that is, $\Sigma_1 = \Sigma_2$, and $R_2 = R_1 - \{(\ell, r)\}$ for some $(\ell, r) \in R_1$ such that $\ell \overset{*}{\longleftrightarrow}_{R_2} r$. Hence, $(\Sigma_1; R_1)$ is obtained by an elementary Tietze transformation of type 1 from $(\Sigma_2; R_2)$, and thus, by (i), $\mathcal{M}_{R_1} \cong \mathcal{M}_{R_2}$.

(iii) $(\Sigma_2; R_2)$ is obtained by an elementary Tietze transformation of type 3, that is, $\Sigma_2 = \Sigma_1 \cup \{a\}$, and $R_2 = R_1 \cup \{(a, u)\}$ for some string $u \in \Sigma_1^*$. Define a homomorphism $\varphi : \Sigma_2^* \to \Sigma_1^*$ through

$$\varphi(b) := \begin{cases} b & \text{if } b \in \Sigma_1 \\ u & \text{if } b = a. \end{cases}$$

Then, for each $w \in \Sigma_2^*$, $w \xleftrightarrow{*}_{R_2} \varphi(w)$. Further, if $(\ell, r) \in R_2$, then $\varphi(\ell) \xleftrightarrow{*}_{R_1} \varphi(r)$. Hence, φ induces a homomorphism from $\mathcal{M}_{R_2}$ onto $\mathcal{M}_{R_1}$. For $x, y \in \Sigma_2^*$, if $\varphi(x) \xleftrightarrow{*}_{R_1} \varphi(y)$, then $x \xleftrightarrow{*}_{R_2} \varphi(x) \xleftrightarrow{*}_{R_2} \varphi(y) \xleftrightarrow{*}_{R_2} y$, and so φ actually induces an isomorphism from $\mathcal{M}_{R_2}$ onto $\mathcal{M}_{R_1}$, that is, $\mathcal{M}_{R_1} \cong \mathcal{M}_{R_2}$.

(iv) (Σ_2, R_2) is obtained by an elementary Tietze transformation of type 4, that is, $\Sigma_1 = \Sigma_2 \cup \{a\}$, and $R_2 = \{(\varphi_a(\ell), \varphi_a(r)) \mid (\ell, r) \in R_1 - \{(a, u)\}\}$, where $u \in \Sigma_2^*$, $(a, u) \in R_1$ and $\varphi_a : \Sigma_1^* \to \Sigma_2^*$ is defined by

$$\varphi_a(b) = \begin{cases} b & \text{if } b \in \Sigma_2 \\ u & \text{if } b = a. \end{cases}$$

For each $w \in \Sigma_1^*$, $w \xleftrightarrow{*}_{R_1} \varphi_a(w)$. Further, if $(\ell, r) \in R_1$, then $\varphi_a(\ell) \xleftrightarrow{*}_{R_2} \varphi_a(r)$. Hence, φ_a induces a homomorphism from $\mathcal{M}_{R_1}$ onto $\mathcal{M}_{R_2}$. For $x, y \in \Sigma_1^*$, if $\varphi_a(x) \xleftrightarrow{*}_{R_2} \varphi_a(y)$, then $x \xleftrightarrow{*}_{R_1} \varphi_a(x) \xleftrightarrow{*}_{R_1} \varphi_a(y) \xleftrightarrow{*}_{R_1} y$, and so φ_a induces an isomorphism from $\mathcal{M}_{R_1}$ onto $\mathcal{M}_{R_2}$, that is, $\mathcal{M}_{R_1} \cong \mathcal{M}_{R_2}$.

□7.2.2

A transformation involving the introduction or deletion of several new rules or new letters is called a **Tietze transformation**. Lemma 7.2.2 also holds in this more general situation.

Examples 7.2.3 Let $(\Sigma_1; R_1) = (a, b; a^3, b^2, ab = ba)$.

(i) *Introduce a new letter c :* $(a, b, c; a^3, b^2, ab = ba, c = ab)$;

(ii) *$bcb \longleftrightarrow babb \longleftrightarrow abbb \longleftrightarrow ab \longleftrightarrow c$; hence, we can introduce a new relation:* $(a, b, c; a^3, b^2, ab = ba, c = ab, c = bcb)$;

(iii) *$a \longleftrightarrow ab^2 \longleftrightarrow cb$; hence, we can introduce a new relation:* $(a, b, c; a^3, b^2, ab = ba, c = ab, c = bcb, a = cb)$;

(iv) *delete the letter a :* $(b, c; (cb)^3, b^2, cb^2 = bcb, c = cb^2, c = bcb)$;

(v) *$cb^2 \longleftrightarrow c \longleftrightarrow bcb$; hence, we can delete the relation (cb^2, bcb) :* $(b, c; (cb)^3, b^2, c = cb^2, c = bcb)$;

(vi) *$cb^2 \longleftrightarrow c$ using the relation (b^2, e); hence, we can delete the relation (c, cb^2), that is, we obtain* $(\Sigma_2; R_2) = (b, c; (cb)^3, b^2, c = bcb)$.

Observe that the (elementary) Tietze transformations of types 1 and 2 are inverses of each other, that the inverse of an (elementary) Tietze transformation of type 3 is one of type 4, and that the effect of a Tietze transformation of type 4 on a monoid-presentation can be reversed by a finite number of Tietze transformations of types 1 to 3. If the monoid-presentation is finite, then an elementary Tietze transformation of type 4 can be reversed by a finite number of elementary Tietze transformations of types 1 to 3. We will use this observation in the proof of the following theorem, which describes the basic reason for considering Tietze transformations.

Theorem 7.2.4 *Let $(\Sigma_1; R_1)$ and $(\Sigma_2; R_2)$ be two finite presentations of the same monoid. Then there exists a finite sequence of elementary Tietze transformations that transforms $(\Sigma_1; R_1)$ into $(\Sigma_2; R_2)$.*

Proof. Without loss of generality we may assume that the sets Σ_1 and Σ_2 of generators are disjoint. Since $(\Sigma_1; R_1)$ and $(\Sigma_2; R_2)$ define the same monoid, we have $\mathcal{M}_{R_1} \cong \mathcal{M}_{R_2}$. Thus, for each $a \in \Sigma_1$, there exists a string $u_a \in \Sigma_2^*$ such that a and u_a describe the same element of this monoid. Also, for each $b \in \Sigma_2$, there exists a string $v_b \in \Sigma_1^*$ such that b and v_b describe the same element. Using these strings the presentation $(\Sigma_1; R_1)$ is transformed by a finite sequence of elementary Tietze transformations as follows:

(a) $(\Sigma_1; R_1) \to (\Sigma_1 \cup \Sigma_2; R_1 \cup \{(b, v_b) \mid b \in \Sigma_2\})$ by $|\Sigma_2|$ elementary Tietze transformations of type 3.

(b) Let $R_0 = R_1 \cup \{(b, v_b) \mid b \in \Sigma_2\}$, and let g denote the isomorphism from $\mathcal{M}_{R_2}$ onto $\mathcal{M}_{R_1}$ that is induced by mapping b onto v_b for all $b \in \Sigma_2$ (see Lemma 7.1.10). Then, for all $(\ell, r) \in R_2$, $g(\ell) \overset{*}{\longleftrightarrow}_{R_1} g(r)$ implying $\ell \overset{*}{\longleftrightarrow}_{R_0} r$. Thus, $(\Sigma_1 \cup \Sigma_2; R_0) \to (\Sigma_1 \cup \Sigma_2; R_0 \cup R_2)$ by $|R_2|$ elementary Tietze transformations of type 1.

(c) Since, for each $a \in \Sigma_1$, a, u_a, and $g(u_a)$ all define the same element of the monoid $\mathcal{M}_{R_1}$, we have $a \overset{*}{\longleftrightarrow}_{R_1} g(u_a) \overset{*}{\longleftrightarrow}_{R_0} u_a$. Thus, we obtain $(\Sigma_1 \cup \Sigma_2; R_0 \cup R_2) \to (\Sigma_1 \cup \Sigma_2; R_1 \cup R_2 \cup \{(b, v_b) \mid b \in \Sigma_2\} \cup \{(a, u_a) \mid a \in \Sigma_1\})$ by $|\Sigma_1|$ elementary Tietze transformations of type 1. Let $\Sigma_3 := \Sigma_1 \cup \Sigma_2$ and $R_3 := R_1 \cup R_2 \cup \{(b, v_b) \mid b \in \Sigma_2\} \cup \{(a, u_a) \mid a \in \Sigma_1\}$. Then $(\Sigma_1; R_1)$ has been transformed into $(\Sigma_3; R_3)$ by a finite sequence of elementary Tietze transformations.

(d) In an analogous manner $(\Sigma_2; R_2)$ can be transformed into $(\Sigma_3; R_3)$, so by the above remark $(\Sigma_3; R_3)$ can be transformed into $(\Sigma_2; R_2)$ by a finite sequence of elementary Tietze transformations.

$\square$7.2.4

Theorem 7.2.4 remains valid also for infinite presentations once we allow Tietze transformations that are not necessarily elementary.

The above construction does not yield an effective process for transforming two finite presentations of the same monoid into each other, since the strings $u_a(a \in \Sigma_1)$ and $v_b(b \in \Sigma_2)$, that are essential to these transformations, are not known in general. In particular, it does not give a solution to the **isomorphism problem**.

Definition 7.2.5 *The* **isomorphism problem** *for finite monoid-presentations is the following decision problem:*

Instance: *Two finite monoid-presentations* $(\Sigma_1; R_1)$ *and* $(\Sigma_2; R_2)$.

Question: *Do these two presentations describe the same monoid, that is, does* $\mathcal{M}_{R_1} \cong \mathcal{M}_{R_2}$ *hold?*

On the other hand, it can be seen easily that if a presentation $(\Sigma_2; R_2)$ is obtained from a finite presentation $(\Sigma_1; R_1)$ by a single application of an elementary Tietze transformation, then a solution to the word problem for $(\Sigma_1; R_1)$ also induces a solution to the word problem for $(\Sigma_2; R_2)$, and vice versa. Hence, from Theorem 7.2.4 we can immediately conclude the following result.

Corollary 7.2.6 *Let* $(\Sigma_1; R_1)$ *and* $(\Sigma_2; R_2)$ *be two finite presentations of the same monoid. Then the word problem for* $(\Sigma_1; R_1)$ *is decidable if and only if the word problem for* $(\Sigma_2; R_2)$ *is decidable.*

Thus, the decidability of the word problem is an invariant of finite presentations. Hence, we can speak of the decidability or undecidability of the word problem for a finitely presented **monoid** $\mathcal{M}$.

7.3   Some Undecidability Results

In Section 3.4 we saw that given a finite string-rewriting system R it is in general not possible to obtain much information on the congruence $\xleftrightarrow{*}_R$. Here we consider the analogous problem of extracting information on the algebraic structure of the monoid $\mathcal{M}_R$ from a given string-rewriting system R. Not surprisingly we will see that almost all properties of interest are undecidable in general. The proof of this fact is based on what is known as Markov's Theorem.

Definition 7.3.1 *Let P be a property that finitely presented monoids may or may not have.*

(a) *Property P is called* **invariant** *if every monoid that is isomorphic to a monoid possessing property P itself possesses this property.*

(b) *Property P is a* **Markov property** *if it satisfies the following three conditions:*

    (0) *P is invariant;*

    (1) *there exists a finitely presented monoid M_1 which does not have property P, and which is not isomorphic to a submonoid of any finitely presented monoid having property P;*

    (2) *there exists a finitely presented monoid M_2 that possesses property P.*

(c) *Property P is called* **hereditary** *if whenever a finitely presented monoid M has P, then so does every finitely presented submonoid of M.*

Whenever P is a hereditary property of finitely presented monoids, then condition (1) in the definition of Markov property can be relaxed to the following condition:

(1′) There exists a finitely presented monoid M_1 not having property P.

Before stating and proving Markov's result we want to give some examples of Markov properties.

Definition 7.3.2 *In what follows let M be a finitely presented monoid. Then the properties $P_1, P_2, \ldots, P_{10}$ are defined as follows:*

(a) $P_1(M)$ *if and only if M is* **trivial**, *that is, $M \cong \{e\}$;*

(b) $P_2(M)$ *if and only if M is finite;*

(c) $P_3(M)$ *if and only if M is* **commutative**, *that is, for all $m_1, m_2 \in M$, we have $m_1 \circ m_2 = m_2 \circ m_1$, where $\circ$ denotes the operation of M;*

(d) $P_4(M)$ *if and only if M is* **cancellative**, *that is, for all $m_1, m_2, m_3 \in M$, $m_1 \circ m_2 = m_1 \circ m_3$ implies $m_2 = m_3$, and $m_1 \circ m_3 = m_2 \circ m_3$ implies $m_1 = m_2$;*

(e) $P_5(M)$ *if and only if M is a free monoid, that is, $M \cong \Sigma^*$ for some finite alphabet Σ;*

(f) $P_6(M)$ *if and only if M is a group, that is, for all $m \in M$, there is an element $m' \in M$ such that $m \circ m' = 1_M$, where 1_M denotes the identity of M;*

(g) $P_7(M)$ *if and only if M does not contain a* **non-trivial idempotent**, *that is, there is no $m \in M$ satisfying $m \neq 1_M$ and $m \circ m = m$;*

(h) $P_8(\mathcal{M})$ *if and only if* $\mathcal{M}$ *does not contain a* **non-trivial element of finite order**, *that is, there is no* $m \in \mathcal{M} - \{1_{\mathcal{M}}\}$ *such that there exist* $k \geq 1$ *and* $n \geq 0$ *satisfying* $m^{k+n} = m^n$, *where* m^i *stands for* $m \circ m \circ \ldots \circ m (i - \text{times});$

(i) $P_9(\mathcal{M})$ *if and only if* $\mathcal{M}$ *does not contain an* **element of infinite order**, *that is, there is no* $m \in \mathcal{M}$ *satisfying* $m^i \neq m^j$ *for all* $i, j \in \mathcal{N}$ *with* $i \neq j;$

(j) $P_{10}(\mathcal{M})$ *if and only if* $\mathcal{M}$ *is a free group.*

All the properties $P_1, P_2, \ldots, P_{10}$ are invariant. As can be seen easily, properties P_1 to P_4 and P_7 to P_9 are hereditary, and they satisfy conditions $(1')$ and (2), that is, they are Markov properties. However, the remaining properties $P_5, P_6,$ and P_{10} are not hereditary as shown by the following examples.

Examples 7.3.3

(a) Let $\Sigma = \{a, b\}$, and let $A = \{ab, aba, bab\}$. Then the monoid $\mathcal{M} = \Sigma^*$ is a free monoid, while its submonoid $\langle A \rangle$ generated by A is not a free monoid. This can be seen from the fact that each set of words that generates $\langle A \rangle$ must contain every element of A.

(b) Let $\Sigma = \{a, \bar{a}\}$, and let $R = \{(a\bar{a}, e), (\bar{a}a, e)\}$. Then the monoid $\mathcal{M}_R$ presented by $(\Sigma; R)$ is the free group F_1 of rank 1. Consider the submonoid $\langle a \rangle$ of $\mathcal{M}_R$ generated by a. This submonoid is isomorphic to the free monoid $\{a\}^*$ and, hence, it is not a group, let alone a free group.

In order to prove that properties $P_5, P_6,$ and P_{10} are in fact Markov properties, we must check conditions (1) and (2) of Definition 7.2.1 Obviously, they all satisfy condition (2), which leaves us with condition (1).

Lemma 7.3.4 *There exists a finitely presented monoid* $\mathcal{M}_1$ *that is not isomorphic to a submonoid of any finitely generated free monoid.*

Proof. Each finitely generated submonoid of a free monoid has a decidable word problem. Now let $\mathcal{M}_1$ be a finitely presented monoid with an undecidable word problem. Since the undecidability of the word problem is an invariant property, we conclude that $\mathcal{M}_1$ is not isomorphic to a submonoid of any finitely generated free monoid.   □7.3.4

This shows that property P_5 is also a Markov property.

Lemma 7.3.5 *There exists a finitely presented monoid* $\mathcal{M}_1$ *that is not isomorphic to a submonoid of any group.*

Proof. Let $\mathcal{M}_1$ be given through the presentation $(\{a, b, c\}; \{(ab, ac)\})$. Then $\mathcal{M}_1$ is not cancellative, and hence, it is not isomorphic to a submonoid of any group.   □7.3.5

This implies that also properties P_6 and P_{10} are Markov properties. We can summarize the results obtained so far as follows.

Theorem 7.3.6 *Properties P_1 to P_{10} are Markov properties of finitely presented monoids.*

The main result of Markov states the following undecidability result.

Theorem 7.3.7 *Let P be a Markov property. Then the following problem is undecidable:*

Instance: *A finite presentation $(\Sigma; R)$.*

Question: *Does the monoid $\mathcal{M}_R$ given by this presentation have property P?*

Because of Theorem 7.3.6, this immediately gives the following.

Corollary 7.3.8 *Properties 1 through 10 are all undecidable in general.*

It remains to prove Theorem 7.3.7.

Definition 7.3.9 *Let $\mathcal{M}_1$ and $\mathcal{M}_2$ be two monoids that are given through presentations $(\Sigma_1; R_1)$ and $(\Sigma_2; R_2)$, respectively, where $\Sigma_1 \cap \Sigma_2 = \emptyset$. Then the **free product** $\mathcal{M}_1 * \mathcal{M}_2$ of the monoids $\mathcal{M}_1$ and $\mathcal{M}_2$ is the monoid $\mathcal{M}_R$ which is defined through the presentation $(\Sigma; R)$, where $\Sigma = \Sigma_1 \cup \Sigma_2$ and $R = R_1 \cup R_2$.*

As can be seen easily, we have $u \longleftrightarrow^*_{R_i} v$ if and only if $u \longleftrightarrow^*_R v$ for all $u, v \in \Sigma_i^*$, $i = 1, 2$. This yields the following fundamental property of the free product.

Theorem 7.3.10 *Let $(\Sigma_1; R_1)$ and $(\Sigma_2; R_2)$ be two presentations such that $\Sigma_1 \cap \Sigma_2 = \emptyset$, and let $(\Sigma; R)$ denote the presentation $(\Sigma_1 \cup \Sigma_2; R_1 \cup R_2)$. Then for $i = 1, 2$, the identity mapping $id_i : \Sigma_i \to \Sigma_i$ induces an embedding of the monoid $\mathcal{M}_{R_i}$ in the monoid $\mathcal{M}_R = \mathcal{M}_{R_1} * \mathcal{M}_{R_2}$.*

In particular, this induces the following corollary we will make use of in the proof of Theorem 7.3.7.

Corollary 7.3.11 *Let $\mathcal{M}_1$ and $\mathcal{M}_2$ be two finitely presented monoids such that the word problem for the free product $\mathcal{M}_1 * \mathcal{M}_2$ is decidable. Then the word problems for $\mathcal{M}_1$ and $\mathcal{M}_2$ are decidable.*

The reverse implication also holds, that is, two finitely presented monoids $\mathcal{M}_1$ and $\mathcal{M}_2$ have decidable word problems if and only if their free product $\mathcal{M}_1 * \mathcal{M}_2$ has a decidable word problem. Finally we are prepared to prove Markov's result.

Proof of Theorem 7.3.7 Let P be a Markov property. Then there are two finitely presented monoids $\mathcal{M}_1$ and $\mathcal{M}_2$ such that

(1) $\mathcal{M}_1$ does not have property P, and $\mathcal{M}_1$ is not isomorphic to a submonoid of any finitely presented monoid having property P, and

(2) $\mathcal{M}_2$ does have property P.

In addition, let $\mathcal{M}_3$ be a finitely presented monoid with an undecidable word problem, and for $i = 1, 2, 3$, let $(\Sigma_i; R_i)$ be a finite presentation of the monoid $\mathcal{M}_i$. Without loss of generality we may assume that the sets of generators Σ_1, Σ_2, and Σ_3 are pairwise disjoint.

The free product $\mathcal{M}_R$ of $\mathcal{M}_1$ and $\mathcal{M}_3$ is given through the presentation $(\Sigma; R)$, where $\Sigma = \Sigma_1 \cup \Sigma_3$ and $R = R_1 \cup R_3$. According to Theorem 7.3.10 $\mathcal{M}_1$ and $\mathcal{M}_3$ are embedded in $\mathcal{M}_R$. Hence, $\mathcal{M}_R$ does not have property P due to the choice of $\mathcal{M}_1$, and its word problem is undecidable due to the choice of $\mathcal{M}_3$ and Corollary 7.3.11. On the other hand, the word problem for $\mathcal{M}_R$ is effectively reducible to the problem of deciding property P as we will see in the following. Hence, the latter problem is in fact undecidable.

Let c and d be two new letters, that are not contained in any of the Σ_i considered so far, and let $\Gamma = \Sigma \cup \{c, d\}$. We will describe an effective process that, given two words $u, v \in \Sigma^*$, yields a finite presentation $(\Sigma_4; R_4)$ satisfying the following equivalence:

(*) The monoid $\mathcal{M}_{R_4}$ presented by $(\Sigma_4; R_4)$ has property P if and only if $u \overset{*}{\longleftrightarrow}_R v$.

Let $u, v \in \Sigma^*$. Using the construction of Lemma 3.4.6 we obtain a finite presentation $(\Gamma; R_{u,v})$ such that either $u \overset{*}{\longleftrightarrow}_R v$ and the monoid $\mathcal{M}_{R_{u,v}}$ is trivial, or $u \overset{*}{\not\longleftrightarrow}_R v$ and the monoid $\mathcal{M}_R$ is embedded in $\mathcal{M}_{R_{u,v}}$. Further, define $\Sigma_4 = \Gamma \cup \Sigma_2$ and $R_4 = R_{u,v} \cup R_2$. Then the finite presentation $(\Sigma_4; R_4)$ describes the free product $\mathcal{M}_{R_4}$ of the monoids $\mathcal{M}_{R_{u,v}}$ and $\mathcal{M}_2$. Obviously, the presentation $(\Sigma_4; R_4)$ can be constructed effectively from u and v, since the presentations $(\Sigma; R)$ and $(\Sigma_2; R_2)$ are given in advance.

It remains to verify that the monoid $\mathcal{M}_{R_4}$ presented by $(\Sigma_4; R_4)$ does indeed satisfy equivalence (*). So assume first that $u \overset{*}{\longleftrightarrow}_R v$. Then the monoid $\mathcal{M}_{R_{u,v}}$ is trivial, that is, $\mathcal{M}_{R_{u,v}} \cong \{e\}$, and hence, $\mathcal{M}_{R_4} = \mathcal{M}_{R_{u,v}} * \mathcal{M}_2 \cong \mathcal{M}_2$. Now $\mathcal{M}_2$ having property P, and P being an invariant property imply that $\mathcal{M}_{R_4}$ does have property P. If on the other hand we have $u \overset{*}{\not\longleftrightarrow}_R v$, Lemma 3.4.6 and Theorem 7.3.10 yield the following chain of embeddings: $\mathcal{M}_1 \to \mathcal{M}_R \to \mathcal{M}_{R_{u,v}} \to \mathcal{M}_{R_4}$. Hence, by the choice of $\mathcal{M}_1$, $\mathcal{M}_{R_4}$ does not have property P. Thus, equivalence (*) is satisfied, and the word problem for $\mathcal{M}_R$ has been reduced effectively to the problem of deciding property P.   □7.3.7

7.4   The Free Monoid Problem

All the algebraic properties listed in Definition 7.3.2 are Markov properties, and therefore they are undecidable in general. As with the word problem we can try to overcome the undecidability of these properties by restricting our attention to finite monoid-presentations that satisfy certain additional restrictions. In this section and the next, we present two decidability results of this form.

We begin with the following decision problem **free monoid**:

> **Instance:** *A finite alphabet* Σ, *and a finite string-rewriting system R on* Σ.

> **Question:** *Is the monoid $\mathcal{M}_R$ given through the presentation* $(\Sigma; R)$ *a free monoid?*

We have seen that this problem is undecidable in general, but we do have the following information on presentations of free monoids.

Lemma 7.4.1 *If the monoid $\mathcal{M}_R$ given through the finite presentation* $(\Sigma; R)$ *is free, then there exists a subset Σ_0 of Σ that freely generates this monoid.*

Proof. Let $\Sigma = \{a_1, a_2, \ldots, a_n\}$, and let R be a finite string-rewriting system on Σ such that the monoid $\mathcal{M}_R$ presented by $(\Sigma; R)$ is free. Then it is free of rank m for some $m \leq n$ by the Defect Theorem. Hence, there exists an alphabet $\Gamma = \{b_1, b_2, \ldots, b_m\}$ of cardinality m such that $\mathcal{M}_R = \Sigma^* / {\longleftrightarrow}_R^* \cong \Gamma^*$. So for each $a_i \in \Sigma$, there exists a string $u_i \in \Gamma^*$ such that a_i and u_i represent the same element of $\mathcal{M}_R$. Analogously, for each $b_j \in \Gamma$, there exists a string $v_j \in \Sigma^*$ such that b_j and v_j represent the same element of $\mathcal{M}_R$. Since $\mathcal{M}_R \cong \Gamma^*$, no $b_j \in \Gamma$ represents the identity of $\mathcal{M}_R$, and so $v_j \neq e$, $j = 1, 2, \ldots, m$. Further, the strings $v_j \in \Sigma^*$ can be chosen in such a way that no v_j contains an occurrence of a letter $a_i \in \Sigma$ with $a_i \overset{*}{\longleftrightarrow}_R e$. On the other hand, $u_i = e$ if and only if $a_i \overset{*}{\longleftrightarrow}_R e$, $i = 1, 2, \ldots, n$.

Let $b_j \in \Gamma$, and assume that $v_j = a_{i_1} a_{i_2} \ldots a_{i_k}$ for some letters $a_{i_1}, a_{i_2}, \ldots, a_{i_k} \in \Sigma$. For each $\ell \in \{1, 2, \ldots, k\}$, u_{i_ℓ} represents the same element of $\mathcal{M}_R$ as a_{i_ℓ}. Hence, b_j and the string $u_{i_1} u_{i_2} \ldots u_{i_k} \in \Gamma^*$ represent the same element of $\mathcal{M}_R$. Since $\mathcal{M}_R \cong \Gamma^*$, this implies that $b_j = u_{i_1} u_{i_2} \ldots u_{i_k}$. By the choice of v_j, we have $u_{i_\ell} \neq e$ for all ℓ implying that $k = 1$, that is, $v_j \in \Sigma$.

Take $\Sigma_0 := \{a \in \Sigma \mid \exists b_j \in \Gamma : a = v_j\}$. Then $\Sigma_0 = \{v_j \mid j = 1, 2, \ldots, m\}$ is a subset of Σ that freely generates $\mathcal{M}_R$.   □7.4.1

Now let R be a string-rewriting system on Σ such that the monoid $\mathcal{M}_R$ presented by $(\Sigma; R)$ is free, and let Σ_0 be a subset of Σ that freely generates this monoid. Then, for each $a \in \Sigma$, there is a unique string $u_a \in \Sigma_0^*$ such that $a \overset{*}{\longleftrightarrow}_R u_a$. We define a homomorphism $\varphi : \Sigma^* \to \Sigma_0^*$ by taking $\varphi(a) := u_a$ for all $a \in \Sigma$. Then the following lemma holds.

Lemma 7.4.2 *For all $u, v \in \Sigma^*$, $u \overset{*}{\longleftrightarrow}_R v$ if and only if $\varphi(u) = \varphi(v)$.*

Proof. Since $\varphi(w) \overset{*}{\longleftrightarrow}_R w$ for all $w \in \Sigma^*$, $u \overset{*}{\longleftrightarrow}_R v$ if and only if $\varphi(u) \overset{*}{\longleftrightarrow}_R \varphi(v)$. But $\varphi(u), \varphi(v) \in \Sigma_0^*$, and Σ_0 freely generates $\mathcal{M}_R$ implying that $\varphi(u) \overset{*}{\longleftrightarrow}_R \varphi(v)$ if and only if $\varphi(u) = \varphi(v)$. $\quad\square$7.4.2

Let R be a finite string-rewriting system on Σ such that the monoid $\mathcal{M}_R$ described by the presentation $(\Sigma; R)$ is free. Then there is a subset Σ_0 of Σ such that the monoid $\mathcal{M}_R$ is freely generated by Σ_0, that is, $(\Sigma_0; \emptyset)$ is another presentation of $\mathcal{M}_R$. Hence, by Theorem 7.2.4 there exists a finite sequence of elementary Tietze transformations that transforms the presentation $(\Sigma; R)$ into the presentation $(\Sigma_0; \emptyset)$. In general this finite sequence of Tietze transformations cannot be determined effectively, since the decision problem **free monoid** is undecidable. In the following we will derive a condition for string-rewriting systems such that, whenever R is a string-rewriting system satisfying this condition, then one can effectively construct a finite sequence of Tietze transformations transforming $(\Sigma; R)$ into $(\Sigma_0; \emptyset)$, if $\mathcal{M}_R$ is a free monoid.

For what follows let R be a fixed finite string-rewriting system on Σ, and let $\mathcal{M}$ be the monoid given through the presentation $(\Sigma; R)$. First we perform a kind of normalization of the given presentation $(\Sigma; R)$ by eliminating some of the letters from Σ that are superfluous.

Take $\Sigma_1 := \{a \in \Sigma \mid a \overset{*}{\longleftrightarrow}_R e\}$, let $\Sigma_2 := \Sigma - \Sigma_1$, and let Π_2 denote the **projection** from Σ^* onto Σ_2^*, that is, Π_2 is the homomorphism defined by

$$\Pi_2(a) = \begin{cases} a & \text{if } a \in \Sigma_2, \\ e & \text{if } a \in \Sigma_1. \end{cases}$$

Finally, let $R_1 := \{(\ell_1, r_1) \mid \exists (\ell, r) \in R \text{ such that } \ell_1 = \Pi_2(\ell), r_1 = \Pi_2(r),$ and $\Pi_2(\ell) \neq \Pi_2(r)\}$.

Lemma 7.4.3 *The presentation $(\Sigma_2; R_1)$ defines the monoid $\mathcal{M}$, that is, $\mathcal{M}_R \cong \mathcal{M}$.*

Proof. The presentation $(\Sigma_2; R_1)$ can be obtained from $(\Sigma; R)$ by a finite sequence of elementary Tietze transformations as follows: $(\Sigma; R) \to (\Sigma; R \cup \{(e, a) \mid a \in \Sigma_1\})$ (by $|\Sigma_1|$ transformations of type 1) $\to (\Sigma_2; \{(\Pi_2(\ell), \Pi_2(r)) \mid (\ell, r) \in R\})$ (by $|\Sigma_1|$ transformations of type 4) $\to (\Sigma_2; R_1)$ (by some transformations of type 2 deleting rules of the form (w, w)). $\quad\square$7.4.3

Then $(\Sigma_2; R_1)$ is a finite presentation of $\mathcal{M}$ such that no letter $a \in \Sigma_2$ represents the identity of the monoid $\mathcal{M}$. However, Σ_2 may still contain superfluous letters, since there may exist letters $a, b \in \Sigma_2$ satisfying $a \xleftrightarrow{*}_{R_1} b$. In a second step we want to get rid of at least some of these superfluous letters.

Assume that there are letters $a, b \in \Sigma_2$ such that $(a, b) \in R_1$. Then by applying an elementary Tietze transformation of type 4, we can transform the presentation $(\Sigma_2; R_1)$ into $(\Sigma_2 - \{b\}; R_1')$, where $R_1' := \{(\Psi_b(\ell), \Psi_b(r)) \mid (\ell, r) \in R_1\}$. Here $\Psi_b : \Sigma_2^* \to (\Sigma_2 - \{b\})^*$ is the homomorphism defined by taking $\varphi_b(b) = a$ and $\Psi_b(c) = c$ for all $c \in \Sigma_2 - \{b\}$. Again we can delete all the rules of the form (w, w) from R_1', thus getting a presentation $(\Sigma_2 - \{b\}; R_1'')$ of the monoid $\mathcal{M}$.

By iterating this process we finally get a finite presentation (Σ_3, R_2) of $\mathcal{M}$ satisfying the following conditions:

(i) No letter $a \in \Sigma_3$ represents the identity of the monoid $\mathcal{M}$;

(ii) $R_2 \cap \{(w, w) \mid w \in \Sigma_3^*\} = \emptyset$;

(iii) $R_2 \cap (\Sigma_3 \times \Sigma_3) = \emptyset$.

Notice that $(\Sigma_3; R_2)$ can be constructed effectively from $(\Sigma_2; R_1)$, while the construction of $(\Sigma_2; R_1)$ from $(\Sigma; R)$ requires the feasibility of checking whether or not a given letter from Σ represents the identity of the monoid $\mathcal{M}$.

Finally, we derive a finite presentation $(\Sigma_3; R_3)$ of $\mathcal{M}$ that does not contain any length-increasing rules by taking $R_3 := \{(\ell, r) \mid (\ell, r) \in R_2 \text{ and } |\ell| \geq |r|\} \cup \{(r, \ell) \mid (\ell, r) \in R_2 \text{ and } |\ell| < |r|\}$. Obviously, the presentation $(\Sigma_3; R_3)$ still satisfies conditions (i) to (iii) stated above.

Now assume that the monoid $\mathcal{M}$ is free. What does this assumption tell us about the form of the rules of R_3? From Lemma 7.4.1 we see that under this assumption there exists a subset Σ_0 of Σ_3 that freely generates the monoid $\mathcal{M}$. Let $\varphi : \Sigma_3^* \to \Sigma_0^*$ be the corresponding homomorphism, and let $\Sigma_4 := \Sigma_3 - \Sigma_0$. Since no letter of Σ_3 represents the identity of $\mathcal{M}$, we have $|\varphi(a)| > 0$ for all $a \in \Sigma_3$. Hence, Lemma 7.4.2 implies the following.

Corollary 7.4.4 For all $a \in \Sigma_3$ and $u \in \Sigma_3^*$ with $|u| \geq 2$, if $u \xleftrightarrow{*}_{R_3} a$, then $|u|_a = 0$.

In addition, $|\varphi(a)| > 0$ for all $a \in \Sigma_3$ means that $|\varphi(u)| \geq |u|$ for all $u \in \Sigma_3^*$. By Lemma 7.4.2 we have $u \xleftrightarrow{*}_{R_3} e$ if and only if $\varphi(u) = \varphi(e) = e$. Thus, $u \not\xleftrightarrow{*}_{R_3} e$ for all non-empty strings $u \in \Sigma_3^*$. In particular, this shows the following.

Corollary 7.4.5 $\text{Range}(R_3) \subseteq \Sigma^* - \{e\}$.

Finally, we can derive the following technical result.

Lemma 7.4.6 $\text{Range}(R_3) \cap \Sigma_3 = \Sigma_4$.

Proof. Let $a \in \Sigma_4$. From the definition of φ we conclude that $\varphi(a) \in \Sigma_0^*$ satisfying $\varphi(a) \overset{*}{\longleftrightarrow}_{R_3} a$. Hence, there exist an integer $n \geq 1$ and strings $u_0, u_1, \ldots, u_n \in \Sigma_3^*$ such that $\varphi(a) = u_0 \longleftrightarrow_{R_3} u_1 \longleftrightarrow_{R_3} \ldots \longleftrightarrow_{R_3} u_n = a$. Since $e \notin \text{range}(R_3)$, this implies that $(u, a) \in R_3$ or $(a, u) \in R_3$ for some string $u \in \Sigma_3^*$. But no rule of R_3 is length-increasing, and $R_3 \cap (\Sigma_3 \times \Sigma_3) = \emptyset$ by condition (iii). Hence, we have $(u, a) \in R_3$ for some $u \in \Sigma_3^*$ with $|u| \geq 2$, and thus, $a \in \text{range}(R_3)$.

Assume that $(u, a) \in R_3$ for some letter $a \in \Sigma_0$. From the construction of R_3 we conclude that $u \in \Sigma_3^*$ satisfies $|u| \geq 2$. Since $u \overset{*}{\longleftrightarrow}_{R_3} a$, Lemma 7.4.2 yields $\varphi(u) = \varphi(a)$. Hence, we get $1 = |a| = |\varphi(a)| = |\varphi(u)| \geq |u| \geq 2$, a contradiction. Therefore, $\Sigma_0 \cap \text{range}(R_3) = \emptyset$, that is, $\text{range}(R_3) \cap \Sigma_3 = \Sigma_4$. □7.4.6

Thus, if the monoid M presented by $(\Sigma_3; R_3)$ is free, then a set Σ_0 of free generators of M can be extracted immediately from the given presentation $(\Sigma_3; R_3)$.

We are now going to present an algorithm *DECIDE-FM* that solves the decision problem **free monoid** under the assumption that given a finite presentation $(\Sigma; R)$, we can determine the set $\Sigma_1 = \{a \in \Sigma \mid a \overset{*}{\longleftrightarrow}_R e\}$. After stating the algorithm we will prove its correctness using the results derived so far.

Algorithm 7.4.7 *DECIDE-FM:*

INPUT: A finite alphabet Σ, and a finite string-rewriting system R on Σ;

      begin
(1) $\Sigma_1 := \{a \in \Sigma \mid a \overset{*}{\longleftrightarrow}_R e\}$;
(2) $\Sigma_2 := \Sigma - \Sigma_1$;
(3) $R_1 := \{(\ell_1, r_1) \mid \exists (\ell, r) \in R : \ell_1 = \Pi_2(\ell),\ r_1 = \Pi_2(r),$
           and $\ell_1 \neq r_1\}$;
(4)   **while** $\exists (a, b) \in R_1 : |a| = |b| = 1$ **do**
(5)   **begin** $\Sigma_2 := \Sigma_2 - \{b\}$;
(6) $R_1 := R_1 - \{(a, b)\}$;
(7)   substitute each occurrence of b in a rule of R_1 by a;
(8) $R_1 := R_1 - \{(\ell, r) \in R_1 \mid \ell = r\}$
        end;
(9) $\Sigma_3 := \Sigma_2$;
(10) $R_3 := \{(\ell, r) \mid (\ell, r) \in R_1 \text{ and } |\ell| \geq |r|\} \cup \{(r, \ell) \mid (\ell, r) \in R_1$
          and $|\ell| < |r|\}$;
(11)   **if** $e \in \text{range}(R_3)$ **then** REJECT;
(12) $\Sigma_4 := \Sigma_3 \cap \text{range}(R_3)$;
(13) $\Sigma_0 := \Sigma_3 - \Sigma_4$;
(14)   **while** $\Sigma_4 \neq \emptyset$ **do**

(15)   **begin** choose a letter $a \in \Sigma_4$ together with a rule
             $(u, a) \in R_3$;
(16)   **if** $|u|_a > 0$ **then** REJECT;
(17) $\Sigma_4 := \Sigma_4 - \{a\}$;
(18) $R_3 := R_3 - \{(u, a)\}$;
(19)   Substitute each occurrence of a in a rule of R_3 by
             the string u;
         end;
(20)   **if** $R_3 \subseteq \{(w, w) \mid w \in \Sigma_0^*\}$ **then** ACCEPT **else** REJECT
    end.

Lemma 7.4.8 *Algorithm DECIDE-FM accepts on input $(\Sigma; R)$, where R is a finite string-rewriting system on Σ such that the set $\Sigma_1 = \{a \in \Sigma \mid a \longleftrightarrow_R^* e\}$ can be determined effectively if and only if the monoid $\mathcal{M}$ presented by $(\Sigma; R)$ is a free monoid.*

Proof. Let Σ be a finite alphabet, and let R be a finite string-rewriting system on Σ such that the set $\Sigma_1 = \{a \in \Sigma \mid a \longleftrightarrow_R^* e\}$ can be determined effectively. By executing statements (1) to (10) *DECIDE-FM* derives a presentation $(\Sigma_3; R_3)$ satisfying:

(i) $\forall a \in \Sigma_3 : a \not\longleftrightarrow_{R_3}^* e$,

(ii) $R_3 \cap \{(w, w) \mid w \in \Sigma_3^*\} = \emptyset$,

(iii) $R_3 \cap (\Sigma_3 \times \Sigma_3) = \emptyset$,

(iv) $\forall (\ell, r) \in R_3 : |\ell| \geq |r|$.

From Lemma 7.4.3 and the considerations following it we see that $(\Sigma_3; R_3)$ is just another presentation of the monoid $\mathcal{M} := \mathcal{M}_R$.

If $\mathcal{M}$ is a free monoid, then by Corollary 7.4.5, $e \notin \text{range}(R_3)$. Thus, *DECIDE-FM* does not reject in line (11). Further, by Lemma 7.4.1 $\mathcal{M}$ is freely generated by some subset Σ_0 of Σ_3. We see from Lemma 7.4.6 that $\Sigma_0 = \Sigma_3 - (\Sigma_3 \cap \text{range}(R_3))$.

Let $a \in \Sigma_4 := \Sigma_3 \cap \text{range}(R_3)$. Then there is a rule of the form (u, a) in R_3. Choose one such rule. Because of (iii) and (iv) we have $|u| \geq 2$, and so by Corollary 7.4.4 $|u|_a = 0$. Hence, *DECIDE-FM* does not reject in line (16). In lines (17) to (19) *DECIDE-FM* performs a Tietze transformation of type 4, thus deleting the letter a and the rule (u, a) from the presentation $(\Sigma_3; R_3)$.

Let $(\Sigma_3'; R_3')$ denote the presentation of $\mathcal{M}$ this Tietze transformation yields. Then for each $b \in \Sigma_4' := \Sigma_4 - \{a\}$, R_3' contains at least one rule of the form (v, b) with $v \in \Sigma_3'^*$ and $|v| \geq 2$. Hence, $v \in \Sigma_3'^* = (\Sigma_0 \cup \Sigma_4')^* \subseteq (\Sigma_0 \cup \Sigma_4)^* = \Sigma_3^*$, and $v \longleftrightarrow_{R_3}^* b$ implying that $|v|_b = 0$. Thus, *DECIDE-FM* performs the loop in lines (14) to (19) until $\Sigma_4 = \emptyset$ without rejecting in line (16).

When this loop is left, the presentation of $\mathcal{M}$ at this point is $(\Sigma_0; R')$ for some $R' \subseteq \Sigma_0^* \times \Sigma_0^*$. Since $\mathcal{M}$ is freely generated by Σ_0, this means that $R' \subseteq \{(w, w) \mid w \in \Sigma_0^*\}$, that is, $DECIDE\text{-}FM$ accepts.

On the other hand, if $DECIDE\text{-}FM$ accepts, then the presentation $(\Sigma_3; R_3)$ is transformed by $DECIDE\text{-}FM$ into a presentation of the form $(\Sigma_0; R')$ for some subset Σ_0 of Σ_3 and some string-rewriting system $R' \subseteq \{(w, w) \mid w \in \Sigma_0^*\}$. During this transformation $DECIDE\text{-}FM$ only applies Tietze transformations to presentations of $\mathcal{M}$ starting with $(\Sigma_3; R_3)$. Hence, $(\Sigma_0; R')$ is a presentation of $\mathcal{M}$ showing that $\mathcal{M}$ is the free monoid generated by Σ_0. $\square$7.4.8

Let **RV-uniform-word-problem** denote the following restricted version of the uniform word problem:

Instance: *A finite presentation $(\Sigma; R)$, and a string $u \in \Sigma^*$.*

Question: *Does $u \xleftrightarrow{*}_R e$ hold?*

Obviously, Lemma 7.4.8 yields the following result.

Theorem 7.4.9 *The decision problem* **free monoid** *is effectively reducible to the problem* **RV-uniform-word-problem**.

Of course, the complexity of the reduction given by algorithm $DECIDE\text{-}FM$ depends on the lengths of the words created by $DECIDE\text{-}FM$ in line (19). As it turns out these words may have exponential length. We conclude this discussion with an example of a non-trivial presentation of a free monoid.

Examples 7.4.10 *Let $\Sigma = \{a, b, c, d_1, \ldots, d_{n+1}, f, g, h_1, h_2, h_3\}$ for some $n \geq 1$, and let $R = \{(a^2ba^2, d_1), (bd_nc, f), (d_2d_{n+1}c, h_3g), (d_nf, g), (a^2ba, h_1),$ $(aba, h_2), (h_1h_2^2a, h_3)\} \cup \{(d_ibd_i, d_{i+1}) \mid i = 1, 2, \ldots, n\}$. Then R already satisfies the conditions (i) to (iv) listed in the proof of Lemma 7.4.8.*

Now $\Sigma_0 = \{a, b, c\}$ and $\Sigma_4 = \{d_1, \ldots, d_{n+1}, f, g, h_1, h_2, h_3\}$. Define $\varphi : \Sigma^* \to \Sigma_0^*$ by $\varphi(a) = a, \varphi(b) = b, \varphi(c) = c, \varphi(d_1) = a^2ba^2, \varphi(d_{i+1}) = \varphi(d_i) b\varphi(d_i)$ for $i = 1, 2, \ldots, n, \varphi(f) = b\varphi(d_n)c, \varphi(g) = \varphi(d_n)\varphi(f), \varphi(h_1) = a^2ba, \varphi(h_2) = aba$, and $\varphi(h_3) = \varphi(h_1)(\varphi(h_2))^2a$.

Applying $DECIDE\text{-}FM$ to the input $(\Sigma; R)$ yields the presentation $(\Sigma_0; \{(\varphi(d_2)\varphi(d_{n+1})c, \varphi(h_3)\varphi(g))\})$. Expanding $\varphi(d_2)\varphi(d_{n+1})c$, we have $a^2ba^2ba^2ba^2\varphi(d_n)b\varphi(d_n)c = \varphi(h_1)(\varphi(h_2))^2a\varphi(d_n)\varphi(f) = \varphi(h_3)\ \varphi(g)$. Thus the monoid $\mathcal{M}$ presented by $(\Sigma; R)$ is free on Σ_0, and $DECIDE\text{-} FM$ accepts. In particular, φ is the homomorphism that, for each string $w \in \Sigma^*$, gives the corresponding string from Σ_0^*. It is easy to see that, for all $i = 1, 2, \ldots, n+1, |\varphi(d_i)| = 6 \cdot 2^{i-1} - 1, |\varphi(f)| = 6 \cdot 2^{n-1} + 1$, and $|\varphi(g)| = 6 \cdot 2^n$. So in fact, the letters f and g do represent extremely long strings from Σ_0^*.

7.5   The Group Problem

The following decision problem will be refered to as the **group problem**:

Instance: *A finite alphabet Σ and a finite string-rewriting system R on Σ.*

Question: *Is the monoid $\mathcal{M}_R$ given by the presentation $(\Sigma; R)$ a group?*

It is shown that the group problem is decidable for rather general classes of monoid-presentations; in particular, the free-monoid problem and the group problem are decidable for the class of finite convergent presentations.

Let R be a finite string-rewriting system on Σ. Then the monoid $\mathcal{M}_R$ given through this presentation is a group if and only if, for each string $w \in \Sigma^*$, there exists some string $w' \in \Sigma^*$ such that $ww' \overset{*}{\longleftrightarrow}_R e$. Obviously, this is equivalent to saying that for each letter $a \in \Sigma$, there exists some string $u_a \in \Sigma^*$ such that $au_a \overset{*}{\longleftrightarrow}_R e$. In general, it is undecidable whether or not such strings $u_a(a \in \Sigma)$ exist, since the **group problem** is undecidable. However, we will see in the following that given a finite presentation $(\Sigma; R)$, one can effectively determine reasonable candidates for these strings. It then remains to check whether they actually satisfy the above congruences.

Let $(\Sigma; R)$ be a finite presentation. As a first step we define a sequence $\Sigma_1, \Sigma_2, \ldots, \Sigma_i, \ldots$ of subsets of Σ inductively by taking

$$\Sigma_1 := \{a \in \Sigma \mid \exists u, v \in \Sigma^* : (uav, e) \in R \text{ or } (e, uav) \in R\} \quad \text{and}$$
$$\Sigma_{i+1} := \{a \in \Sigma - \Sigma_i \mid \exists u, v \in \Sigma^* \exists w \in \Sigma_i^* : (uav, w) \in R \quad \text{or}$$
$$(w, uav) \in R\} \cup \Sigma_i.$$

Obviously we have $\Sigma_1 \subseteq \Sigma_2 \subseteq \ldots \subseteq \Sigma_i \subseteq \Sigma_{i+1} \subseteq \ldots \subseteq \Sigma$. Furthermore, if $\Sigma_i = \Sigma_{i+1}$ for some $i \geq 1$, then $\Sigma_i = \Sigma_{i+k}$ for all $k \geq 0$. Since Σ is finite, we conclude that the above chain of inclusions is finite. Thus, it suffices to construct $\Sigma_1, \Sigma_2, \ldots, \Sigma_n$, where n is the cardinality $|\Sigma|$ of Σ, and this can be done effectively.

Now for each letter $a \in \Sigma_n$, we determine a string $u_a \in \Sigma^*$ as follows. If $a \in \Sigma_1$, then $(uav, e) \in R$ or $(e, uav) \in R$ for some strings $u, v \in \Sigma^*$. We choose one such rule, and take $u_a := vu$. If $a \in \Sigma_{i+1} - \Sigma_i$ for some $i \geq 1$, then $(uav, w) \in R$ or $(w, uav) \in R$ for some strings $u, v \in \Sigma^*$ and $w \in \Sigma_i^*$. Again we choose one such rule. Let $w = a_{i_1} a_{i_2} \ldots a_{i_m} \in \Sigma_i^*$. Then strings $u_{a_{i_1}}, \ldots, u_{a_{i_m}} \in \Sigma^*$ have already been chosen. Now we take $u_a := vu_{a_{i_m}} \ldots u_{a_{i_2}} u_{a_{i_1}} u$. Notice that in this way, for each letter $a \in \Sigma_n$, a corresponding string u_a is determined effectively.

Lemma 7.5.1 *The monoid $\mathcal{M}_R$ given through the presentation $(\Sigma; R)$ is a group if and only if the following two conditions are satisfied:*

(i) $\Sigma_n = \Sigma$, *where* $n = |\Sigma|$;

(ii) $au_a \overset{*}{\longleftrightarrow}_R e$ *for all* $a \in \Sigma_n$.

Proof. If conditions (i) and (ii) are satisfied, then the monoid $\mathcal{M}_R$ is obviously a group. Thus, it remains to prove the converse implication. So assume that $\mathcal{M}_R$ is a group.

Let $a \in \Sigma$. Since $\mathcal{M}_R$ is a group, there exists a string $w \in \Sigma^*$ such that $aw = v_k \longleftrightarrow_R v_{k-1} \longleftrightarrow_R \ldots \longleftrightarrow_R v_1 \longleftrightarrow_R e$. Since $v_1 \longleftrightarrow_R e$, we have $(v_1, e) \in R$ or $(e, v_1) \in R$ implying $v_1 \in \Sigma_1^*$. For each $i \geq 1$, $v_{i+1} \longleftrightarrow_R v_i$ means that $v_{i+1} = xuy$ and $v_i = xvy$ for some strings $x, y, u, v \in \Sigma^*$ with $(u, v) \in R$ or $(v, u) \in R$. If $v_i \in \Sigma_i^*$, we have $v \in \Sigma_i^*$, which in turn gives $u \in \Sigma_{i+1}^*$. Hence, if $v_i \in \Sigma_i^*$, then $v_{i+1} \in \Sigma_{i+1}^*$. By induction this implies that $aw = v_k \in \Sigma_k^*$, that is, $a \in \Sigma_k$. But $\Sigma_1 \subseteq \Sigma_2 \subseteq \ldots \subseteq \Sigma_n = \cup_{j \geq 1} \Sigma_j \subseteq \Sigma$, and so we actually have $a \in \Sigma_n$. Thus, condition (i) is satisfied.

In addition, we must show that condition (ii) also holds. To do so, we prove by induction on i, that for each $i \geq 1$ and each $a \in \Sigma_i$, $au_a \overset{*}{\longleftrightarrow}_R e$ holds. Let $a \in \Sigma_1$. Then $u_a = vu$, where $u, v \in \Sigma^*$ are strings such that $(uav, e) \in R$ or $(e, uav) \in R$. This gives $uav \overset{*}{\longleftrightarrow}_R e$, which in turn implies $au_a = avu \overset{*}{\longleftrightarrow}_R e$, since $\mathcal{M}_R$ is a group. If $a \in \Sigma_{i+1} - \Sigma_i$, then $u_a = vxu$, where $u, v \in \Sigma^*$ and $x = u_{a_{i_m}} \ldots u_{a_{i_2}} u_{a_{i_1}}$ with $a_{i_1}, a_{i_2}, \ldots, a_{i_m} \in \Sigma_i$ such that $(uav, a_{i_1} a_{i_2} \ldots a_{i_m}) \in R$ or $(a_{i_1} a_{i_2} \ldots a_{i_m}, uav) \in R$. Hence, $uavx \longleftrightarrow_R a_{i_1} a_{i_2} \ldots a_{i_m} x = a_{i_1} a_{i_2} \ldots a_{i_m} u_{a_{i_m}} \ldots u_{a_{i_2}} u_{a_{i_1}} \overset{*}{\longleftrightarrow}_R e$ by the induction hypothesis. This implies that $au_a = avxu \overset{*}{\longleftrightarrow}_R e$, since $\mathcal{M}_R$ is a group. $\qquad \square 7.5.1$

Since the set Σ_n and the strings u_a for $a \in \Sigma_n$ can be determined effectively, Lemma 7.5.1 induces the following result.

Theorem 7.5.2 *The* **group problem** *is effectively reducible to the problem* **RV-uniform-word-problem**.

Given a finite presentation $(\Sigma; R)$, the set Σ_n can be determined in polynomial time. Thus, the complexity of this reduction depends on the lengths of the strings $u_a (a \in \Sigma_n)$. As it turns out these strings may have exponential length. We close this consideration with an example of a monoid presentation defining a group.

Examples 7.5.3 *Let* $\Sigma = \{a, b_1, b_2, \ldots, b_{m+1}\}$ *for some* $m \geq 1$, *and let* $R = \{(b_1 a, e), (ab_1, e)\} \cup \{(b_i^2, b_{i+1}) \mid i = 1, 2, \ldots, m\}$. *Then we have* $\Sigma_1 = \{a, b_1\}$, $\Sigma_2 = \{a, b_1, b_2\}, \ldots, \Sigma_{m+1} = \{a, b_1, b_2, \ldots, b_{m+1}\} = \Sigma$. *Further, we get* $u_a = b_1, u_{b_1} = a, u_{b_2} = a^2, \ldots, u_{b_{m+1}} = a^{2^m}$. *Obviously, the monoid* $\mathcal{M}_R$ *presented by* $(\Sigma; R)$ *is a group. But* $|u_{b_i}| = 2^{i-1}$ *for* $i = 1, 2, \ldots, m + 1$, *that is, the candidate* $u_{b_{m+1}}$ *for the inverse of the letter* b_{m+1} *is of exponential length.* $\qquad \square 7.5.3$

So far we have seen that both the problems **free monoid** and **group** are effectively reducible to the problem **RV-uniform-word-problem**. However, all these problems are undecidable in general.

Now assume that $\mathcal{C}$ is a class of finite presentations such that there exists an algorithm $A(\mathcal{C})$ satisfying

$$A(\mathcal{C})((\Sigma; R), u) = \begin{cases} 1 & \text{if } u \xleftrightarrow{*}_R e, \\ 0 & \text{if } u \not\xleftrightarrow{*}_R e, \end{cases}$$

for all presentations $(\Sigma; R)$ from $\mathcal{C}$ and all strings $u \in \Sigma^*$, that is, $A(\mathcal{C})$ solves the problem **RV-uniform-word-problem** when restricted to $\mathcal{C}$. Then Theorem 7.4.9 and Theorem 7.5.2 yield the following result.

Theorem 7.5.4 *Let $\mathcal{C}$ be a class of finite presentations as described above. Then the problems **free monoid** and **group** are decidable, when they are restricted to presentations from $\mathcal{C}$.*

Lemma 7.4.8 shows that in order to decide whether or not the monoid $\mathcal{M}_R$ given through the presentation $(\Sigma; R)$ from $\mathcal{C}$ is a free monoid, we must determine the set $\Sigma_1 = \{a \in \Sigma \mid a \xleftrightarrow{*}_R e\}$. This is the only point, where algorithm $A(\mathcal{C})$ is applied. Similarly, given a presentation $(\Sigma; R)$ from $\mathcal{C}$, we can effectively determine the subset Σ_n of Σ, and for each letter $a \in \Sigma$, we can compute a candidate u_a for the right-inverse of a modulo R. Now algorithm $A(\mathcal{C})$ is only used to check whether or not the string u_a actually is a right-inverse of a modulo R, that is, whether or not $a u_a \xleftrightarrow{*}_R e$ holds.

As an application let us consider the class $\mathcal{C}_c$ of all presentations of the form $(\Sigma; R)$, where R is a finite noetherian and confluent string-rewriting system on Σ. Obviously, the problem **RV-uniform-word-problem** is decidable for this class. Hence, we can conclude the following from Theorem 7.5.4.

Corollary 7.5.5 *The problems **free monoid** and **group** are decidable, when they are restricted to presentations involving finite, noetherian and confluent string-rewriting systems.*

7.6   Bibliographic Remarks

In a paper dealing with presentations of fundamental groups of closed orientable surfaces, Dehn [Deh11] introduced the following three fundamental decision problems: the **word problem**, the **conjugacy problem**, and the **isomorphism problem**. Using the transformations introduced by Tietze [Tie08] it is not hard to see that for finitely generated groups, the decidability or the undecidability of these problems, which are defined in terms of a fixed presentation, is in fact a property of the group presented (see Corollary 7.2.6). These problems have been generalized to semigroups and monoids, and various decidability and undecidability results have been derived during the 1940's and 1950's. Here we mention Markov's undecidability result [Mar51, Mos52], presented as Theorem 7.3.7. As a general reference for combinatorial semigroup theory, we would like to point the interested reader to Lallement's book [Lal79]. Adjan [Adj66] is another very interesting, though very technical, treatment of many combinatorial aspects of semigroup and group theory. Concerning the very active field of combinatorial group theory, we point to the two standard monographs in this field: [MKS76, LySc77]. In the following we will restrict our attention to the developments since the late 1970s regarding the problem of deciding algebraic properties of monoids (and groups) that are given through certain classes of finite string-rewriting systems.

For groups the word problem reduces to the conjugacy problem, that is, if the conjugacy problem for a group $\mathcal{G}$ is decidable, then so is the word problem for $\mathcal{G}$. For monoids in general, the situation is different. First of all, we have various different notions of conjugacy in monoids.

Let $(\Sigma; R)$ be a monoid-presentation. Two strings $u, v \in \Sigma^*$ are called **cyclically equal** ($u \approx_R v$) if there exist strings $x, y \in \Sigma^*$ such that $u \leftrightarrow_R^* xy$ and $v \leftrightarrow_R^* yx$. Cyclic equality is a reflexive and symmetric relation that need not be transitive. The strings $u, v \in \Sigma^*$ are called **left-conjugate** ($u \sim_R^L v$), if there exists a string $w \in \Sigma^*$ such that $uw \leftrightarrow_R^* wv$, and they are **conjugate** if $u \sim_R^L v$ and $v \sim_R^L u$. Left-conjugacy is reflexive and transitive, but in general not symmetric. Thus, these notions, which coincide in case the monoid $\mathcal{M}$ presented by $(\Sigma; R)$ is a free monoid or a group, are in general different. In fact, the problem of cyclic equality, the left-conjugacy problem and the word problem are algorithmically independent for finitely presented monoids [Osi73].

We have seen that the word problem for a monoid $\mathcal{M}$ is decidable, whenever $\mathcal{M}$ has a presentation by some finite, noetherian, and confluent string-rewriting system. What can we say in this situation about the variants of the conjugacy problem introduced above? In [Ott84b] it is shown that cyclic equality and conjugacy coincide for monoids that are presented by finite special and confluent string-rewriting systems. In addition, it is shown that these problems are decidable in this setting. Recently, these results have been extended by Zhang [Zha91] who proves that for all monoids that are presented by special string-rewriting systems the various notions of conjugacy coincide, and that the conjugacy problem for such a monoid is decidable if and only if the conjugacy problem for the group of units of this monoid is decidable. On the other hand, for monoids that are presented by finite, noetherian and confluent string-rewriting systems, the conjugacy problem is undecidable in general [NaOt86]. The uniform version of the conjugacy problem for finite, length-reducing and confluent string-rewriting systems is NP-complete [NOW84], while for a fixed finite, length-reducing and confluent string-rewriting system this problem can be solved nondeterministically in linear time [NaOt85]. Contrasting this result it is shown in [NaOt86] that there exists a finite, length-reducing and confluent string-rewriting system for which the problem of deciding cyclic equality is undecidable. Finally, when we restrict our attention to monoids that are presented by finite, monadic, and confluent string-rewriting systems, then the uniform versions of the left-conjugacy and the conjugacy problems become tractable, that is, decidable in polynomial time [NaOt89]. However, it is still an open problem whether or not cyclic equality is decidable for all finite, monadic, and confluent string-rewriting systems.

While the conjugacy problem asks whether certain given elements have a particular property, many decision problems asking about algebraic properties of finitely presented monoids like the problems **free monoid** and **group** have also received much attention. One of these problems is the problem of **cancellativity**. It asks whether a monoid given through a finite presentation $(\Sigma; R)$ is **(left-, right-) cancellative**. Since the property of being (left-, right-) cancellative is a Markov property, this problem is undecidable in general (Corollary 7.3.8). Narendran and Ó'Dúnlaing have investigated this problem for the class of presentations involving finite, length-reducing and confluent string-rewriting systems [NaÓ'Dú89]. They proved that even in this restricted setting this problem remains undecidable in general. It is only for finite, monadic and confluent systems that it becomes decidable [NaÓ'Dú89]; in fact, then it becomes even tractable [NaOt89]. In [Ott86c] two problems are investigated that are closely related to cancellativity. Actually, these problems can be seen as encodings of the problem of unification modulo an equational theory. As for cancellativity these problems are undecidable for finite, length-reducing and confluent string-rewriting systems in general, and they become decidable when being restricted to the class of finite, monadic and confluent systems. Again for the latter class they are even tractable [NaOt89].

The problem of deciding whether a monoid is free was considered by Book [Boo83]. For a cancellative monoid freeness can be expressed through a linear sentence, and thus for finite, monadic, and confluent systems freeness can be decided by the algorithm presented in the proof of Theorem 4.3.1 provided it is already established that the monoid presented is cancellative. In [Ott86a] it was then shown that the problem **free monoid** becomes decidable when it is restricted to presentations that involve finite, length-reducing and confluent string-rewriting systems. The technique developed there was then extended in [Ott86b] in the way presented here (Theorem 7.4.9). The problem **group** was first solved in [Boo82b] for the class of finite, monadic, and confluent systems. In fact, the following more general problem was shown there to be tractable:

Instance: *A finite, monadic, and confluent string-rewriting system R on some alphabet Σ, and a finite subset $U \subset \Sigma^*$.*

Question: *Is the submonoid of M_R that is generated by U a group?*

The solution to the problem **group** presented here (Theorem 7.5.2) is from [Ott86b]. On the other hand it has been shown recently that this problem remains undecidable when it is restricted to presentations involving finite special string-rewriting systems [NÓO91]. This is very interesting since the original proof of Markov's undecidability result, which is essentially the one presented here, rests on the construction described in Lemma 3.4.6, and this construction does not preserve the property of being a finite special system. In fact, it can be shown that all Markov properties remain undecidable when they are restricted to monoids presented by finite special string-rewriting systems [Zha94].

Finally, the problems of deciding whether the monoid given through a finite presentation $(\Sigma; R)$ contains a non-trivial idempotent or whether it contains a non-trivial element of finite order have been shown to be decidable when the systems R considered are finite, monadic and confluent [Ott85]. Later these results have been extended to all finite, length-reducing and confluent systems R, and it has been shown that they are in fact tractable in this setting [NaOt88a].

All the results mentioned so far can be seen as partial answers to the following general question: What is the *algorithmic power* of a particular class of finite string-rewriting systems? Since finite string-rewriting systems are a way to present monoids and groups, it is natural to ask for an algebraic characterization for those monoids (or groups) that can be presented through the systems of a particular class. This problem can be described through the following general question: What is the *descriptive power* of a particular class of finite string-rewriting systems? Concerning this problem there have been many investigations. Most results obtained are however about groups.

Cochet [Coc76] has shown that a group G has a presentation (Σ, R), where R is a finite, special and confluent system, if and only if the group G is the free product of finitely many (finite or infinite) cyclic groups. Squier [Squ87a] has investigated the class of monoids that can be presented by this class of string-rewriting systems. He proved that the group of units of a monoid that has a presentation of this form has itself a presentation of this form. However, an algebraic characterization for this class of monoids has not yet been obtained.

On the other hand, it has been shown that a group G has a presentation $(\Sigma; R)$, where R is a finite, monadic and confluent string-rewriting system on Σ such that each letter from Σ has an inverse of length one, or the left-hand side of each rule of R has length 2, if and only if G is a **plain** group, that is, G is the free product of a free group of finite rank and finitely many finite groups [AvMa83, AMO86]. These groups have been receiving attention since Haring-Smith [Har83] charactized them in terms of language-theoretical properties of finite presentations. It has been conjectured that by finite, monadic and confluent string-rewriting systems only plain groups can be presented [Gil84], but this conjecture is still open.

However, it has been shown that with finite, length-reducing and confluent systems, only a proper subclass of the **context-free groups** can be presented [Die87, MaOt88a, MaOt88b]. Here the group G presented by $(\Sigma; R)$ is called **context-free** if the congruence class $[e]_R$ is a context-free language. Analogously, the class of **regular groups** can be considered. It is known that a group is regular if and only if it is a finite group [Ani71], and the context-free groups have received much attention [AnSe75]. Finally, Muller and Schupp [MuSc83] succeeded in giving an algebraic characterization for the class of context-free groups. They showed that a finitely generated group is context-free if and only if it is **virtually free**, a result which was completed through a technical result of Dunwoody [Dun85]. On the other, Autebert, Boasson and Senizergues [ABS87] proved that a group is context-free if and only if it has a presentation through some finite monadic string-rewriting system R that is **e-confluent**, that is, confluent on the congruence class $[e]_R$.

Finally, Squier [Squ87b] established that there are finitely presented monoids and groups with decidable word problems that cannot be presented by any finite, noetherian and confluent string-rewriting systems by showing that each monoid that admits such a presentation must satisfy the homological finiteness condition FP_3. In fact, all these monoids must already satisfy the condition FP_∞ [Kob90].

A detailed account of the results on the descriptive power of various classes of finite string-rewriting systems can be found in [MaOt89]. Further, algorithmic properties of finite string-rewriting systems that are special or monadic and that are only confluent on certain congruence classes have been investigated in several papers (see, for example, [MaOt91, OtZh91]). However, we must refer the reader to the references for these results since discussing these topics here would surely exceed the space available.

References

[Adj66]   S.I. Adjan, *Defining Relations and Algorithmic Problems for Groups and Semigroups*, Proc. Steklov Institute Mathematics 85, American Mathematical Society, Providence, RI, 1966.

[Ani71]   A.V. Anissimov, Group languages, *Cybernetics* 7 (1971), 594–601.

[AnSe75]   A.V. Anissimov and F.D. Seifert, Zur algebraischen Charakteristik der durch kontext-freie Sprachen definierten Gruppen, *Elektronische Informationsverarbeitung und Kybernetik* 11 (1975), 695–702.

[ABS87]   J.-M. Autebert, L. Boasson, and G. Senizergues, Groups and NTS languages, *J. Computer System Sciences* 35 (1987), 243–267.

[AvMa83]   J. Avenhaus and K. Madlener, On groups defined by monadic Thue systems, in *Algebra, Combinatorics and Logic in Computer Science*, Proc. Colloquium Mathematical Society, Janos Bolyai 42, Hungary (1983), 63–71.

[AMO86]   J. Avenhaus, K. Madlener, and F. Otto, Groups presented by finite two-monadic Church-Rosser Thue systems, *Transactions American Mathematical Society* 297 (1986), 427–443.

[Bau81]   G. Bauer, *Zur Darstellung von Monoiden durch konfluente Regelsysteme*, Doctoral Dissertation, Universität Kaiserslautern, Kaiserslautern, Germany, 1981.

[BaOt84]   G. Bauer and F. Otto, Finite complete rewriting systems and the complexity of the word problem, *Acta Informatica* 21 (1984), 521–540.

[Ber77]   J. Berstel, Congruences plus que parfaites et langages algébriques, *Seminaire d'Informatique Théorique*, Institute de Programmation (1976–77), 123–147.

[Ber79]   J. Berstel, *Transductions and Context-free Languages*, Teubner Studienbücher, Stuttgart, Germany, 1979.

[BlLo83]   W. Bledsoe and D. Loveland (eds.), *Automated Theorem Proving: After 25 Years*, Contemporary Mathematics Vol. 29, American Mathematical Society, Providence, RI, 1983.

176   References

[Boo69]   R. Book, *Grammars with Time Functions*, Ph.D. Dissertation, Harvard University, Cambridge, MA, 1969.

[Boo82a]   R. Book, Confluent and other types of Thue systems, *J. Association Computing Machinery* 29 (1982), 171–182.

[Boo82b]   R. Book, When is a monoid a group? The Church-Rosser case is tractable, *Theoretical Computer Science* 18 (1982), 325–331.

[Boo83]   R. Book, Decidable sentences of Church-Rosser congruences, *Theoretical Computer Science* 24 (1983), 301–312.

[Boo84]   R. Book, Homogeneous Thue systems and the Church-Rosser property, *Discrete Mathematics* 48 (1984), 137–145.

[Boo92]   R. Book, A note on confluent Thue systems, in K.U. Schulz (ed.), *Word Equations and Related Topics, Lecture Notes in Computer Science* 572, Springer-Verlag, Berlin, Heidelberg, 1992, 231–236.

[BJMO'DW81] R. Book, M. Jantzen, B. Monien, C. Ó'Dúnlaing, and C. Wrathall, On the complexity of word problems in certain Thue systems, in J. Gruska and M. Chytil (eds.), *Mathematical Foundations of Computer Science, Lecture Notes in Computer Science* 118, Springer-Verlag, Berlin, Heidelberg, 1981, 216–223.

[BJW82]   R. Book, M. Jantzen, and C. Wrathall, Monadic Thue systems, *Theoretical Computer Science* 19 (1982), 231–251.

[BoLi87]   R. Book and H.-N. Liu, Rewriting systems and word problems in a free partially commutative monoid, *Information Processing Letters* 26 (1987), 29–32.

[BoÓ'Dú81a]   R. Book and C.Ó'Dúnlaing, Thue congruences and the Church-Rosser property, *Semigroup Forum* 22 (1981), 367–379.

[BoÓ'Dú81b]   R. Book and C.Ó'Dúnlaing, Testing for the Church-Rosser property, *Theoretical Computer Science* 16 (1981), 223–229.

[BoOt85a]   R. Book and F. Otto, Cancellation rules and extended word problems, *Information Processing Letters* 20 (1985), 5–11.

[BoOt85b]   R. Book and F. Otto, On the security of name-stamp protocols, *Theoretical Computer Science* 39 (1985), 319–325.

[BoOt85c]   R. Book and F. Otto, On the verifiability of two-party algebraic protocols, *Theoretical Computer Science* 40 (1985), 101–130.

[Buc87]   B. Buchberger, History and basic features of the critical-pair/completion procedure, *J. Symbolic Computation* 3 (1987), 3–38.

[CaFo69]   P. Cartier and D. Foata, *Problèmes Combinatoires de Commutation et Rèarrangements, Lecture Notes in Mathematics* 85, Springer-Verlag, Berlin, Heidelberg, 1969.

[ChRo39]   A. Church and J. Rosser, Some properties of conversion, *Transactions American Mathematical Society* 39 (1939), 472–482.

[Coc76]   Y. Cochet, Church-Rosser congruences on free semigroups, *Proc. Colloquium Mathematical Society Janos Bolyai: Algebraic Theory of Semigroups* 20 (1976), 51–60.

[Cum83]   L. Cummings (ed.), *Combinatorics on Words: Progress and Perspectives*, Academic Press, Don Mills, Ontario, Canada, 1983.

[Dav58]   M. Davis, *Computability and Unsolvability*, McGraw-Hill, 1958. Reprinted by Dover, New York, 1982.

[Deh11]   M. Dehn, Über unendliche diskontinuierliche Gruppen, *Mathematische Annalen* 71 (1911), 116–144.

[Der82]   N. Dershowitz, Orderings for term-rewriting systems, *Theoretical Computer Science* 17 (1982), 279–301.

[Der87]   N. Dershowitz, Termination of rewriting, *J. Symbolic Computation* 3 (1987), 69–116.

[DeJo90]   N. Dershowitz and J.-P. Jouannaud, Rewrite systems, in J. van Leeuwen (ed.), *Handbook of Theoretical Computer Science, Volume B: Formal Models and Semantics*, Elsevier, Amsterdam, 1990, 243–320.

[DeMa79]   N. Dershowitz and Z. Manna, Proving termination with multiset orderings, *Communications Association Computing Machinery* 22 (1979), 465–476.

178   References

[Die86]   V. Diekert, Complete semi-Thue systems for abelian groups, *Theoretical Computer Science* 44 (1986), 199–208.

[Die87]   V. Diekert, Some remarks on Church-Rosser Thue presentations, in F.J. Brandenburg, G. Vital-Naquet, and M. Wirsing (eds.), *Proc. STACS 87, Lecture Notes in Computer Science* 247, Springer-Verlag, Berlin, Heidelberg, 1987, 272–285.

[DoYa83]   D. Dolev and A. Yao, On the security of public key protocols, *IEEE Transactions Information Theory*, IT-29 (1983), 198–208.

[Dun85]   M.J. Dunwoody, The accessibility of finitely presented groups, *Inventiones Mathematicae* 81 (1985), 449–457.

[Gil79]   R. Gilman, Presentations of groups and monoids, *J. Algebra* 57 (1979), 544-554.

[Gil84]   R. Gilman, Computations with rational subsets of confluent groups, in J. Fitch (ed.), *Proc. EUROSAM 84, Lecture Notes in Computer Science* 174, Springer-Verlag, Berlin, Heidelberg, 1984, 207–212.

[Gill91]   R. Gilleron, Decision problems for term rewriting systems and recognizable tree languages, in C. Choffrut and M. Jantzen (eds.), *Proc. STACS 91, Lecture Notes in Computer Science* 480, Springer-Verlag, Berlin, Heidelberg, 1991, 148–159.

[Har83]   R.H. Haring-Smith, Groups and simple languages, *Transactions American Mathematical Society* 279 (1983), 337–356.

[HoUl79]   J. Hopcroft and J. Ullman, *Introduction to Automata Theory, Languages, and Computation*, Addison-Wesley, Reading, MA, 1979.

[Hue80]   G. Huet, Confluent reductions: abstract properties and applications to term rewriting systems, *J. Association Computing Machinery* 27 (1980), 797–821.

[HuLa78]   G. Huet and D. Lankford, *On the uniform halting problem for term rewriting systems*, Lab. Report No. 283, INRIA, Le Chesnay, France, March 1978.

[HuOp80]   G. Huet and D. Oppen, Equations and rewrite rules: a survey, in R. Book (ed.), *Formal Language Theory: Perspectives and Open Problems*, Academic Press, New York, 1980, 349–405.

[Jan81]   M. Jantzen, On a special monoid with a single defining relation, *Theoretical Computer Science* 16 (1981), 61–73.

[Jan85]   M. Jantzen, A note on a special one-rule semi-Thue system, *Information Processing Letters* 21 (1985), 135–140.

[Jan88]   M. Jantzen, *Confluent String Rewriting*, EATCS Monograph Number 14, Springer-Verlag, Berlin, Heidelberg, 1988.

[Jou87]   J.-P. Jouannaud (ed.), *Rewriting Techniques and Applications*, Academic Press, London, 1987.

[JoKi86]   J.-P. Jouannaud and H. Kirchner, Completion of a set of rules modulo a set of equations, *SIAM J. Computing* 15 (1986), 1155–1194.

[KKMN85]   D. Kapur, M. Krishnamoorthy, R. McNaughton, and P. Narendran, An $O(|T|^3)$ algorithm for testing the Church-Rosser property of Thue systems, *Theoretical Computer Science* 35 (1985), 109–114.

[KaNa85a]   D. Kapur and P. Narendran, A finite Thue system with decidable word problem and without equivalent finite canonical system, *Theoretical Computer Science* 35 (1985), 337–344.

[KaNa85b]   D. Kapur and P. Narendran, The Knuth-Bendix completion procedure and Thue systems, *SIAM J. Computing* 14 (1985), 1052–1072.

[KnBe70]   D. Knuth and P. Bendix, Simple word problems in universal algebras, in J. Leech (ed.), *Computational Problems in Abstract Algebra*, Pergamon Press, New York, 1970, 263–297.

[Kob90]   Y. Kobayashi, Complete rewriting systems and homology of monoid algebras, *J. Pure Applied Algebra* 65 (1990), 263–275.

[Lal79]   G. Lallement, *Semigroups and Combinatorial Applications*, Wiley-Interscience, New York, 1979.

[Lot83]   M. Lothaire, *Combinatorics on Words*, Addison-Wesley, Reading, MA, 1983.

[LySc77]   R.C. Lyndon and P.E. Schupp, *Combinatorial Group Theory*, Springer-Verlag, Berlin, Heidelberg, 1977.

[MNOZ93]   K. Madlener, P. Narendran, F. Otto, and L. Zhang, On weakly confluent monadic string-rewriting systems, *Theoretical Computer Science*, to appear, 1993.

[MaOt85]   K. Madlener and F. Otto, Pseudo-natural algorithms for the word problem for finitely presented monoids and groups, *J. Symbolic Computation* 1 (1985), 383–418.

[MaOt88a]   K. Madlener and F. Otto, Commutativity in groups presented by finite Church-Rosser Thue systems, *RAIRO Informatique Théorique et Appl* 22 (1988), 93–111.

[MaOt88b]   K. Madlener and F. Otto, On groups having finite monadic Church-Rosser presentations, in H. Jürgensen, G. Lallement, and H.J. Weinert (eds.), *Semigroups, Theory and Applications, Lecture Notes in Mathematics* 1320, Springer-Verlag, Berlin, Heidelberg, 1988, 218–234.

[MaOt89]   K. Madlener and F. Otto, About the descriptive power of certain classes of finite string-rewriting systems, *Theoretical Computer Science* 67 (1989), 143–172.

[MaOt91]   K. Madlener and F. Otto, Decidable sentences for context-free groups, in C. Choffrut and M. Jantzen (eds.), *Proc. STACS 91, Lecture Notes in Computer Science* 480, Springer-Verlag, Berlin, Heidelberg, 1991, 160–171.

[MKS76]   W. Magnus, A. Karrass, and D. Solitar, *Combinatorial Group Theory*, 2nd revised edition, Dover, New York, 1976.

[Mar51]   A. Markov, Impossibility of algorithms for recognizing some properties of associative systems, *Doklady Adakemii Nauk SSSR* 77 (1951), 953–956.

[Maz77]   A. Mazurkiewicz, Concurrent program schemes and their interpretations, DAIMI Report PB 78, Aarhus University, Aarhus, Denmark, 1977.

[MNO88]   R. McNaughton, P. Narendran, and F. Otto, Church-Rosser Thue systems and formal languages, *J. Association Computing Machinery* 35 (1988), 324–344.

[Mos52]   A. Mostowski, Review of [Mar51], *J. Symbolic Logic* 17 (1952), 151–152.

[MuSc83]   D.E. Muller and P.E. Schupp, Groups, the theory of ends, and context-free languages, *J. Computer System Sciences* 26 (1983), 295–310.

[NaMc84]   P. Narendran and R. McNaughton, The undecidability of the preperfectness of Thue systems, *Theoretical Computer Science* 31 (1984), 165–174.

[NaÓ'Dú89]   P. Narendran and C. Ó'Dúnlaing, Cancellativity in finitely presented semigroups, *J. Symbolic Computation* 7 (1989), 457–472.

[NÓO91]   P. Narendran, C. Ó'Dúnlaing, and F. Otto, It is undecidable whether a finite special string-rewriting system presents a group, *Discrete Mathematics* 98 (1991), 153–159.

[NOR85]   P. Narendran, C. Ó'Dúnlaing, and H. Rolletschek, Complexity of certain decision problems about congruential languages, *J. Computer System Sciences* 30 (1985), 343–358.

[NaOt85]   P. Narendran and F. Otto, Complexity results on the conjugacy problem for monoids, *Theoretical Computer Science* 35 (1985), 227–243.

[NaOt86]   P. Narendran and F. Otto, The problems of cyclic equality and conjugacy for finite complete rewriting systems, *Theoretical Computer Science* 47 (1986), 27–38.

[NaOt88a]   P. Narendran and F. Otto, Elements of finite order for finite weight-reducing and confluent Thue systems, *Acta Informatica* 25 (1988), 573–591.

[NaOt88b]   P. Narendran and F. Otto, Preperfectness is undecidable for Thue systems containing only length-reducing rules and a single commutation rule, *Information Processing Letters* 29 (1988), 125–130.

[NaOt89]   P. Narendran and F. Otto, Some polynomial-time algorithms for finite monadic Church-Rosser Thue systems, *Theoretical Computer Science* 68 (1989), 319–332.

[NOW84]   P. Narendran, F. Otto, and K. Winklmann, The uniform conjugacy problem for finite Church-Rosser Thue systems is NP-complete, *Information Control* 63 (1984), 58–66.

[New43]   M.H.A. Newman, On theories with a combinatorial definition of "equivalence," *Annals Mathematics* 43 (1943), 223–243.

[NiBe72]   M. Nivat and M. Benois, Congruences parfaites et quasi-parfaites, *Seminaire Dubreil* 25 (1971–72), 7–01–09.

182   References

[Ó'Dú81]   C. Ó'Dúnlaing, *Finite and Infinite Regular Thue Systems*, Ph.D. Dissertation, University of California, Santa Barbara, 1981.

[Ó'Dú83a]   C. Ó'Dúnlaing, Undecidable questions related to Church-Rosser Thue systems, *Theoretical Computer Science* 23 (1983), 339–345.

[Ó'Dú83b]   C. Ó'Dúnlaing, Infinite regular Thue systems, *Theoretical Computer Science* 25 (1983), 171–192.

[Osi73]   V.A. Osipova, On the conjugacy problem in semigroups, in S.I. Adjan (ed.), *Mathematical Logic, the Theory of Algorithms and the Theory of Sets*, Proc. Steklov Institute Mathematics 133, American Mathematical Society, Providence, RI, 1973, 169–182.

[Ott84a]   F. Otto, Some undecidability results for non-monadic Church-Rosser Thue systems, *Theoretical Computer Science* 33 (1984), 261–278.

[Ott84b]   F. Otto, Conjugacy in monoids with a special Church-Rosser presentation is decidable, *Semigroup Forum* 29 (1984), 223–240.

[Ott85]   F. Otto, Elements of finite order for finite monadic Church-Rosser Thue systems, *Transactions American Mathematical Society* 291 (1985), 629–637.

[Ott86a]   F. Otto, Church-Rosser Thue systems that present free monoids, *SIAM J. Computing* 15 (1986), 786–792.

[Ott86b]   F. Otto, On deciding whether a monoid is a free monoid or is a group, *Acta Informatica* 23 (1986), 99–110.

[Ott86c]   F. Otto, On two problems related to cancellativity, *Semigroup Forum* 33 (1986), 331–356.

[Ott87]   F. Otto, On deciding the confluence of a finite string-rewriting system on a given congruence class, *J. Computer System Sciences* 35 (1987), 285–310.

[OtZh91]   F. Otto and L. Zhang, Decision problems for finite special string-rewriting systems that are confluent on some congruence class, *Acta Informatica* 28 (1991), 477–510.

[Pan86]   L. Pan, *Applications of Rewriting Techniques*, Ph.D. Dissertation, University of California, Santa Barbara, 1986.

[Pan88]   L. Pan, On the security of p-party algebraic protocols, *Discrete Applied Mathematics* 20 (1988), 127–144.

[Pos46]   E. Post, A variant of a recursively unsolvable problem, *Bulletin American Mathematical Society* 52 (1946), 264–268.

[Ros73]   B. Rosen, Tree-manipulating systems and the Church-Rosser property, *J. Association Computing Machinery* 20 (1973), 160–187.

[Sal73]   A. Salomaa, *Formal Languages*, Academic Press, New York, 1973.

[SiWr83]   J. Siekmann and G. Wrightson (eds.), *Automation of Reasoning, Vol. 1 and 2*, Springer-Verlag, Berlin, Heidelberg, 1983.

[Squ87a]   C. Squier, Units of special Church-Rosser monoids, *Theoretical Computer Science* 49 (1987), 13–22.

[Squ87b]   C. Squier, Word problems and a homological finiteness condition for monoids, *J. Pure Applied Algebra* 49 (1987), 201–217.

[Thu14]   A. Thue, Probleme über Veränderungen von Zeichenreihen nach gegebenen Regeln, *Skr. Vid. Kristiania, I Mat. Natuv. Klasse*, No. 10 (1914), 34 pp.

[Tie08]   H. Tietze, Über die topologischen Invarianten mehrdimensionaler Mannigfaltigkeiten, *Monatshefte für Mathematik und Physik* 19 (1908), 1–118.

[Wra88]   C. Wrathall, The word problem for free partially commutative groups, *J. Symbolic Computation* 6 (1988), 99–104.

[Zha91]   L. Zhang, Conjugacy in special monoids, *J. Algebra* 143 (1991), 487–497.

[Zha94]   L. Zhang, Some properties of finite special string-rewriting systems, *J. Symbolic Computation*, to appear, 1994.

Index

Texts and Monographs in Computer Science

(continued from page ii)

Edsger W. Dijkstra and Carel S. Scholten
Predicate Calculus and Program Semantics
1990. XII, 220 pages

W.H.J. Feijen, A.J.M. van Gasteren, D. Gries, and J. Misra, Eds.
Beauty Is Our Business: A Birthday Salute to Edsger W. Dijkstra
1990. XX, 453 pages, 21 illus.

P.A. Fejer and D.A. Simovici
Mathematical Foundations of Computer Science, Volume I:
Sets, Relations, and Induction
1990. X, 425 pages, 36 illus.

Melvin Fitting
First-Order Logic and Automated Theorem Proving
1990. XIV, 242 pages, 26 illus.

Nissim Francez
Fairness
1986. XIII, 295 pages, 147 illus.

R.T. Gregory and E.V. Krishnamurthy
Methods and Applications of Error-Free Computation
1984. XII, 194 pages, 1 illus.

David Gries, Ed.
Programming Methodology: A Collection of Articles by Members of IFIP WG2.3
1978. XIV, 437 pages, 68 illus.

David Gries
The Science of Programming
1981. XV, 366 pages

John V. Guttag and James J. Horning
Larch: Languages and Tools for Formal Specification
1993. XIII, 250 pages, 76 illus.

Micha Hofri
Probabilistic Analysis of Algorithms
1987. XV, 240 pages, 14 illus.

A.J. Kfoury, Robert N. Moll, and Michael A. Arbib
A Programming Approach to Computability
1982. VIII, 251 pages, 36 illus.

Texts and Monographs in Computer Science

Texts and Monographs in Computer Science

(continued)

J.T. Schwartz, R.B.K. Dewar, E. Dubinsky, and E. Schonberg
Programming with Sets: An Introduction to SETL
1986. XV, 493 pages, 31 illus.

Alan T. Sherman
VLSI Placement and Routing: The PI Project
1989. XII, 189 pages, 47 illus.

Santosh K. Shrivastava, Ed.
Reliable Computer Systems
1985. XII, 580 pages, 215 illus.

Jan L. van de Snepscheut
What Computing Is All About
1993. XII, 468 pages, 78 illus.

William M. Waite and Gerhard Goos
Compiler Construction
1984. XIV, 446 pages, 196 illus.

Niklaus Wirth
Programming in Modula-2, 4th Edition
1988. II, 182 pages

Study Edition

Edward Cohen
Programming in the 1990s: An Introduction to the Calculation of Programs
1990. XV, 265 pages